art / shop / eat
ROME

Alexandra Massini

Campidoglio Forum

Navona Pantheon

Trevi Spagna

Villa Borghese

Vatican St Peter's

introduction

Divina natura dedit agros, ars humana aedificavit urbes
'Divine Nature gave the country, human skill built the cities'
(Varro, Roman Republic, 3.1)

'Rome is yet the capital of the world. It is a city of palaces and temples, more glorious than those which any other city contains, and of ruins more glorious than they' (Percy Bysshe Shelley)

The capital of an empire and then of a religion, with over 2750 years of history, Rome is justly known as the Eternal City and the Caput Mundi (Head of the World). From Classical antiquity to the Middle Ages and the Renaissance, from the Baroque age to that of Neoclassicism and the Grand Tour, nowhere else is there such comprehensive evidence of the past. Rome is one great museum with an unparalleled collection of art.

'All streets lead to Rome' and there are many different ways of approaching the city. This guide is intended to give the visitor an introductory taste of its beauty, dividing the city into five art areas. Campidoglio Forum focuses on ancient Rome; Navona Pantheon and Trevi Spagna feature some of the galleries, piazzas and churches of Renaissance and Baroque Rome; Villa Borghese describes a beautiful park with three wonderful museums; and Vatican St Peter's explores the city's most celebrated collections of fabulous art treasures.

Eating and shopping can be high art in Rome and a favourite pastime, too. In this book, each museum district is accompanied by a selection of the best restaurants, cafés and bars as well as the finest shops listed by theme. You will also find a section on entertainment, and practical details to help with planning your trip (including a list of recommended hotels). The art glossary at the back will keep you up-to-date with Rome's key artistic personalities.

CAMPIDOGLIO
FORUM

Piazza del Campidoglio

The Capitoline Hill – the Campidoglio – is the location of the Musei Capitolini. In ancient times it was the religious centre of Rome, with the most important sanctuaries. The **Temple of Jupiter Optimus Maximus**, built on its southern summit, was dedicated in the first year of the Republic (509 BC) and became the symbol of Roman civilization. The northern part of the hill was occupied by the **Arx**, the citadel of Rome, and later by the **Temple of Juno Moneta** (343 BC). In the 1c BC, the **Tabularium**, or state-archive, rose above the Etruscan temple of Veiovis, on the slopes of the hill facing the Forum. With the fall of the Roman Empire (AD 476) and the suppression of pagan cults, the Capitoline Hill was gradually abandoned.

Recovery came in the Middle Ages when the church of **Santa Maria in Aracoeli** was built above the ruins of the Temple of Juno and the Senate was re-instituted (1144) as the centre of civic government. The ancient Tabularium was chosen as its seat and rebuilt. The **Palazzo dei Conservatori** (for the city magistrates), was built in the 15c and the esplanade in the centre was embellished with sculptures brought here from the Lateran palace at the order of Sixtus IV (1471).

In 1538 the Farnese pope Paul III transferred the statue of *Marcus Aurelius* from the Lateran to the Capitoline Hill (what you see here is a copy, the original is in the Palazzo Nuovo). He also commissioned Michelangelo to design a new square and rebuild the medieval palaces. The new **Campidoglio**, the first monumental square of modern Rome, faced towards St Peter's rather than the Forum of the ancient city.

On the balustrade at the top of the access ramp are the late Roman statues of the *Dioscuri* (the twin heroes Castor and

Piazza del Campidoglio *Marcus Aurelius* (copy of 2c AD statue)

Pollux) with their horses. The statues of *Constantine* and his son *Constans II* came from the Baths of Constantine on the Quirinal and were placed here in 1653.

Closing the piazza, the **Palazzo Senatorio** (the Mayor's office) was rebuilt by Giacomo della Porta and Girolamo Rainaldi in 1582-1605). Beneath the double staircase (by Michelangelo), are a statue of *Minerva* (1c AD), adapted by Rainaldi to symbolize Roma, and two river-gods representing the *Nile* and the *Tiber*, which were found in the Baths of Constantine.

Michelangelo's **Palazzo dei Conservatori** was finished by Giacomo della Porta. Its highly innovative design features huge pilasters to tie the two storeys together. Known as the 'giant order' they were repeated by Michelangelo on the exterior of St Peter's. The balustrade crowned with statues had never appeared on a Roman palace before and became a distinctive feature of Palladio's architecture in the Veneto. Opposite is the **Palazzo Nuovo**, begun in 1603 and finished by Carlo Rainaldi in 1655. The Palazzi dei Conservatori and Nuovo house the Capitoline Museums. The star-shaped pavement design was laid in 1940 and follows a famous engraving by Etienne Dupérac (1567) after Michelangelo's plans.

The Capitoline Museums

OPEN	Tues-Sun 9.00-20.00
CLOSED	Mon; 1/1, 1/5, 25/12
CHARGES	€6.20; Reduced €4.20. Free to under 18s and over 65s who are citizens of countries with a reciprocal agreement
RECORDED INFO	06 3996 7800
WWW.	museicapitolini.it

MAIN ENTRANCE	Piazza del Campidoglio
BUS	All buses to Piazza Venezia, 60 express (64, 87, 117, 119, 186, 492)

There are bookshops in Palazzo Nuovo and Palazzo dei Conservatori. The museum café is in Palazzo Caffarelli. Access for disabled visitors is via a ramp in via del Tempio di Giove; telephone in advance to make arrangements.

The collections date from 1471 when Sixtus IV returned to the citizens of Rome a group of bronzes (including the *Spinario* and the *She-wolf*) hitherto kept in the Lateran Palace. During the 16c this collection was added to by finds made in the city and by Pius V's donation of 1566, which was intended to 'purge the Vatican of its pagan statues'. Cardinal Alessandro Albani's collection of 418 pieces was purchased in 1733 and the Palazzo Nuovo became a museum of Classical sculpture. Further finds, acquisitions and donations made during the 18c and 19c resulted in the opening of a second museum in the Palazzo dei Conservatori. In 1990 the Centrale di Montemartini, a former electrical plant, was converted into a superb exhibition space to house a part of the collection. It is on the outskirts of town in Via Ostiense, south of Stazione Ostiense. The Pinacoteca Capitolina was founded by Benedict XIV in 1748. It contains 16c and 17c paintings from the collections of Cardinal Sacchetti and Prince Gilberto Pio of Savoy, 14c-15c works from the Sterbini collection and the Cini bequest of 18c porcelain.

THE PALAZZO NUOVO
HIGHLIGHTS

Marcus Aurelius	Courtyard
Capitoline Venus	Room 3
Cicero	Room 5
Centaurs, Wounded Amazon	Room 6
Silenus	Room 7
Dying Gaul, Hermes, Resting Satyr	Room 8

Beyond the entrance, to the left, is a giant statue of *Athena* (Minerva) after Phidias' original executed in gold and ivory for the Parthenon in Athens (mid 5c BC).

COURTYARD Here is a colossal statue of a *River-god* (1c AD) found at the foot of the Campidoglio and incorporated into the present fountain by Giacomo della Porta (1596). Known as *Marforio*, it was believed to have come from the Forum of Augustus (dedicated to Mars). As one of Rome's 'talking statues', it displayed satirical comments and 'conversed' with another statue, *Madama Lucrezia* (possibly Isis), at the bottom of the hill (in the corner of Piazza San Marco).

To the right is the equestrian statue of *Marcus Aurelius*, moved here from Piazza del Campidoglio after its restoration in the 1980s. A masterpiece of Roman art, it is one of the few bronzes and the only equestrian statue of an emperor to have survived from the 2c AD - it was held to represent Constantine, the first Christian Emperor.

The three rooms on the ground floor, displaying portraits of Roman citizens, funerary reliefs and a great marble sarcophagus with portraits of the deceased and the stories of Hercules (2c AD), are presently closed.

At the foot of the stairs leading to the upper floor is a giant statue of *Mars* dating from the Flavian period (1c AD).

FIRST FLOOR
GALLERIA Here the statues, busts and inscriptions are arranged as they were in the 18c, according to symmetry and aesthetics rather than archaeological or historical principles. The statue of *Hercules* (2c AD) was altered in the 17c by the sculptor Alessandro Algardi to show him slaying the Hydra. The fine *Cupid with a Bow* is one of the best Roman copies (early 1c AD) of a celebrated work by Lysippos. Beside it, the Roman copy of Myron's *Discobolos* (460 BC) was restored in the 17c as a falling soldier. Opposite is *Leda with the Swan*, a replica of a work by Timotheos of the 4c BC.

ROOM 2 has a number of busts and inscriptions as well as two fine 2c mosaics featuring theatrical masks and doves at a fountain. The latter copies a work by Sosias of Pergamon (2c BC) and was discovered in the 18c in a pavement of Hadrian's villa at Tivoli. Beneath the far window is the *Tabula Iliaca*, a plaque with minute reliefs of the Trojan cycle executed by Theodorus (1c AD). Just outside, in the Galleria, is a seated statue of a *Drunken Old Woman* after an original by Myron the Younger (late 3c BC).

ROOM 3 (off the far end of the Galleria) has the celebrated *Capitoline Venus*, a superb replica in Parian marble of a Hellenistic variation on Praxiteles' *Aphrodite of Knidos* (360 BC). It was re-discovered in the 17c, and when it was purchased by Benedict XIV in 1752 it was one of the most famous statues in Rome.

ROOM 4 has Roman Imperial busts arranged chronologically (clockwise from the top shelf in the corner by the door to Room 5), starting with portraits of *Augustus* and his wife *Livia*. On a pedestal in front of the window is the *Young Marcus Aurelius*. Along the next wall are portraits of the Flavian dynasty and, on a pedestal, a fine *Bust of a Woman* with a complex hairstyle typical of that time. On the opposite wall is the bearded *Marcus Aurelius* (161-180) and, on the shelf below, *Trajan Decio* (249-251), strikingly realistic, with a worried expression. The young *Honorius* (384-217) closes the series introducing the modes of Byzantine art. In the centre is a seated figure of *Helena*, mother of Constantine (early 4c AD).

ROOM 5 displays busts of philosophers and poets, including *Homer, Socrates, Sophocles, Euripides, Pythagoras*, and a fine 1c BC bust of *Cicero* (in the right corner opposite the window).

ROOM 6 is the *Salone*. Among the statues exhibited here are the *Infant Hercules* in basanite (a volcanic rock) and two 2c *Centaurs* in dark marble, found in Hadrian's villa and signed by Aristeas and Papias from Aphrodisias (in Asia Minor). Along the walls are statues of *Apollo playing the Lyre*, after an original by Praxiteles (4c BC), and a replica, signed by Sosikles, of a *Wounded Amazon* by Polykleitos (5c BC).

ROOM 7 In the centre is a statue of a *Silenus* in red marble, derived from a Hellenistic bronze original. On the walls are inscriptions including Vespasian's *Lex de Imperio*, a bronze plaque conferring power on the Emperor. Beyond are a *Boy Strangling a Goose* (after an original by Boethus of Chalcedon, 2c BC) and a playful *Boy with a Mask*.

ROOM 8 has the famous *Dying Gaul*, a Roman copy of one of the bronze statues made for Attalos I of Pergamon to commemorate his victory over the Gauls (239 BC). It was found in 1622 in the grounds of the Villa Ludovisi (see p 141). By the window is the famous 2c marble group of *Eros and Psyche*. To the left stands an *Amazon*, after an original by Phidias (5c BC), extensively restored in the 18c. The fine statue representing *Hermes* or Antinous, is a Hadrianic version of an original of the 4c BC. It was found in the Emperor's villa at Tivoli and was purchased from Cardinal Albani. Also from Hadrian's villa is the *Resting Satyr*, after Praxiteles (4c BC).

Stairs lead down to the underground tunnel leading to the **Tabularium** (with spectacular views over the Forum) and the Palazzo dei Conservatori.

THE PALAZZO DEI CONSERVATORI
HIGHLIGHTS

Fragments of a colossal statue of *Constantine*	Courtyard
Reliefs from a monument to *Marcus Aurelius*	Staircase
Bronze head of *Constantine*	Room 1
Spinario, Junius Brutus	Room 3
She-wolf of Rome	Room 4
Commodus as Hercules	Room 10

COURTYARD Here are the marble fragments of a colossal statue of *Constantine* (c 12m high) including the head, parts of the arms, a hand and foot, brought here from the Basilica of Constantine in

Head of Constantine

1486. The bare extremities were made of marble, while the rest of the body was of wood covered with gilded bronze or stucco drapery. Opposite, reliefs representing the Roman provinces were taken from the Temple of Hadrian at Piazza di Pietra (AD 145). Beneath the portico at the far end are a seated statue of *Roma* and two statues of *Barbarians* in grey marble, dating from the time of Trajan (AD 98-117).

Stairs lead up to the first floor past four reliefs: three of these celebrate *Marcus Aurelius and his Triumph* (AD 176). Together with the other eight now incorporated in the Arch of Constantine (p 33) they once formed part of a triumphal monument. The fourth relief (to the left) belonged to an arch dedicated to Hadrian in Via di Pietra. From the same arch are two reliefs exhibited on the next two landings illustrating the *Adlocutio of Hadrian* and the *Apotheosis of his wife Sabina*.

SALA DEGLI ORAZI E CURIAZI *Room 1* The meeting place of the Roman council was frescoed by Cavalier d'Arpino with episodes from the reigns of the early kings. The statues of *Urban VIII* (in marble) and *Innocent X* (in bronze) are respectively by Bernini (and workshop) and Alessandro Algardi. The bronze statue of *Hercules*, after a Greek original, was found in the Forum Boarium during the time of Sixtus IV, who also donated, in 1471, the head, hand and globe of *Constantine* (all belonging to a lost statue).

SALA DEI CAPITANI *Room 2* The frescoes by Tommaso Laureti (1594) imitate Raphael's work in the Vatican Stanze and illustrate examples of Roman virtue and courage as narrated by Livy. Along the walls are inscriptions and statues dedicated to illustrious captains of the Papal State.

SALA DEI TRIONFI *Room 3* has a frieze of 1569 representing the *Triumph of Emilius Paulus* which took place in 167 BC. The *Battle between Alexander the Great and Darius* is by Pietro da Cortona. The famous **Spinario** - a statue of a boy plucking a thorn from his foot - is a late Hellenistic work of the 1c BC that was frequently copied in the Renaissance. The **Camillus**, or statue of an acolyte, is a work of the 1c AD imitating Classical Greek sculpture. A fine portrait bust has been identified as **Junius Brutus**, the first Roman consul, which dates from the 3c BC.

SALA DELLA LUPA *Room 4* Here are the **Fasti Consulares et Triumphales**, records of Roman consuls between 483 and 19 BC and of victorious captains between 753 and 19 BC; they once decorated the Arch of Augustus in the Forum (later destroyed). Also here is the famous **She-wolf of Rome**, an Etruscan bronze of the early 5c BC given to the city by Sixtus IV. Originally symbolizing strength, the image was altered in the late 15c to refer to the legendary foundation of Rome by the addition of the twins Romulus and Remus.

SALA DELLE OCHE *Room 5* contains antique bronzes of two ducks, a marble head of **Medusa** by Bernini, and a bronze **Portrait of Michelangelo** (a replica of a work by Daniele da Volterra in Florence).

SALA DELLE AQUILE *Room 6* Like the previous room, this retains its 16c decoration and displays fine Roman sculpture including two eagles and a **Diana of Ephesus**.

SALA VERDE *Room 7* has busts of Roman emperors, including a fine portrait of **Hadrian** in green alabaster from Egypt.

Stairs to the left lead to a terraced **café** with wonderful views over the city.

SALA DEGLI ARAZZI *Room 10* The tapestries were made in Rome in the 18c after works preserved in the Capitoline Museums. The frescoes and ceiling date from 1544. Also here is a fine bust of **Commodus as Hercules** (AD 180-192).

SALA DI ANNIBALE *Room 11* Has frescoes of **Hannibal and the Punic Wars** by the Bolognese Jacopo Ripanda (1508-23). A bronze *krater*, which belonged to Mithridates VI, King of Pontus, in the 1c BC, was found in Nero's villa at Anzio.

CHAPEL *Room 12* was decorated with frescoes and stuccoes in 1578. The paintings of the *Evangelists* and *Saints* are by Giovan Francesco Romanelli (1645-8). On the left is a 15c *Madonna and Child with Angels* by Andrea d'Assisi (l'Ingegno), formerly in the loggia of the palace.

SALE DEI FASTI MODERNI *Rooms 13-15* To the right of the staircase, these rooms contain lists of the chief magistrates of Rome since 1640. Also here is an impressive statue of *Marsyas* who dared Apollo to a music competition and was flayed alive as punishment. The anguished expression of the *Silenus* follows a Hellenistic original and provided the inspiration for many a Crucifixion.

The stairs continue up to the second floor past two splendid panels in *opus sectile* showing a bull attacked by a tigress from the Basilica of Junius Bassus on the Esquiline (4c AD).

PINACOTECA CAPITOLINA
HIGHLIGHTS

Titian, *Baptism of Christ*	Room 3
Guercino, *Burial of St Petronilla*	Room 7
Caravaggio, *Fortune Teller, St John the Baptist*	
Pietro da Cortona, *Rape of the Sabines*	Room 8
Velázquez, *Self-portrait*	Room 9
Van Dyck, *Portrait of the Brothers de Wael*	
Giovanni Bellini, *Portrait of a Young Man*	

ROOMS 1-2 contain paintings from central Italy and 16c Ferrara.

ROOM 3 Venetian painting in the 16c. Here are **Titian**'s early *Baptism of Christ,* executed c 1512 for Giovanni Ram who appears on the right; a fine *Portrait of a Lady* by Girolamo Savoldo (c 1525); the *Rape of Europa* by Paolo Veronese (1580), and paintings by Domenico Tintoretto, son of Jacopo.

ROOMS 5 AND 6 To follow a chronological sequence around the gallery, return to Room 2 to enter Room 5 dedicated to painting in Emilia and Rome between the 16c and 17c. Room 6 has works by the Bolognese school including the Carracci and Guido Reni.

ROOM 7 has paintings from early 17c Rome. There are a number of paintings by **Guercino**, including his huge canvas of the *Burial of St Petronilla* (1623) made for an altar in St Peter's. Also here are **Caravaggio**'s *Fortune Teller*, an early work (1595) formerly in the collection of Cardinal Del Monte, as well as his revolutionary *St John the Baptist*, painted in 1602 for the Mattei family and highly unusual in its representation of the saint (inspired by Michelangelo's *Ignudi* in the Sistine Chapel). More classical is the work of Annibale Carracci's follower Domenichino, whose *Sybil* of 1622 looks back to Raphael. The painting of *Romulus and Remus fed by the She-wolf* was begun by Peter Paul Rubens and finished by his pupils.

ROOMS 4 AND 8 Room 4 features Baroque painting in Rome between 1630 and 1660, while the adjoining Room 8 is dedicated to **Pietro da Cortona** and the paintings he executed for the Sacchetti family, including the *Rape of the Sabines* (c 1630).

ROOM 9 contains the Cini collection of fine Chinese, Japanese and Meissen porcelain, and Italian ceramics (Capodimonte and Doccia). On the walls are Flemish tapestries of the mid 17c from Antwerp. Down the steps are the *Portrait of the Brothers de Wael* by **Anthony van Dyck** (1621), a *Self-portrait* by **Velázquez**, made during his second visit to Rome (1649-51), and **Giovanni Bellini**'s *Portrait of a Young Man* (c 1500). At the end of the gallery hangs a portrait of *Cardinal Silvio Valenti Gonzaga*, who was involved in the foundation of the Pinacoteca, by Pierre Subleyras (c 1750).

The adjoining Palazzo Caffarelli contains the **Medagliere**, an extensive collection of Roman, medieval and modern coins and medals.

The Forum Romanum

OPEN	Daily, 9.00 to one hour before sunset
CLOSED	1/1, 25/12
CHARGES	Free entrance
TELEPHONE	**06 699 0110**
MAIN ENTRANCE	From the Capitoline Hill or the gate beyond the Arch of Titus
METRO/BUS	Line B to Colosseo. All buses through Piazza Venezia and Via dei Fori Imperiali (85, 87, 175, 186)

Originally a marshy valley used during the Iron Age (9c BC) as a necropolis, by c 600 BC this area was paved as a market place or forum. The first structures to be erected here were the Comitium (a square reserved for legislative assemblies), the Curia, or senate house (where the council of the elders met), the Regia, seat of the Pontifex Maximus (who presided over the state cult), and the Temple of Vesta, linked to the worship of fire. The Forum was divided into three areas: the political centre at the foot of the Capitoline Hill, the religious centre to the south, and the commercial centre (the Forum proper) in the middle.

In the course of time it lost its importance as a market (which was moved to the area closest to the Tiber) and became the scene of public functions and ceremonies. After the institution of the Republic (509 BC) new temples were erected. By the 2c BC Rome had become the undisputed ruler of the Western Mediterranean and this was reflected in the increasing grandeur of its political centre. At about the same time, a new form of building, the basilica, was introduced to hold judicial hearings, trade negotiations and public meetings. Later, in the 1c BC, the decline of the Republic and the ascendance of dictatorial power were accompanied by an extensive building campaign. The Forum was re-organized and enlarged by Julius Caesar, who began the reconstruction of the Curia and the Rostra (the speaker's tribune), as well as the basilica bearing his name. He also built his own Forum. His successor Octavian completed his work and assumed absolute power as Augustus, the first Roman Emperor, in 27 BC. Augustus was the first to build in the area of the Imperial Fora, and the first to erect monuments for his own dynastic propaganda. This trend continued throughout the Empire with the dedication of temples, triumphal arches, columns and statues.

Repeatedly devastated by fires, the Forum was systematically restored (the last time in AD 284 by Diocletian) until the capital of the Empire was moved to Constantinople (AD 330) and Rome generally declined. In AD 391 pagan rites were abolished: as a result the temples closed down and were robbed of their treasures. The barbarian invasions of the 5c and 6c despoiled what was left and earthquakes further damaged the abandoned buildings. Some of the ruins were used as foundations for fortresses, while others made useful stone quarries.

THE SITE

From the Piazza del Campidoglio, the short Via del Campidoglio (to the right of Palazzo Senatorio) leads to a terrace and to Via di Monte Tarpeo which runs uphill to an entrance to the Forum. From here the ancient road, the **Clivus Capitolinus**, descends to the Forum. Paved in the 2c BC, it was also used for triumphal processions to the Temple of Jupiter Capitolinus.

On the side of the Capitoline Hill are the walls of the **Tabularium**, the State archive erected in 78 BC to preserve the tabulae (wax tablets) inscribed with the laws of the Republic. Below are three tall columns, all that remains of the **Temple of Vespasian**, dedicated by his sons Titus and Domitian after his death in AD 79. Beside it is the platform where once stood the **Temple of Concord**, built by Camillus in 366 BC to commemorate the peace between patricians and plebeians and reconstructed by Tiberius (7 BC-AD 10). Part of the frieze is in the Tabularium.

To the right of the Clivus Capitolinus are eight columns of the **Temple of Saturn**. Founded in 498 BC, it was rebuilt in 42 BC and restored by Diocletian after the fire of AD 283 (as mentioned in the inscription on the frieze). Beyond the temple to the right are the steps and column bases of the **Basilica Julia**, begun in 54 BC by Julius Caesar and completed by Augustus in AD 12. It had a large central hall and was surrounded by a double row of columns forming aisles. On the long side facing the Forum was a portico containing shops.

To the right of the triumphal arch is a cylindrical construction, the **Umbilicus Urbis** (3c AD), marking the centre (navel) of the city. Behind it is a semicircular stepped platform that was part of the **Imperial Rostra**, the orator's tribune where magistrate's edicts, legal decisions and official communications were published, and which dates from the time of Julius Caesar.

ARCH OF SEPTIMIUS SEVERUS This arch was erected in AD 203 on the tenth anniversary of the emperor's ascendancy and dedicated by the Senate and People of Rome (S.P.Q.R.) to Severus and his sons Caracalla and Geta to commemorate their military victories in Parthia (Iran). The name of Geta was erased after he was murdered by Caracalla (AD 212). To the left of the arch is another entrance to the Forum from Via San Pietro in Carcere, where the **Carcer Tullianum**, the ancient prison, is still to be seen beneath the church of San Giuseppe dei Falegnami. The oldest part of it dates back to the 6c BC.

CURIA JULIA The brick building beyond the triumphal arch, to the left, is the Curia Julia, or Senate House. Begun by Sulla in 80 BC, it was rebuilt after a fire (52 BC) by Julius Caesar and completed by Augustus. The brick façade was originally covered in marble (on the lower part) and stucco. Twice restored, it was converted into a church in AD 630. The bronze doors are copies of the originals, moved in the 18c to San Giovanni in Laterano. Inside, three broad steps along the side walls provided seats for 300 senators whose

ROMAN FORUM
West

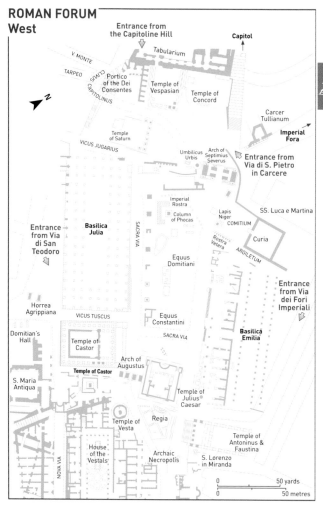

Entrance from
the Capitoline Hill

Capitol

V. MONTE
TARPEO

CLIVUS CAPITOLINUS

Tabularium

Portico
of the Dei
Consentes

Temple of
Vespasian

Temple of
Concord

Carcer
Tullianum

Imperial
Fora

Temple
of Saturn

VICUS JUGARIUS

Umbilicus
Urbis

Arch of
Septimius
Severus

Entrance from
Via di S. Pietro
in Carcere

Imperial
Rostra

Column
of Phocas

Lapis
Niger

COMITIUM

SS. Luca e Martina

Basilica
Julia

SACRA VIA

Rostra
Vetera

ARGILETUM

Curia

Entrance
from Via
di San
Teodoro

Equus
Domitiani

Entrance
from Via
dei Fori
Imperiali

Horrea
Agrippiana

VICUS TUSCUS

Equus
Constantini

SACRA VIA

Basilica
Emilia

Domitian's
Hall

Temple of
Castor

Arch of
Augustus

S. Maria
Antiqua

Temple of Castor

Temple of
Julius
Caesar

NOVA VIA

Temple of
Vesta

Regia

House
of the
Vestals

Archaic
Necropolis

Temple of
Antoninus &
Faustina

S. Lorenzo
in Miranda

0   50 yards

0   50 metres

speeches were amplified by the height of the building. The porphyry statue of *Trajan* or *Hadrian* on the president's tribune was discovered in excavations behind the building. The *Plutei of Trajan*, two finely carved parapets found in 1872 in the central square of the Forum, illustrate ceremonies which took place during the reign of Trajan (AD 98-117).

In front of the Curia are the remains of the **Comitium**, a stepped circular platform which served as a meeting place for the *Comitia Curiata*, representing the 30 districts or *curiae* of the city. The centre of the earliest political activity of the Republic and the original site of the Rostra, it was suppressed by Julius Caesar to make way for the new Curia. Nearby is the **Lapis Niger**, an underground sanctuary with a pavement in black marble, traditionally held to be the tomb of Romulus, but now considered to be a sanctuary of Vulcan. Inside is the oldest Latin inscription (6c BC), identifying the place as a sacred spot that should not be profaned.

The open space stretching beyond the Curia was the original Forum or market-place where all important ceremonies and meetings were held. During the Empire it became an official centre displaying a number of commemorative monuments. Across the street from the Lapis Niger is the **Plinth of the Decennalia**, celebrating the tenth anniversary of the Tetrarchy (instituted in AD 293 by Diocletian to divide the empire into four parts). It is decorated with reliefs showing a procession of senators and scenes of sacrifice. Beyond rises the **Column of Phocas**, the last monument to be erected in the Forum (AD 608) and commemorating the emperor's gift of the Pantheon to the pope (the Pantheon was the first pagan temple to be converted into a church). Close by is an unpaved space with a fig and olive tree and a vine, which were sacred to the Romans.

BASILICA EMILIA Facing the Forum are the remains of the **Tabernae Novae**, a row of shops that stood beneath the portico of the **Basilica Emilia**. The basilica was constructed in 179 BC and rebuilt during the time of Julius Caesar. Alaric's sack of Rome in

410 nearly destroyed it and then much of its marble was used in Renaissance buildings leaving only poor remains. It consisted of a great rectangular hall divided by columns into a central nave and three aisles and was paved in coloured marble.

TEMPLE OF JULIUS CAESAR Just beyond the central square the path joins the **Via Sacra**. To the right of the crossing are the few remains of the Temple of Julius Caesar. After his assassination on 15 March 44 BC his body was brought to the Forum. An altar (protected by a wall and covered by a roof) marks the spot where he was cremated and his will read by Mark Antony. Caesar was deified by his adoptive son Augustus and a temple erected to his name in 29 BC (behind the altar). Unfortunately only the central block of the podium survives. A terrace in front of the podium once exhibited the prows of Antony and Cleopatra's ships, captured at Actium in 31 BC.

TEMPLE OF CASTOR AND POLLUX Further on rise three columns and the podium of the Temple of Castor and Pollux. This was built in 484 BC in honour of the Dioscuri ('sons of God'), brothers of Helen and Clytemnestra, born from Leda and Jupiter (transformed into a swan), who, according to a legend, granted the Romans an important victory at the Battle of Lake Regillus (in the hills south of Rome) in 496 BC. The temple had three cellae (sanctuaries) and a deep pronaos (porch) and was approached by a steep flight of steps. Fragments of statues of the Dioscuri were found here and are now in the Antiquarium (p 24).

DOMITIAN'S HALL Behind the temple are the ruins of Domitian's Hall, a large rectangular brick building, planned as the monumental vestibule of Domitian's palace on the Palatine. To the side of it, a late Imperial hall was transformed in the 6c into the church of **Santa Maria Antiqua**, and decorated with wonderful frescoes in the 7c-9c. Unfortunately it is closed to the public.

Up above, along the sides of the hill, are the imposing walls that were added by Domitian and Hadrian to the Domus Tiberiana, the first imperial palace to be erected on the Palatine.

TEMPLE OF VESTA The Vicus Tuscus returns to the Via Sacra past the circular Temple of Vesta, one of the first temples to be built in the Forum. Its design is thought to have been based on the circular huts of the ancient Latin people. It burned down in 64 and AD 191 and was last rebuilt by Septimius Severus (193-211) and his wife Julia Domna. The temple was in ruins by the early 20c when it was partially reconstructed. It was dedicated to Vesta, an archaic goddess of the family hearth, and housed the sacred fire which was guarded by six Vestal Virgins and kept perpetually alight in order to grant the safety of the State.

Inside was the *Palladium*, a statue of Pallas Athena supposedly brought from Troy by Aeneas. No-one was allowed in the temple except the Vestals and the Pontifex Maximus, the highest religious authority whose official seat was in the Regia. Opposite the temple of Vesta are the ruins of the **House of the Vestals** (presently closed). This large building was constructed around a courtyard and a two-storeyed portico. During the Republic it also included the living quarters of the Pontifex Maximus.The complex dates from Republican times but was rebuilt after the fire of Nero in AD 64 and was last restored by Septimius Severus (AD 193-211).

TEMPLE OF ANTONINUS AND FAUSTINA Facing the Regia, scant remains of which lie behind the Temple of Vesta, on the other side of the Via Sacra is the Temple of Antoninus and Faustina dedicated in AD 141 to the deceased Empress Faustina and, after his death in AD 161, also to her husband Antoninus Pius. One of the best preserved temples in the Forum, its pronaos (porch) features 10 huge columns. In the 11c it was converted into the church of San Lorenzo in Miranda; its Baroque façade was added in 1602.

TEMPLE OF ROMULUS On the left is the so-called Temple of Romulus, a 4c brick building, circular in plan, preceded by a curving porch with niches for statues.The bronze doors are original. At the back, a long hall, once the library of the Forum of Peace built by Vespasian in AD 70, was transformed in the 6c into the church of Santi Cosma e Damiano.

ROMAN FORUM
East

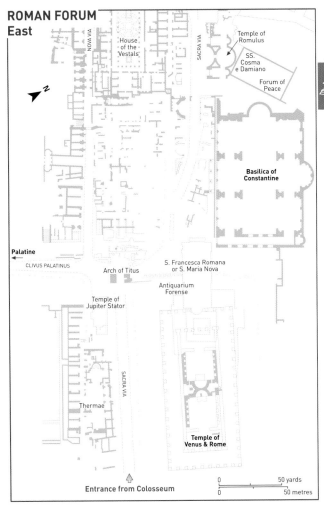

NOVA VIA

House of the Vestals

SACRA VIA

Temple of Romulus

SS. Cosma e Damiano

Forum of Peace

Basilica of Constantine

Palatine

CLIVUS PALATINUS

Arch of Titus

S. Francesca Romana or S. Maria Nova

Antiquarium Forense

Temple of Jupiter Stator

Thermae

SACRA VIA

Temple of Venus & Rome

Entrance from Colosseum

0   50 yards
0   50 metres

BASILICA OF CONSTANTINE A path on the left leads to the impressive remains of the Basilica of Constantine, the last and biggest to be built in the Forum. Begun by Maxentius (AD 306-310), it was completed by Constantine. The rectangular hall, 100m long and 65m wide, was divided into a nave and two aisles by massive piers and arches. Only the northern aisle survives with its huge barrel vaults. The walls were decorated with coloured marbles and stucco. Fragments of a colossal statue of Constantine (now in the Capitoline Museums) were found in the west apse in 1487.

ANTIQUARIUM OF THE FORUM Returning to the Via Sacra, on the left is the church of Santa Francesca Romana. The adjoining convent is now the seat of the Antiquarium (officially open 9.00-18.00, but often closed). The four rooms presently on view contain finds from the nearby Archaic necropolis, which dates back to the 9c BC, as well as vases, votive objects and glassware from excavations in the Forum. Room 4 looks into one cella of the **Temple of Venus and Roma** (otherwise not visible). Rome's largest temple, it had two sanctuaries placed back to back to hold the shrines of the two goddesses. It was erected by Hadrian c 125-135 AD on the site of the vestibule of Nero's Domus Aurea.

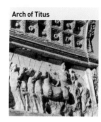

Arch of Titus

ARCH OF TITUS The Arch of Titus was erected by Domitian to commemorate the victories of his father Vespasian and his brother Titus in the Judaean War. Both emperors are identified in the inscription as '*Divus*', indicating that the arch was dedicated after their death (respectively in AD 79 and 81). The reliefs on the inside walls of the arch depict the Emperor guided by the goddess Roma, with winged Victory and a triumphal procession. On the vault is the Apotheosis of Titus, with the Emperor mounted on an eagle. The arch, which had been incorporated into a fortress in the Middle Ages, was restored by Valadier in the early 19c.

The ruins on the northern slopes of the Palatine belong to the substructures of the Domus Tiberiana and a series of shops. An extension of the Via Sacra continues beyond the exit gate towards the Colosseum, passing the Baths of Elagabalus (early 3c) on the right and the Temple of Venus and Roma on the left.

The Palatine Hill

OPEN	Daily, 9.00 to one hour before sunset
CLOSED	1/1, 25/12
CHARGES	Combined ticket with the Colosseum: €8 Reduced €4
MAIN ENTRANCE	Near the Arch of Titus in the Forum, or Via di San Gregorio 30
TELEPHONE	06 699 0110
METRO/BUS	Line B to Colosseo. Buses to Colosseum (85, 87, 175, 186)

According to legend the twins Romulus and Remus, founders of Rome, were nursed by a she-wolf at the foot of the Palatine Hill. When they grew up they held a competition to decide where a new city should be erected - Remus favoured the Aventine while Romulus the Palatine. The decisive omen was a flight of twelve vultures over the Palatine. Romulus killed his brother and became the first king of Rome on 21 April 753 BC. The city was surrounded by a rectangular wall, a stretch of which has been identified on the southwest part of the hill. Traces of huts from the 9c-8c BC have been discovered there, too.

By the time of the Republic, the Palatine had become a popular residential area with many prominent citizens building their houses here. Subsequently the emperors, starting with Augustus, turned pre-existing houses into their own living quarters. In the 1c AD the Flavian emperors' grand residence dominated the summit of the hill, the Palatium, from which the word palace derives. After the fall of the Roman Empire in AD 476, the victorious king Odoacer lived on the Palatine, as did Theodoric, king of the Ostrogoths, who ruled Italy from 493 to 526. During the Middle Ages, the Frangipani and other noble

THE PALATINE HILL

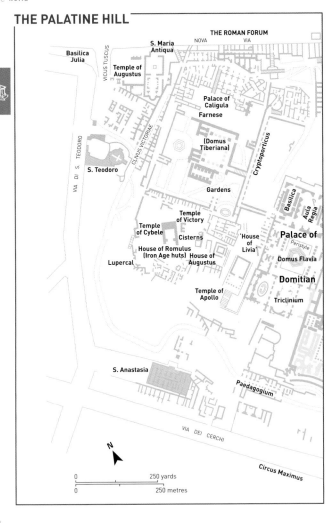

THE ROMAN FORUM

NOVA VIA

Basilica Julia

S. Maria Antiqua

VICUS TUSCUS

Temple of Augustus

Palace of Caligula

Farnese

CLIVUS VICTORIAE

(Domus Tiberiana)

VIA DI S. TEODORO

S. Teodoro

Cryptoporticus

Gardens

Basilica

Aula Regia

Temple of Victory

Temple of Cybele

Cisterns

'House of Livia'

Palace of

Peristyle

House of Romulus (Iron Age huts)

House of Augustus

Domus Flavia

Lupercal

Domitian

Temple of Apollo

Triclinium

S. Anastasia

Paedagogium

VIA DEI CERCHI

N

Circus Maximus

0   250 yards

0   250 metres

THE PALATINE HILL

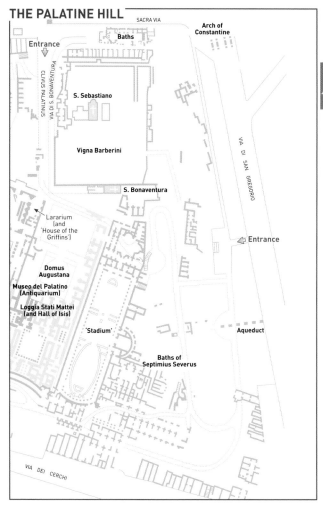

SACRA VIA

Arch of
Constantine

Entrance

Baths

CLIVUS PALATINUS

VIA DI S. BONAVENTURA

S. Sebastiano

Vigna Barberini

VIA DI SAN GREGORIO

S. Bonaventura

Lararium
(and
'House of the
Griffins')

Entrance

Domus
Augustana

Museo del Palatino
(Antiquarium)

Loggia Stati Mattei
(and Hall of Isis)

'Stadium'

Aqueduct

Baths of
Septimius Severus

VIA DEI CERCHI

families built their castles over the ruins, and in the 16c the Farnese laid out a villa with beautiful gardens.

THE SITE

The site is entered from the Nova Via, a street lined with shops which runs parallel to the Via Sacra. Steps lead up to the **Farnese Gardens** (Orti Farnesiani), laid out in the middle of the 16c for Cardinal Alessandro Farnese, nephew of Pope Paul III. They were designed by Vignola and completed by Girolamo Rainaldi and are arranged on a series of terraces.

DOMUS TIBERIANA The gardens at the top cover the site of the so-called Domus Tiberiana. This palace was built by the successors of Augustus on top of late Republican houses and later incorporated into Nero's Domus Aurea. It was subsequently modified by Domitian, who built a ramp on four levels to connect it with the Forum.

TEMPLES OF CYBELE AND VICTORY Pathways lead to the western end of the gardens where steps (presently closed) descend to the ruins of the **Temple of Cybele**, goddess of fertility and mother of the gods. The temple was built between 204 and 191 BC and was reconstructed after fires in 111 BC and AD 3.

HOUSE OF AUGUSTUS The House of Augustus is closed for restoration. It consisted of late Republican houses, including that of the wealthy orator Hortensius (the rival of Cicero who also lived on the Palatine), which were purchased by Augustus around 30 BC and adapted as his residence. Some of the rooms have refined wall-paintings, mosaic floors and stucco vaults; these date from 25 BC–AD 25.

TEMPLE OF APOLLO Beyond the House of Augustus you can see the basement of the Temple of Apollo, erected by Augustus in 36 BC and dedicated in 28 BC. The temple was surrounded by a portico and linked to the house by a corridor.

HOUSE OF LIVIA To the north is the House of Livia, wife of Augustus. It is decorated with wall-paintings in the Second Pompeian style (late 1c BC), with imitation marbles, figures and mythological subjects. It can only be visited by special appointment, *T* 06 3996 7700.

The Palatine Hill The Stadium

PALACE OF DOMITIAN The various buildings of this vast palace were planned in AD 81-96 by the architect Rabirius who levelled the centre of the hill and demolished or covered a number of earlier constructions.

The entrance to the complex was from the north, by a monumental staircase that linked it to the Forum. To the southwest was the official part of the complex, the so-called **Domus Flavia**, praised in antiquity for its splendour and structured around a central courtyard framed by a portico (peristilium). In the middle is a fountain in the form of an octagonal maze. To the north are the ruins of three large halls, the one in the centre being the **Aula Regia**, or throne room, used for public audiences and ceremonies and originally decorated with 16 marble columns and 12 black basalt statues. Adjacent to it, to the west, is the **Basilica**, where the emperor held administrative councils. To the east is the so-called **Lararium**, from the Lares, or household gods. This may have been the guard-room of the praetorians, the soldiers who protected the emperor.

HOUSE OF THE GRIFFINS Beneath the Lararium is the House of the Griffins (open by appointment, *T* 06 3996 7700), named after two griffins in stucco which decorate one of the rooms. It dates from the end of the 2c BC and is the oldest Republican building discovered on the Palatine. The house was built on two levels using the natural slope of the hill and was decorated with precious mosaics and wall paintings in the Second Pompeian style (late 1c BC) representing columns and walls of coloured marble in a false perspective. The fact that it lay buried beneath Domitian's palace helped to preserve the astonishing brightness of the paintings.

AULA ISIACA Another Republican structure was discovered below the Basilica, the so-called Hall of Isis (Aula Isiaca). This was decorated with Second Pompeian style frescoes of fantastical architecture and scenes of the cult of Isis, which were painted just before an edict in 21 BC banned the worship of the Egyptian goddess. The frescoes have been moved to a room that is visible from the Loggia Stati-Mattei (see p 31).

TRICLINIUM This banqueting hall stands to the south of the Domus Flavia. It was paved with coloured marbles and had an ingenious system of floor heating. On either side was a court with an oval fountain - the one to the west has a fine pavement belonging to the earlier Domus Transitoria of Nero (AD 54). The pavilion here, with a double loggia and decorations attributed to the Zuccari, was built in the 16c for the Farnese. A staircase (presently closed) leads down from the Triclinium to a **nymphaeum** which was also part of Nero's first palace. The 1c AD frescoes are now exhibited in the Palatine Museum. They are among the first examples of the Fourth Pompeian style in Rome.

DOMUS AUGUSTANA Adjoining the Domus Flavia is the so-called Domus Augustana, the private section of Domitian's palace, which was built on two levels against the slope of the hill. On the upper level are the remains of a peristyle (a court surrounded by a columned portico), with a water basin in the centre and a small temple of Minerva that was reached by a bridge.

CIRCUS MAXIMUS The southern end of the Domus Augustana overlooks the Circus Maximus, which was probably built in the early 4c BC, although it was subsequently restored and enlarged several times. By the 3c AD it could hold more than 350,000 spectators. The chariots raced seven times around the *spina*, a low wall placed in the centre of the oblong and terminating at either end with a *meta*, a conical pillar marking the turnings of the course. The spina was decorated by two Egyptian obelisks now in Piazza del Popolo and Piazza del Laterano, placed there respectively by Augustus (at the end of the 1c BC) and Constans II (AD 357).

MUSEO PALATINO The Palatine Museum houses finds from excavations on the hill including materials from the earliest settlements as well as sculptures, frescoes, marble and stucco decorations from Republican and Imperial buildings.

Close to the museum is the **Loggia Stati-Mattei**. Built in 1520 on the ruins of the Domus Augustana, it was decorated with grotesques and the Signs of the Zodiac by the circle of Peruzzi. The impressive frescoes of the Aula Isiaca are visible from the loggia. Ask for admission at the museum.

STADIUM The eastern part of the Palace of Domitian is at a much lower level than the rest and has the so-called stadium, a 160m-long garden with a series of rooms at the north end and a curved wall at the south, once surrounded by a two-storeyed portico. It may have been used for athletic contests and horse riding. In the middle of the east wall is a high recess (exedra) from where the emperor watched the races.

DOMUS SEVERIANA AND SEPTIZODIUM East of the stadium was the Domus Severiana, a monumental wing which Septimius Severus (AD 193-211) annexed to the Imperial palace. It extended beyond the edges of the hill and was supported by enormous arches. In the southeastern corner is the site of the Septizodium, a much admired three-storeyed nymphaeum, built in AD 203 and demolished by Sixtus V who used its marble for the construction of his chapel in Santa Maria Maggiore.

You can find your way out of the Palatine via the exit on Via di San Gregorio (to the east), or by returning to the Arch of Titus in the Forum.

The Colosseum

OPEN	Daily, 9.00 to one hour before sunset
CLOSED	1/1, 25/12
CHARGES	Combined ticket with the Palatine: €10; reduced €4
TELEPHONE	**06 700 4261** or **06 700 5469**
METRO/BUS	Metro Line B to Colosseo. Buses 85, 87, 175, 186

The Colosseum has for centuries been the symbol of Rome. It was illustrated in the first city maps and mentioned in the earliest guidebooks, its popular name referring to a colossal bronze statue of Nero which stood nearby.

The Flavian Amphiteatre (as it is more appropriately called after the family name of the emperors who built it) was begun by Vespasian in AD 70 on the site of an artificial lake that was part of Nero's Domus Aurea. The Colosseum was completed by Titus in AD 80 and inaugurated with 100 days of gladiatorial games during which 5000 beasts were killed. Domitian, brother of Titus, built the structures beneath the arena, and Alexander Severus (222-235) restored it after a fire.

The Colosseum is the largest amphitheatre ever built in the Roman world. It measures 545m in circumference (the ellipse is 189m long, 156m wide and nearly 50m high) and held more than 50,000 spectators.

During the Middle Ages it fell into disuse and was heavily damaged by fires and earthquakes. It became a source of building material - the Palazzi Venezia, Cancelleria, Barberini and St Peter's all benefited from its marble. More than two thirds of the original masonry had been removed when in 1749 Benedict XIV dedicated the amphitheatre to the Passion of Jesus and the memory of the martyrs.

The outer wall and load-bearing pillars of the Colosseum are built of travertine, while brick-faced concrete and tufa were used for the interior. The holes that you see on the outside once held iron clamps which were melted down in the Middle Ages. The four storeys are articulated by engaged columns of the three orders:

Tuscan Doric below, Ionic in the middle and Corinthian at the top, forming a decorative scheme that inspired a number of Renaissance architects from Raphael onwards. Statues originally decorated the arches of the second and third register. The corbels projecting from the topmost storey supported 240 wooden poles which held in place a giant awning. This was pulled into position by a system of cords, operated by the sailors of the fleet of Cape Misenus. The 80 arches on the ground floor were numbered and served as entrances for the spectators. The corridors beyond gave access to the staircases and the seats of the cavea. The entrance on the northeast, which was wider than the others, opened into a hall decorated with stuccoes and was reserved for the emperor.

The Colosseum

The arena inside, where the combats took place, has been partially reconstructed. Beneath are underground passages and substructures for cages of animals and scenery which were hoisted up through openings in the floor. Beyond the arena was the podium, a broad terrace reserved for the emperor, the senators and the vestals. The vast cavea, with seats now missing, was divided into three tiers which were separated by landings and reached by staircases. In the lowest tier sat the knights, in the middle the Roman citizens, and at the top, on wooden steps, women and slaves.

East of the Colosseum are the ruins of the Ludus Magnus, a training school for gladiators.

THE ARCH OF CONSTANTINE

The tripartite arch commemorates Constantine's victory over Maxentius in the battle on the Milvian bridge (AD 312). It is decorated mainly with reliefs and sculptures taken from earlier monuments. The large reliefs decorating the top of the short sides

Arch of Constantine

and the central archway, as well as the figures of captive Dacians, come from the Forum of Trajan (p 36). The eight large medallions of the two façades belong to the time of Hadrian and illustrate hunting scenes and sacrifices. The eight rectangular high-reliefs of the upper level were taken from a monument to Marcus Aurelius. The narrow friezes surrounding the arch, the two roundels with the personifications of the sun and the moon on the short sides, the spandrel figures as well as the victories and captives at the base of the columns were all carried out at the time of Constantine and are considered to be of lesser quality.

The Imperial Fora

Along the north side of Via dei Fori Imperiali (the road laid out by Mussolini in 1933 to stage military parades) is the impressive series of fora built by the emperors Augustus, Vespasian, Nerva and Trajan to celebrate their victories and mythical ancestors.

FORUM OF CAESAR The first to build a forum with a temple celebrating his own ancestry was Julius Caesar. He erected a temple to Venus Genetrix, mother of Aeneas from whom his family (the Julii) claimed to descend. Only a third of the original forum, which was completed by Augustus, is visible today.

FORUM OF AUGUSTUS The Forum of Augustus centred around the **Temple of Mars Ultor**, the 'Avenger', and commemorated the battle of Philippi (42 BC) where Caesar's assassins, Cassius and Brutus, were defeated. In the cella (sanctuary) were statues of

IMPERIAL FORA

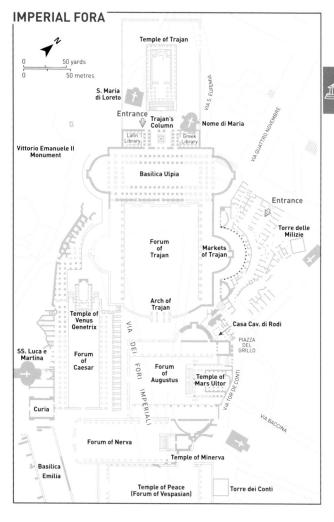

0 — 50 yards
0 — 50 metres

Temple of Trajan

VIA S. EUFEMIA

S. Maria di Loreto

VIA QUATTRO NOVEMBRE

Entrance
Trajan's Column
Nome di Maria

Latin Library
Greek Library

Vittorio Emanuele II Monument

Basilica Ulpia

Entrance

Torre delle Milizie

Forum of Trajan

Markets of Trajan

Arch of Trajan

Casa Cav. di Rodi

PIAZZA DEL GRILLO

Temple of Venus Genetrix

VIA DEI FORI IMPERIALI

SS. Luca e Martina

Forum of Caesar

Forum of Augustus

Temple of Mars Ultor

VIA TOR DE CONTI

Curia

VIA BACCINA

Forum of Nerva

Temple of Minerva

Basilica Emilia

Temple of Peace (Forum of Vespasian)

Torre dei Conti

Venus, Mars and the deified Julius Caesar. The colonnaded porticoes at the sides of the forum ended with large exedrae (semicircular recesses) and were decorated with statues of Roman heroes including Aeneas and Romulus, the legendary ancestors of Caesar and Augustus. A colossal image of Augustus, of which only the podium survives, once stood in a room in the left portico. The grey peperino wall behind the temple separated the Forum from the Subura, the poorest district of the city.

FORUM OF NERVA There are only scant remains of this forum which lies buried beneath the modern roads. Begun by Domitian, it was completed in AD 97 by his successor, Nerva. What survives is the massive basement of the **Temple of Minerva** which was torn down at the beginning of the 17c. Two giant Corinthian columns (the so-called Colonnacce) belonged to the portico surrounding the central square. They are decorated with a splendid frieze of Minerva and Arachne.

FORUM OF VESPASIAN Further east was the Forum of Vespasian, also called Forum of Peace since it celebrated the end of the civil wars which ensued after the death of Nero (AD 68). It exhibited the treasures of the Temple of Jerusalem (spoils from the Judaean War) and numerous statues taken from Nero's Golden House. Described by Pliny as the most magnificent edifice in Rome, it was destroyed by fire in AD 192 and reconstructed by Septimius Severus (193-211). Today very little survives. The hall to the south, across Via dei Fori Imperiali, was transformed into the 6c church of Santi Cosma e Damiano and decorated with superb mosaics.

FORUM OF TRAJAN Closer to Piazza Venezia is the Forum of Trajan, the last and grandest of the Imperial fora, built between 107 and 113 by the architect Apollodorus of Damascus to celebrate the emperor's victories. It was entered from the east by a triumphal arch and had an equestrian statue in the centre. To the west was the **Basilica Ulpia** (from Trajan's family name Ulpius) and two libraries, respectively for Latin and for Greek texts, with Trajan's Column in between. The complex ended with a temple erected by Hadrian in honour of his deceased and deified predecessor. The site is now covered by the churches of Santa Maria di Loreto (by Giuliano da Sangallo, 1534) and the Santo Nome di Maria (by Antoine Dérizet, 1738).

Forum of Trajan

A masterpiece of Roman art, **Trajan's Column** commemorates the emperor's conquest of Dacia (modern day Romania). The marble shaft, 30m high, is entirely covered by a spiral frieze, 200m long, that narrates the various episodes of Trajan's campaigns (AD 101-102 and 105-106). The carving was roughed out on the ground and finished on site by an unknown master who completed the entire work within four years. The extraordinarily skilful work pays particular attention to naturalistic detail and foreshortening. It is known that the ashes of the Emperor (d. AD 117) and his wife Plotina were kept in the base. Inside the shaft, a staircase climbs to the top where the original statue of the Emperor was replaced in 1587 by that of St Peter.

MARKETS OF TRAJAN To the north of the forum is the arcaded brick hemicycle of the Markets of Trajan, a complex of 150 shops arranged on different levels on the slopes of the Quirinal Hill. The entrance is in Via Quattro Novembre (open Tues-Sun 9.00-1hr before sunset). Steps descend to the Via Biberatica, running past the shops overlooking the Forum and named after the taverns and bars once lining the street. Behind the markets is the Torre delle Milizie, a massive tower erected in the 13c as a defensive stronghold against the Colonna family whose residence was just opposite (p 87).

on route

The Domus Aurea Above Via Labicana, at the northeast corner of the Colosseum, Viale Domus Aurea leads to the underground remains of Nero's Golden House. This was built after AD 64 and encompassed the Palatine, Celian, and part of the Esquiline hills. The various wings were connected through corridors and terraces overlooking an artificial lake and splendid gardens. After his death in AD 68 Nero's successors quickly demolished or built over the enormous edifice.

The section that survives was discovered by chance in the 1490s. The fine stuccoes and wall paintings found underground became famous and were extensively copied during the Renaissance. They introduced the Fourth Pompeian style, heavily criticized by Vitruvius for its daintiness. 9.00-19.45, closed Tues, 1/1, 25/12. Booking essential, *T* 06 3996 7700.

Palazzo Venezia, Piazza Venezia. The first grand palace of Renaissance Rome was built (with stone from the Colosseum) in 1455 for the Venetian cardinal Pietro Barbo and enlarged when he became Pope Paul II (1464-71). The building now houses the Museo di Palazzo Venezia exhibiting decorative arts including medieval ivories, ceramics and porcelain, silver, paintings, wood sculptures, bronzes and terracotta models by Bernini and Algardi. Tues-Sun 9.00-19.00.

San Clemente, Via di San Giovanni in Laterano, east of the Colosseum. One of the most interesting medieval basilicas, it consists of two churches, one above the other. The 4c church was destroyed by fire in the Sack of Rome in 1084. The new building was erected in the early 12c by Paschal II. The magnificent **apse** mosaic of the *Triumph of the Cross* dates from this period. The **Chapel of St Catherine**, in the left aisle, contains important frescoes (the *Lives of St Catherine* and *St Ambrose*), painted in 1428-31 by Masolino da Panicale and, possibly, Masaccio.

Steps descend from the Sacristy to the **lower church** with frescoes of the 9c and 11c. 9.00-12.30 and 15.00-18.00, Sun 10.00-12.30 and 15.00-18.00. Further down are also a 3c mithraeum and the remains of a 2c Roman house.

Santa Maria in Aracoeli, Piazza del Campidoglio. The church stands on the site of the Arx, or Roman citadel, where, according to medieval tradition, the Tiburtine Sibyl foretold the coming of Christ to Augustus. Built in the 7c as a Greek foundation, it was rebuilt by the Franciscans in Romanesque style in 1285-7. The interior is divided by 22 columns taken from Roman buildings and contains important funerary monuments of the early 14c to 15c. The first chapel in the right aisle has magnificent frescoes of the *Life of St Bernardino* by Pinturicchio, c 1486. Daily 7.00-18.00.

Santa Maria in Cosmedin, Piazza della Bocca della Verità. Founded as a chapel in the 3c, it was rebuilt as a basilica in the late 8c and assigned to Greek refugees escaping iconoclastic persecution. 'Cosmedin' comes from the Greek term '*kosmidion*' (jewel) which described the beauty of its decorations. The Cosmati family (12c) produced the fine schola cantorum (an enclosure for choristers), pavement and episcopal throne. Beneath the portico, to the left, is the famous **Bocca della Verità** (mouth of truth), believed to close on the hands of perjurers, but actually just the top of an ancient drain. Daily 10.00-13.00 and 14.30-18.30.

San Pietro in Vincoli, on the Esquiline Hill. The basilica (reached by a flight of steps from Via Cavour) was built in 442 by Eudoxia, wife of Valentinian III, and is named after the chains with which St Peter is said to have been bound while imprisoned in the Carcer Tullianum (p 18). At the end of the right aisle is the *Tomb of Julius II*, a much smaller and incomplete version of the huge monument commissioned from **Michelangelo** in 1513, which was originally planned to have some 40 statues. All that is left by Michelangelo's hand are the majestic figure of *Moses*, and the statues of *Leah* and *Rachel*, finished by Raffaello di Montelupo. Daily 7.00-12.30 and 15.30-18.00.

Michelangelo *Moses* (San Pietro in Vincoli)

Teatro di Marcello At the western foot of the Capitoline Hill, along Via del Teatro Marcello, are the remains of the theatre begun by Julius Caesar and dedicated by Augustus (13 BC) to the memory of his nephew Marcellus.

Just beyond lies the **Ghetto**, one of the most characteristic quarters of Rome, still preserving its popular traditions and cuisine. It was created in 1556 when Paul IV issued a decree segregating the Jews of the city. Quiet piazzas and cooling fountains, fine 16c-17c palaces and churches, delicious restaurants and patisseries add to its unspoilt charm.

Il Vittoriano The incongruous white monument overlooking Piazza Venezia celebrates the achievement of Italian unity under King Victor Emmanuel II in 1870. Begun in 1885 by Giuseppe Sacconi, it was finally completed in 1935. Popularly called the 'wedding cake' or 'the typewriter', its construction entailed the destruction of an entire Renaissance district. The fine interior was decorated by Armando Brasini (1924-35) and houses the Museo del Risorgimento illustrating the history of Italy's independence. Tues-Sun 10.00-18.00.

FURTHER UPHILL

Museo Nazionale Romano The main section of the museum of Classical sculpture is housed in Palazzo Massimo near the central station. On the second floor are superb wall-paintings, stuccoes and mosaics. You must book to see the frescoes (**T** 06 4890 3500). 9.00-19.45, closed Mon. Important sculptures are exhibited in the Octagonal Hall of the **Baths of Diocletian** (9.00-13.00 except Mon).

San Giovanni in Laterano, Piazza San Giovanni in Laterano, southeast of the Colosseum. The Cathedral of Rome, bishop see of the Pope, was built in 314-318 on the property of the Laterani family and given to the popes by Constantine. The basilica owes its present interior to Francesco Borromini who reconstructed the nave and four side aisles in 1646-9 and 1656-7.

The fine **cloister**, entered from the left aisle, is a masterpiece of Cosmatesque art by Jacopo and Pietro Vassalletto (1215-32). Behind the apse, and entered from Piazza San Giovanni, is the octagonal **baptistery**, remodelled in the 5c-7c and again in 1657 by Borromini. Fine Byzantine mosaics decorate the chapels of San Giovanni Evangelista and San Venanzio.

Off Piazza San Giovanni, incorporated into a building by Domenico Fontana, are the remains of the old Lateran palace, the residence of the popes until their move to Avignon in 1305.

The basilica is open daily in summer, 7.00-18.00 and 7.00-19.00. The baptistery is open Sun-Wed 9.00-13.00 and 17.00-19.00 (16.00-18.00 in winter) and Fri-Sat 9.00-13.00.

Santa Maria Maggiore, near the central station. Founded by Pope Liberius (352-366) on the site of a miraculous snowfall, it was rebuilt in the mid 5c. Nicholas IV (1288-92) was reponsible for the apse, transepts, and the façade decorated with mosaics signed by Filippo Rusuti. The late Baroque entrance portico was added by Ferdinando Fuga in 1741-3.

Inside are important 5c **mosaics** from the time of Sixtus III, including 36 Old Testament scenes in the nave and the Life of Christ over the triumphal arch. The Cosmatesque pavement dates from c 1150. The apse mosaic of the *Coronation of the Virgin* by Jacopo Torriti (1295) was inspired by the one in Santa Maria in Trastevere (c 1140). The Cappella Sistina, at the of the right aisle, was built by Domenico Fontana for Sixtus V (1587), and frescoed by late 16c Mannerists. The Cappella Borghese, opposite, was erected by Flaminio Ponzio for Paul V (1611) and decorated by early Baroque artists including Guido Reni. Daily 7.00-18.00 or 19.00.

Santa Prassede, near Santa Maria Maggiore. This small church was built by St Paschal I (817-24) on the site of a 2c oratory. It was restored in the 15c and 16c (the trompe l'oeil frescoes in the nave date from that time) and again in the 19c. The apse and triumphal arch are decorated with fine 9c mosaics. The **Chapel of St Zeno**, in the right aisle, was built by Paschal I as a mausoleum for his mother Theodora and decorated with magnificent mosaics. Daily 7.30-12.00 and 16.00-18.30.

commercial galleries

Autori Cambi, Via San Martino ai Monti 21a (Santa Maria Maggiore), *T* 06 4782 4613. The owner, Matteo Boetti, is the son of the artist Alighiero Boetti. Open 11.30-19.30.

Galleria Valentina Bonomo, Via del Portico d'Ottavia 13 (Ghetto), *T* 06 683 2766, www.galleriabonomo.com. Among the artists who have exhibited here are the Austrian Franz West, Enzo Cucchi, and L. Moro.

Sala 1, Piazza di Porta San Giovanni 10, *T* 06 700 8691, www.salauno.com. Housed in the crypt of an unfinished church of the 1940s, this gallery represents international avant-garde artists. Recent exhibitions have included the work of 12 women artists from Iran, as well as a beautiful photographic exhibition on monasteries.

eating and drinking

Since this area covers mainly archaeological sites, shopping is fairly limited. However, there are a number of good stores, restaurants, wine bars, etc, in the Ghetto (at the foot of the Capitoline Hill) and in the districts northeast and south of the Forum. The Ghetto, a maze of narrow streets and tiny squares, can be reached via buses running to Piazza Venezia (nos 30, 40, 60, 62, 64, 81, 117, 119, 186, 492) or on foot from Campo de' Fiori and Largo Argentina. The Rione Monti, adjoining the Forum to the northeast, is a favourite with students and young people.

The Celio (or Caelian Hill), south of the Colosseum, has a few restaurants for a well deserved break after intensive archaeology sessions. Besides walking, you can get there on metro Line B (Colosseo) or any bus running along Via dei Fori Imperiali (nos 60, 85, 87,117, 175, 186, 810 etc). Avoid the bars facing the Colosseum where the food is bad and the prices high.

AT THE MUSEUMS

Caffè del Vittoriano, *T* 06 678 0905. A terrace at the back of the Victor Emmanuel monument has been turned into a good café-bistro with a stunning view over the Fora. Entrance from the Museo del Risorgimento or Piazza dell'Ara Coeli (from the loggia behind the church by the same name).

Caffè Capitolino, *T* 06 678 8821. On the roof terrace of Palazzo Caffarelli is the cafeteria of the Capitoline Museums. Go there for the view rather than their dry sandwiches and limp salads. Entrance from Palazzo dei Conservatori or Piazza Caffarelli 4.

RESTAURANTS

€   **Divinare**, Via Ostilia 4 (Celio), *T* 06 709 6381; 9.00-22.00, closed Sunday. A deli with tables where you can sip wine and taste cold meats, cheeses, smoked seafood and more.

Le Naumachìe, Via Celimontana (Celio); open until late. An informal place serving huge portions of pasta. Small but with outdoor seating in summer.

Pane Vino e San Daniele, Piazza Mattei 16 (Ghetto), *T* 06 687 7147. The name is a lunch menu (bread, wine and prosciutto San Daniele). Great ambience in one of the most beautiful piazze of the Ghetto.

Sora Margherita, Piazza delle Cinque Scole 30 (Ghetto), *T* 06 687 4216; closed Monday and August. A typical Roman *trattoria*. Home cooking *alla romana* with generous portions of freshly made pasta.

€€ **Ai Tre Scalini**, Via dei SS. Quattro 30 (Celio), *T* 06 709 6309; closed Sunday and August. A small but comfortable place with a tasty and inventive cuisine.

F.I.S.H., Via dei Serpenti 16 (Monti), *T* 06 4782 4962; evenings only; closed Monday and August. The Fine International Seafood House is a high-tech fish bar with four menus: Japanese, Oriental, Mediterranean and Oceanian.

Il Sanpietrino, Piazza Costaguti 15 (Ghetto), *T* 06 6880 6471; evenings only; closed Sunday, 1-8 January and 10-31 August. Seasonal foods and Roman specialities.

La Taverna degli Amici, Piazza Margana 36-37 (Ghetto), *T* 06 6992 0637. Traditional Roman cuisine in a charming square (tables outside).

La Taverna del Ghetto, Via del Portico d'Ottavia 7b (Ghetto), *T* 06 6880 9771; closed Friday evening and Saturday lunch; open in August. One of the best addresses for Kosher cuisine. Tables outside.

La Taverna dei Quaranta, Via Claudia (Celio), in the Colosseum vicinity. Tables outside in summer.

Monti, Via di San Vito 13a (Santa Maria Maggiore), *T* 06 446 6573; closed Sunday evening and Monday. A long established restaurant with delicious regional specialities from the Marche.

Olivella e Mariarosa, Via del Boschetto 73 (Monti), *T* 06 486 781; closed Sunday. Charming setting (including a terrace) and good food.

€€€ **Agata e Romeo**, Via Carlo Alberto 45 (Santa Maria Maggiore), *T* 06 446 6115; closed Sunday. Comfortable ambience and high quality cooking. Try their *millefoglie* for dessert.

Crab, Via Capo d'Africa 2 (Celio), *T* 06 7720 3636; closed Sunday evening and Monday. As the name suggests, everything here (except dessert) has to do with seafood.

Hasekura, Via dei Serpenti 27 (Monti), *T* 06 483 648. Excellent Japanese food with set menus around €30. Prices much higher when ordering à la carte.

Kisso, Via Firenze 30 (Teatro dell'Opera), *T* 06 4782 4677; closed Sunday. A Japanese restaurant on two floors, with a bargain menu for a kaiten sushi over lunch. Booking essential.

Sora Lella, Via di Ponte Quattro Capi 16 (Isola Tiberina), *T* 06 686 1601; closed Sunday and August. Very good traditional cuisine.

COFFEE BARS

Antico Caffè del Brasile, Via dei Serpenti 22, *T* 06 488 2319. Established in 1908, this store sells freshly roasted coffee in various blends including 'the Pope's', which Wojtyla would buy here in his student days in Rome. Espresso and cappuccinos at the counter.

Il Chiosco, in the Colle Oppio Park above the Domus Aurea. Sip your coffee under umbrella pines.

PATISSERIES

Dagnino, Via Vittorio Emanuele Orlando 75 (Galleria Esedra-Piazza della Repubblica), *T* 06 481 8660. Get a bus and come up here for a real Sicilian *cassata*, a ricotta-filled *cannolo* or some marzipan fruits, a delight for the eye and palate.

Il Forno del Ghetto, Via del Portico d'Ottavia 1, *T* 06 687 8637; closed Saturday. Traditional Roman Jewish pastries, from *torta di ricotta* (with choc-chip or sour cherries) to *mostaccioli* with candied and dried fruits and almond cookies. Expensive.

La Dolce Roma, Via del Portico d'Ottavia 20b (Ghetto), *T* 06 689 2196; closed Monday and Sunday afternoon. Austrian and American cakes including strudels, Sacher Torten, apple, cherry and pecan pies as well as chocolate chip or peanut butter cookies. Expensive.

PIZZA (TAKE AWAY)

Nadia e Davide, Via Milano 33 (Monti), *T* 06 488 2842. A tiny place with good pizza, *supplì* (deep fried rice balls), etc.

Florida, Via Florida 25 (Largo Argentina), *T* 06 6880 3236. Excellent pizza, from the classics with tomato and buffalo mozzarella to the most inventive combinations.

Zi' Fenizia, Via Santa Maria del Pianto 64 (Ghetto), *T* 06 689 6976. Try the pizza with artichokes.

WINE BARS

Al vino Al vino, Via dei Serpenti 19 (Monti), *T* 06 485 803; closed August. A pretty wine bar with good wine, charcuterie and cheeses, soups, soufflés and more.

Anacleto Bleve, Via Santa Maria del Pianto 9a-11 (Ghetto), *T* 06 686 5970; closed Sunday, Monday and August. Anacleto is a real institution here, serving tasty lunches and great wines.

Antica Locanda, Via del Boschetto 85 (Monti), *T* 06 4788 1729; open 23.00-2.00 except Monday. 500 wines and good appetizers.

Cavour 313, the name is also the address of this charming wine bar in Via Cavour (close to the Imperial Fora); closed Sunday and August. Good light food for lunch and dinner.

Trimani, Via Cernaia 37b (Baths of Diocletian), *T* 06 446 9630; closed Sunday and 10-24 August. Run by the oldest wine merchants in Rome (their shop is next door), it also offers good food.

LATE-NIGHT BARS

BarTaruga, Piazza Mattei 7 (Ghetto), *T* 06 689 2299; open 15.00-2.00. Artists, intellectuals and show biz people meet in this fine cocktail bar with Venetian-style furnishings.

Too.Bar, Largo Angelicum 7 (Salita del Grillo, Monti); open 23.00-3.00. A club specializing in African and Black music and live concerts.

Vicolo de'Musici, Via Madonna dei Monti 28, *T* 06 678 6188; open 21.00-2.00; closed Monday and Tuesday. A small pub with live music by traditional Italian artists. Cabaret on Wednesdays. Home cooking from 19.00.

Villa Celimontana Jazz, Piazza della Navicella (Celio). *T* 06 589 7807. Set in the fine park of Villa Celimontana, this is one of the events you shouldn't miss if you're in Rome during the summer: live concerts (jazz, fusion, ethnic) every night from mid-June to September.

shopping

Trendy boutiques are in Via del Boschetto, Via dei Serpenti, and Via degli Zingari. These are best reached on foot from the Imperial Fora. Alternatively take metro line B to Cavour or any bus running to Via Cavour (nos 84, 75) and Via Nazionale (nos 40, 60, 64, 70), the two large 19c roads that enclose the district.

BOOKS

Appunti di Viaggio, Via Urbana 130 (Monti), **T** 06 4782 5030. Art, narrative, essays, spirituality, etc.

Ellediemme, Via Baccina 30 (Monti), **T** 06 678 9567. The name stands for 'Libri dal mondo', literally 'Books from the world'.

Itinerando, Via Madonna dei Monti 97, **T** 06 6992 3533. Art, architecture, archaeology, history and books on Rome.

Mel Bookstore, Via Nazionale 254 (Piazza della Repubblica), **T** 06 488 5405; open Sunday. A well-stocked bookshop with an international section.

Libri necessari, Via Madonna dei Monti 112, **T** 06 678 6385. New and secondhand books. Michelle, the owner, also organizes readings of international poetry.

Voland, Via del Boschetto 129. An independent publisher and bookshop specializing in literature from Eastern Europe and, recently, Latin America.

CHOCOLATE

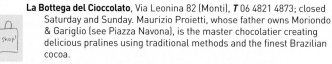

La Bottega del Cioccolato, Via Leonina 82 (Monti), **T** 06 4821 4873; closed Saturday and Sunday. Maurizio Proietti, whose father owns Moriondo & Gariglio (see Piazza Navona), is the master chocolatier creating delicious pralines using traditional methods and the finest Brazilian cocoa.

CLOTHES

La Brebis Noire, Via del Boschetto 1d (Monti), **T** 06 482 0357. A wizard at the loom, Florence Quellien, owner of this small shop, produces wonderful fabrics for clothes or home furnishings.

De Grillis, Via Campo Carleo 26 (Piazza del Grillo, Monti). Wonderful clothes.

François Boutique, Via del Boschetto (Monti). Look out for this lovely shop run by three guys named Francesco: one designs the clothes, the second sells them, the third organizes his companions.

Le Gallinelle, Via del Boschetto 76 (Monti), **T** 06 488 1017. Designs by the owners (for men and women); they also hire and sell period clothes.

Kaja, Via degli Zingari 62 (at the corner with Via del Boschetto). 'Hecho a mano en Buenos Aires' is the logo of this shop selling handmade clothes from Argentina.

LOL – Spazio in Metamorfosi, Piazza degli Zingari 11 (Monti), *T* 06 481 4160. Fashion meets art and design in this unique place that holds a weekly art exhibition.

Via degli Zingari 10, *T* 06 4782 3889. The name is also the address of this store selling shoes and clothes by fashion houses and lesser-known designers.

FLOWERS

Pastore & T Jader, Via Madonna dei Monti 62a, *T* 06 4782 2332. Two uncommon girls, like the shop they run, create unusual flower compositions, bouquets, natural furnishings and objects for the home.

FOOD

Delizie di Calabria, Via Baccina 63 (Monti), *T* 06 678 2499. The name says it all: delicious specialities from Calabria (truffles, dried porcini, savoury olive oil preserves with sun-dried tomatoes, chilli peppers, etc).

Il Giardino del Tè, Via del Boschetto 107 (Monti), *T* 06 474 6888. An infinite variety of teas, herbal infusions, sugar sticks, candies and aromatic coffees.

La Tana dei Golosi, Via San Giovanni in Laterano 220 (Celio), *T* 06 7720 3202; open 15.00-24.00 except Sunday. Gourmet specialities including preserves (sweet and savoury), olive oils, wines, etc. Inside are tables where you can taste it all: they offer thematic menus concentrating on regional cuisines or seasonal products.

Panella, Via Merulana 54 (Santa Maria Maggiore), *T* 06 487 2435. A little outside the area but an amazing bakery with over 100 types of bread. Aperitifs on Sunday morning.

HOMES

Fausto Barberini, Piazza Margana 40 (Ghetto), *T* 06 6788 8002. Beyond a signless door is the workshop of this glass specialist and restorer.

La Vetrata, Via del Boschetto 94, *T* 06 474 7022. A laboratory and shop producing all sorts of glass objects from rings and necklaces to vases and larger items.

Via del Boschetto 12 Roberto's handmade glass shop has no sign, but he sells lovely objects that make fine gifts or collectables.

Yaky, Via Santa Maria del Pianto 55 (Ghetto), *T* 06 6880 7724; open
Sunday. Antique furniture and objects from China (early 1900s),
Japan, Mongolia and Tibet. Reproductions available too. Their other
outlet is at Via Silla 32-34, *T* 06 360 04525.

JEWELLERY

Agau, Via dei Serpenti 25, *T* 06 488 2067. Jewels in silver and fine stones.

Fabio Piccioni, Via del Boschetto 148, *T* 06 474 1697. An artisan's
bijouterie.

MUSIC

Lo Spartito, Via Cavour 135. No records but instruments and sheet
music.

Metropoli Rock, Via Cavour 72, *T* 06 488 0934. For vinyl lovers, 300,000
albums. New and secondhand CDs.

Nuova Rinascita Musica e Film, Via Botteghe Oscure 4 (Piazza Venezia),
T 06 678 1777. Part of a bookshop selling CDs of various genres.

ORGANIC

L'Albero del Pane, Via Santa Maria del Pianto 19 (Ghetto), *T* 06 686 5016.
Bread, cheeses, pasta, cosmetics, stationery and books.

Bio Dispensa, Via Santa Maria Maggiore 118, *T* 06 482 7958. Organic food
and vitamins.

SHOES

Santini Yesterday's, Via Cavour 106, *T* 06 488 0934. A good place to find
bargain shoes (for men and women) from past (or last season's)
collections. Bags and suitcases are on sale, too.

WINE

Trimani, Via Goito 20 (Termini station), *T* 06 446 9661. The oldest wine
store in the city also has one of the biggest selections as well as
wine accessories (glasses, decanters, bottle openers, etc), specialist
books and magazines.

NAVONA
PANTHEON

Piazza Navona

The piazza's elliptical shape and impressive dimensions derive from the underlying Stadium of Domitian of AD 86, which could hold some 30,000 spectators. From the mid 13c houses and towers were built on top of its ruins, followed by palaces and churches in the 15c-17c.

The name of the piazza comes from the races, the *Agoni*, which were held here in antiquity. The term was gradually corrupted to *'in agone'*, *'nagone'* and *'navona'*. *Navona* suggests a large ship and has been mistakenly related to the practice in the 17c-19c of flooding the piazza on hot August weekends for the entertainment of the Romans and the parades of princes and prelates.

Bernini *Fontana dei Quattro Fiumi* (detail)

In the mid 17c, Innocent X Pamphilj ordered the construction of a large palace (Palazzo Pamphilj) and the transformation of the piazza. Although **Bernini** was recognized as one of the best sculptors in Rome, Innocent X was reluctant to employ him as he had been the favourite artist of his predecessor, Urban VIII. However, the pope could not resist Bernini's designs for the piazza, and the commission was given in 1648.

Three fountains decorate the piazza. The **Fontana del Moro**, at the south end, was planned by Giacomo della Porta in 1576 and altered by Bernini in 1653 - he designed the central figure of a Moor. The **Fontana del Nettuno**, to the north, was also designed by Giacomo della Porta, although its sculptures were added only in 1878.

In the centre is one of Bernini's masterpieces, the theatrical **Fontana dei Quattro Fiumi**. Like the Trevi fountain, it is fed by the Roman aqueduct, the Acqua Vergine (p 86). Four allegorical figures, updating antique images of river gods, represent the largest known rivers of the time: the Danube, the Ganges, the Nile (shown as a Moor), and the Rio de la Plata (depicted with his head covered as the river's origins were unknown). The obelisk was cut in Egypt and is inscribed with hieroglyphs which refer to the emperors Domitian, Vespasian and Titus. Innocent X moved it here from the Circus of Maxentius on the Via Appia. He added the dove at the top, emblem of the Pamphilj family.

Palazzo Altemps

OPEN	Tues–Sun 9.00-19.45
CLOSED	Mon; 1/1, 25/12
CHARGES	€5; €2.50 for18-25-year-olds; free for under 18s and over 65s
TELEPHONE	**06 683 3759**
MAIN ENTRANCE	Piazza Sant'Apollinare 44
BUS	Nos 70 Via Piazza Cavour to Termini, 81 Via Colosseum to Piazza Risorgimento, 87 and 186 Via Colosseum to Piazza Cavour, 492 Via Piazza Risorgimento and Piazza Venezia

The palace was bought in 1982 by the Italian state and restored to contain a section of the Museo Nazionale Romano devoted to the Ludovisi collection of Classical sculpture. This was begun in 1621-3 by Cardinal Ludovico Ludovisi, nephew of Gregory XV, to decorate his villa and garden near Porta Pinciana (Via Veneto). Many of the pieces were fragmentary and the cardinal employed Bernini and Algardi to restore them. The collection became famous among travellers and a fashion grew up of making copies and casts of the sculptures. Goethe owned a cast of the colossal head of Juno, while his friend Johann Joachim Winckelmann, the 18c historian of Classical art, studied the statues in detail.

The palace was begun in the 15c by Girolamo Riario and completed after 1568 by Cardinal Marco Sittico Altemps and his descendants. The courtyard is attributed to Antonio da Sangallo the Elder (1513-7) and Baldassarre Peruzzi.

HIGHLIGHTS

GROUND FLOOR

ATRIUM Statue of *Antoninus Pius* (AD 140-147) found in the 16c in the Mausoleum of Augustus and restored in 1621.

ROOM 5 Portrait busts, including a bronze head of *Marcus Aurelius*, frequently mentioned in the diaries of Grand Tour travellers and actually a 17c copy of the head of the equestrian statue of *Marcus Aurelius* in the Capitoline Museums. Also here is a 16c bust of *Julius Caesar*, and portraits of *Matidia* (c 120 AD), mother-in-law of the Emperor Hadrian, and *Giulia*, daughter of the Emperor Titus, whose hairstyle is typical of the Flavian era and dates the portrait to 80 AD.

ROOM 6 shows the remains of a medieval tower as well as 2c Roman wall paintings found here during excavations.

ROOMS 7-9 have Roman statues with extensive 17c additions, including two versions of *Apollo with the Lyre* and a copy after Praxiteles' *Venus of Cnidos* (360 BC).

ROOM 10 has a 1c copy of the colossal statue of *Athena* made by Phidias around 438 BC for the cella of the Parthenon, Athens. It is signed at the bottom with the name of Antiokos, the Athenian.

ROOMS 11 has 3c sarcophagi, one with the *Labours of Hercules* (the head in the centre is a portrait of the deceased), the other decorated with *Dionysiac scenes* (AD 190-220).

ROOM 14 has a colossal group representing *Dionysos, a Satyr and Panther* found in the 16c on the Quirinal Hill, on the site of the ancient Baths of Constantine. The *Satyr* and torso of *Dionysos* are mostly original and date to AD 160-180.

The exit leads into the northern portico displaying funerary reliefs and an impressive statue of a *Dacian Prisoner* in *giallo antico*. The black marble face and hands are later restorations.

The **Teatro Goldoni**, downstairs to the left, is one of the oldest in the city. It was rebuilt in 1575, restored in 1890, and housed one of the first cinemas of Rome in 1905.

FIRST FLOOR

LOGGIA Cross the courtyard and reach the loggia upstairs. The reliefs exhibited here were known in the 15c and were published by Winckelmann in 1767. At the end are two Greek *reliefs* of the 4c BC: one illustrating a funerary banquet, including the horse of the deceased; the other of the Dioscuri (Castor and Pollux) and their sister Helena, which was found in 1885 on the Esquiline Hill.

ROOM 35 To the left are two statues of *Bacchus*: the one with the panther was reconstructed in the 17c from antique fragments; the other is an imitation dating entirely from the 17c. The *Satyr* is a late 2c copy after an original by Praxiteles.

ROOMS 36-37 contain Egyptian pieces, including a *Bull* in green serpentine which represents the god Apis and was made in Egypt in the Ptolemaic period (2c BC).

ROOM 19 On the walls are the remains of 16c painted landscapes and perspectives. The statue of *Hermes*, god of travel, commerce and eloquence, is dated to the end of the 1c and derives from a 5c BC bronze original by Phidias. Alessandro Algardi added the nose, feet and raised arm. Also here are *Hercules*, copied from a 4c BC original ascribed to Lysippos; *Asclepios*, god of medicine, restored by Algardi; and a beautiful grey marble bust of a *Satyr*, thought to have been restored by Bernini. They all date from the 2c AD.

ROOM 20 is decorated with a fresco attributed to the circle of Melozzo da Forlì (1477). The sculpture group of *Achilles with his mother, Thetis,* dating from the late 2c BC, was described by Pliny who saw it in the Temple of Neptune, in the 'Mars field'. Bernini restored the *Achilles* in 1622. The standing group identified by Winckelmann as *Orestes and Electra* is signed by the Greek artist Menelaos, active in the 1c AD.

ROOM 21 displays the famous *Ludovisi Throne*, found at the end of the 19c in the Villa Ludovisi (p 141). Dated to 460 BC, it might have been an altar or a base for a statue of Aphrodite (Venus). On the front is a relief of the Birth of Venus, who rises from the sea supported by personifications of the seasons. On the right side a clothed woman is taking incense grains from a box and burning them in a brazier, while on the left a naked girl plays a double pipe.

The colossal head of *Juno* was greatly admired by Winckelmann, Schiller and Goethe (whose cast of it is now in the Casa di Goethe). It is now understood to be a mid 1c AD portrait of Antonia, mother of Claudius.

ROOMS 34 AND 33, formerly the apartment of the duchess, these rooms contain a 3c statue of a *Boy with a Goose*, after an original by Boethos of Chalcedon (180 BC), and two variations on Doidalsas' *Venus at her Bath* (a third one is exhibited in Room 18). The charming frieze in Room 33 is by Francesco Romanelli (1654).

ROOM 23 A pre-existing 16c frieze was painted over in the 17c with battle scenes to designs by Antonio Tempesta. Here are also a red marble relief of a mask of *Bacchus* (once used as a fountain), two colossal *busts* and a fragment with the *Judgement of Paris*, all dating from the 2c AD.

LOGGIA The loggia has beautiful frescoes of a pergola and putti holding garlands (1595).

ROOM 26 In the centre is the impressive *Galatian committing Suicide*, which once formed part of the same group as the *Dying Gaul*, now in the Capitoline Museums. It is a 1c BC replica of a bronze group made in 239 BC for Attalos I of Pergamon to commemorate a victory over the Gauls. Also in this room is a splendid 3c marble sarcophagus showing a *Battle between Romans and Barbarians*, and a high-relief head of *Mars* (2c AD, with 16c bust).

ROOMS 31-32 have a fine sarcophagus with a *Battle Scene* (AD 180), a statue of a seated *Man in a Toga*, signed in Greek by Zeno of Aphrodisia (1c BC) and a 2c sculptural group of a *Nymph and Satyr* (with reconstructions by Bernini). The *Dadoforo*, or torch-bearer, was created by Algardi from an antique torso.

San Luigi dei Francesi

OPEN	7.30-12.30 and 15.30-19.00; closed Thur afternoon
BUSES	Along Corso Rinascimento, nos 70, 81, 87, 186, 492

San Luigi dei Francesi (Largo Toniolo), the French national church, was begun in 1518 by Giacomo della Porta (he designed the façade) and completed in 1589 by Domenico Fontana.

The interior is heavily decorated with 18c stuccoes and polychrome marbles, and the central vault fresco, by Charles-Joseph Natoire (1756), illustrates the *Death and Apotheosis of St Louis*. The second chapel to the right has Domenichino's frescoes of the *Stories of St Cecilia* (1616-7).

The last chapel on the left contains three masterpieces by **Caravaggio**. Painted in 1599-1602, they were the artist's first public work. On the left is the *Calling of St Matthew*, illustrating the conversion of the former tax collector who is shown amidst his companions counting money. He points at himself while his questioning look leads our eyes towards Christ who has appeared to indicate him as his choice. Unusually, Christ is not immediately recognizable: he is obscured by the figure of St Peter and is only identified by a thin halo and his commanding gesture. As in all Caravaggio's works, the source of light is outside the painting and seems to underline the religious significance of the events, in this case as an allusion to divine grace illuminating the sinner's mind. The figures crowd the shallow picture plane in a frieze-like composition and, with the exception of Christ and St Peter, are dressed in contemporary costumes (including Caravaggio's ubiquitous feathered hats).

Over the altar is *St Matthew and the Angel*, with the Evangelist in the act of writing the Gospels. This was Caravaggio's second attempt at this subject - the first was rejected for lack of decorum because it represented the saint as a humble illiterate. The San Luigi version is also unconventional - St Matthew has just reached his desk and seems eager to capture what the angel is dictating to him; the setting is uncertain, with the table projecting beyond the picture plane and the bench in an unsteady position. The angel is depicted with masterly foreshortening and a strong sense of movement (the fluttering wings and white drapery), a delicate counterpoint to the static and earthy figure of the saint (still shown as a barefooted, simple man).

Opposite the silent drama and the ordered structure of the conversion is the unrestrained violence of *St Matthew's Martyrdom*. X-rays have revealed that this is the third version of an increasingly agitated composition, and show that Caravaggio experimented directly on the canvas, without preparatory drawings. Set in an indefinable space, the dramatic character of the scene is enhanced by the strong chiaroscuro effect. As if on a theatre stage, the light focuses only on the central action, creating a wedge-shaped composition. The screaming assassin has just stabbed the saint and stops him from reaching the palm of martyrdom, which is being handed down by an angel. All of the figures are shown in disquietingly unstable positions, from the saint about to fall into an obscure abyss, to the angel who leans down perilously, and the naked youths in the foreground inspired by Michelangelo's *Ignudi* in the Sistine. The drama is commented on by the frightened boy fleeing on the right and the various reactions of the onlookers on the left. Curiously, they are the only ones to wear contemporary dress. The man peering at the scene in the far background is thought to be Caravaggio's self-portrait.

The Pantheon

OPEN   Mon-Sat 8.30-19.30, Sun 9.00-18.00, **T 06 6830 0230**

Dedicated to all the gods, the original temple was built in 27 BC. It was rectangular in shape, built of travertine and faced the opposite way to the building we see today. Damaged by fires, it was entirely rebuilt in brick and concrete by Hadrian in AD 118-125. The new, much larger, Pantheon retained the inscription M. AGRIPPA L.F. COS. TERTIUM FECIT (Marcus Agrippa, son of Lucius, consul for the third time had this made) in honour of its original builder.

Restored by Septimius Severus (AD 202), it was abandoned under the first Christian emperors and pillaged by the Goths. In AD 608 the Byzantine Emperor Phocas donated the temple to Pope Boniface IV who consecrated it as a Christian church. In 667, on a 12-day visit to Rome, Constans II stripped it bare, taking away the gilded bronze tiles that covered the roof (these were replaced by lead in 735). It later served as a fortress.

During the Renaissance period it was restored and became greatly admired. Pius IV recast the bronze doors in 1563, although in 1625 Pope Urban VIII melted down the bronze ceiling of the portico to make the baldachin in St Peter's and 80 cannon for Castel Sant'Angelo.

Despite its chequered history, the Pantheon is the most celebrated monument of Roman antiquity, prized for its magnificence, state of preservation, and the techniques used in its construction. The combination of a traditional temple front with a

The Pantheon

domed rotunda (derived from Roman baths) was a radical new design type. The portico has 16 monolithic columns of grey and pink granite (three on the east side are 17c replacements). The height and diameter of the interior are the same (43.3m), giving the impression of a spherical space. The diameter of the dome - the largest masonry vault ever built - exceeds by more than 1m that of the dome of St Peter's. It is cast of concrete and volcanic stone (to make it lighter) and is lit by an opening in the roof. The five rows of coffers that articulate its surface were once decorated with gilded rosettes.

The cylindrical drum, of brick and concrete, is 6m thick and has aedicules and niches to lighten the structure. Originally displaying statues, these were transformed into chapels with monuments and royal tombs - kings Victor Emmanuel I and Humbert I are both buried here. The third aedicule to the left holds the tomb of Raphael (d. 1520). Among other artists buried in the Pantheon are Giovanni da Udine, Perin del Vaga, Taddeo Zuccari, Baldassarre Peruzzi and Annibale Carracci. The polychrome marble decoration on the wall was restored in 1747, partially using original pieces. The floor, though restored, retains its original design.

Galleria Doria Pamphilj

OPEN	Fri-Wed 10.00-17.00
CLOSED	Thur; 1/1, Easter Sunday, 1/5, 15/8, 25/12
CHARGES	€8; €5.70 for students, under 18s and over 65s
TELEPHONE	06 679 7323
WWW.	doriapamphilj.it
ENTRANCE	Piazza del Collegio Romano no. 2
BUS	All buses via Piazza Venezia: 60 express from Termini to Colosseum; 64 from Termini to Largo Porta Cavalleggeri (St Peter's); 85, 87 or 117 from Piazza San Giovanni in Laterano (via Colosseum); 95 from Via Veneto

The gallery contains an important collection formed by the Pamphilj family. It was begun in 1651 by the Pamphilj pope Innocent X (1644-55) and inherited by his nephew Camillo. A passionate art lover and collector, Camillo also added, by marriage, the riches of the Aldobrandini.

The palace is among the largest in Rome and one of the few still owned by the descendants of its original owners. It is the result of various phases of building carried out between the 15c and the 19c.

In the early 16c the palace passed to the family of Julius II Della Rovere, and in 1601 to Cardinal Pietro Aldobrandini who endowed it to his niece and only heir, Olimpia. In 1647 Olimpia Aldobrandini married Camillo Pamphilj. The couple moved into the Aldobrandini palace on the Corso and started its refurbishment as well as the construction of a new wing (the present entrance) facing the Collegio Romano. The architect was Antonio del Grande. In the 18c were added the south wing and the main façade on Via del Corso. The façade is among the finest examples of Roman Rococo, designed in 1731-4 by the architect Gabriele Valvassori, who was also responsible for covering the loggia on the first floor and creating a picture gallery around the inner courtyard.

In 1760, the Doria Pamphilj, a Genoese branch of the family, inherited the property. The Appartamento di Rappresentanza was

re-decorated in 1767-9 under Andrea IV and the collection was
arranged as it is seen today.

HIGHLIGHTS

Annibale Carracci, *Flight into Egypt*	First Gallery
Claude Lorrain, *Landscape with Dancing Figures* and *View of Delphi with a Procession*	
Guercino, *Erminia and Tancredi*	
Velázquez, *Innocent X*	
Bernini, *Innocent X*	
Caravaggio, *Rest on the Flight into Egypt* and *Penitent Magdalene*	Sala del Seicento
Raphael, *Double Portrait*	Sala del Cinquecento
Titian, *Salome with the Head of St John the Baptist*	
Hans Memling, *Deposition*	Sala del Quattrocento
Correggio, *Allegory of Virtue*	Third Gallery
Pieter Bruegel the Elder, *Battle in the Port of Naples*	
Alessandro Algardi, *Bust of Olimpia Maidalchini Pamphilj*	Fourth Gallery
Parmigianino, *Nativity* and *Madonna and Child*	
Jan Bruegel the Elder, *Earthly Paradise*	

The grand staircase leads up to the first floor. The first series of
rooms forms part of the **Appartamento di Rappresentanza**, or
official apartment. The rooms facing the inner courtyard are
closed and due to re-open only for guided visits in 2004.

The exhibition of paintings begins with the **Sala del Poussin**,
named after the 17c landscapes by Gaspard Dughet, brother-in-
law of Nicolas Poussin.

The room beyond has 17c paintings by Pasquale Chiesa,
Niccolo Tornioli, and Mattia Preti (*Agar and the Angel*). The fine
busts of *Innocent X* and his brother *Benedetto Pamphilj* are by
Alessandro Algardi.

Off the ballroom, decorated with19c silk hangings, is the **chapel** that was designed by Carlo Fontana (1691) and altered in the 18c-19c. It contains precious church furnishings and relics.

The vestibule of the Gallery, hung with 16c and 17c paintings, is also a bookshop.

The Gallery proper is arranged in the four arms of the courtyard restructured by Gabriele Valvassori in 1731-4. (Inventory numbers are included in the description of the Gallery to help with the indentification of the paintings.)

FIRST GALLERY This features paintings of the Bolognese school and important landscapes. Domenichino's *Landscape with a River* (S 4) hangs to the left of the entrance, close to Bernini's first version of a bust of *Innocent X*. Beyond are the famous 'Aldobrandini Lunettes', a series of six landscapes with the *Stories of the Virgin* commissioned by Pietro Aldobrandini from Annibale Carracci but largely executed by his pupils (1605-13). The *Flight into Egypt* (i5) is entirely by the master's hand and became a model of the idealized landscape in the 17c. Here are also four paintings by Claude Lorrain, including a *Landscape with Dancing Figures* (i4) and a *View of Delphi with a Procession* (i 32), of 1646-7, displayed in the upper register.

Other masterpieces are *Galatea and Polyphemus* (i8) by Giovanni Lanfranco (1609); *Venus, Mars and Cupid* (i15) by the Venetian Paris Bordon (mid 16c); *Erminia and Tancredi* (i28) by Guercino, painted in 1618-9 before his arrival in Rome. On the wall by the windows is the *Usurers* (i47) by Quinten Massys.

In the small room at the end of the gallery is **Velázquez**'s portrait of *Innocent X* (1650). The astounding realism and psychological characterization, as well as the fine colour scale (derived from Venetian art) and the study of the different textures, make this the absolute highlight of the collection. Also here is **Bernini**'s bust of the same pope, showing greater idealization and aiming above all at rendering the social image of the sitter. The sculpture was made twice as the first, now exhibited at the beginning of the first gallery, was damaged during transportation.

GALLERIA DEGLI SPECCHI The Gallery of Mirrors was created in the 18c by Gabriele Valvassori, with ceiling frescoes of the *Labours of Hercules* by Aureliano Milani. Beyond are four rooms containing works divided by period, but exhibited in reverse chronological order.

SALA DEL SETTECENTO This room is dedicated to Italian views of the 18c, an extremely popular genre during the age of the Grand Tour, providing visitors with mementoes to take home. Among the great '*Vedutisti*' whose paintings are exhibited here are Gaspard van Wittel and Hendrick Frans van Lint from the Netherlands, who specialized in views of Venice and Rome.

SALA DEL SEICENTO Here are some of the greatest masterpieces of the collection, including two paintings by **Caravaggio**. The innovative composition of the *Rest on the Flight into Egypt* was severely criticized for its lack of decorum. The naked angel, shown with black wings and his back to the viewer, was unacceptable in Rome after the Counter-Reformation. Yet Caravaggio's intentions were to illustrate the angel's purity and ethereal nature by portraying him as a divine messenger playing music in honour of the Madonna. The score held up by Joseph has been identified as a motet written by the Flemish composer Noel Bauldewijn after the text of the Song of Songs (allegorical of the mystic union of Christ and Mary). The painting was made around 1596, possibly for Cardinal Del Monte, a music expert and Caravaggio's first patron. The style of the background and the treatment of light (as yet devoid of the dramatic chiaroscuro for which he became famous) are linked to Caravaggio's training in Lombardy. The same northern heritage appears in his precise observation of nature. Details such as plants, trees, stones and the flask in the foreground also testify to his beginnings in Rome as a painter of still lifes.

The features of the *Penitent Magdalene* are very similar to those of the Madonna in the *Rest on the Flight*, and seem to be drawn from the same model. Although it dates from Caravaggio's early period, the composition is radical, isolating the figure in the centre of a bare room. From an invisible window high above comes a ray of light as if to symbolize the divine grace that descends upon the regretful sinner.

Also in this room is a *St Sebastian* by Ludovico Carracci (1599) and a painting of the *Sleeping Endymion* (1647) by Guercino, the most Caravaggesque among the followers of Annibale Carracci. The handsome shepherd loved by Selene/Diana, goddess of the moon, is shown with a telescope, a reference to Galileo Galilei's invention at the beginning of the 17c.

SALA DEL CINQUECENTO Many of the paintings exhibited here and in the next room belonged to Lucrezia d'Este, Duchess of Urbino. They were acquired by Cardinal Pietro Aldobrandini and passed by marriage to the Pamphilj. Among these is the *Double Portrait* by **Raphael** representing two humanists of the court of Leo X: Andrea Navagero and Agostino Beazzano. The chromatic choice, with a predominance of black and green, was inspired by the Venetian Sebastiano del Piombo whom Raphael met in 1515. At about the same time **Titian** painted his *Salome with the Head of St John the Baptist*, clearly showing his training under Giorgione. The disquieting *Portrait of a Gentleman* is by Jacopo Tintoretto (mid 16c).

SALA DEL QUATTROCENTO Rare and interesting are three paintings by Bernardo Parentino (c 1494), strongly influenced by Mantegna and northern European painting as seen in the *Temptations of St Anthony*. **Hans Memling**'s *Deposition*, painted between 1475 and 1485, recalls Rogier van der Weyden's *Pietà* in London (National Gallery). It entered the collection in the 19c at a time when late medieval art was highly valued for its sincere devotional qualities. Also in this room are Quinten Massys' *Hypocrites* and works by Giovanni di Paolo.

THIRD GALLERY On the left wall is **Correggio**'s *Allegory of Virtue* (q2), an unfinished study for a painting now in the Louvre that was commissioned by Isabella d'Este (1532-4). Close by is Lorenzo Lotto's *St Jerome* (q10) and the splendid *Penitent Magdalene* (q7), painted by Domenico Fetti around 1621 and derived from a similar composition by Correggio.

The *Battle in the Port of Naples* by **Pieter Bruegel the Elder** (q21) is a rare document of the artist's trip to Italy, undertaken around 1551-4 in the company of the geographer Ortelius, who may have inspired this topographical view and aerial perspective.

Among the 17c paintings are four works by Guercino, including the *Martyrdom of St Agnes* (q14) and *St John the Baptist* (q23), which were given to Pope Innocent X by Cardinal Ludovico Ludovisi in 1652 and show a classicism typical of the artist's late style. The same spirit pervades Guido Reni's *Madonna in Adoration of the Child* (q19).

SALONE ALDOBRANDINI Steps lead down from the beginning of the fourth gallery to this room which displays antique sculptures, including a large sarcophagus of AD 240 decorated with the myth of *Selene and Endymion*. In the centre is a porphyry statue of the young *Bacchus*, restored in the 17c by Alessandro Algardi, and a *Centaur* in red and black marble that was put together from 25 fragments shortly after its discovery in the mid 19c.

FOURTH GALLERY At the beginning of this gallery is the renowned bust of *Olimpia Maidalchini Pamphilj*, sister-in-law of Innocent X and mother of Camillo Pamphilj, carved by **Alessandro Algardi** in 1650. The Bolognese artist skilfully captured the resolute and despotic character of the sitter and rendered, with masterly technique, the widow's mantle swelling behind her head. Among the most important paintings are a good 17c copy (long considered an original) after Caravaggio's *St John the Baptist* in the Capitoline Museums (s57), Jusepe de Ribera's *St Jerome* (s70) and Domenichino's early *Susannah and the Elders* (s67). The fine *Nativity* (s59) and *Madonna and Child* (s71) by **Parmigianino** (1525), strongly influenced by Correggio, once formed a single altar, painted on both sides, that was used for private devotion.

Well represented in the gallery is **Jan Bruegel the Elder**, the son of Pieter, who travelled to Rome in 1593-4 and became fashionable for his rich narratives and skilful portrayal of nature. Camillo Pamphilj acquired 14 of his paintings, including the *Earthly Paradise* (s83) and the *Madonna and Child with Animals* (s43, which follows a Dürer prototype). His famous *Allegories of the Four*

Elements (s95, s96, s111, s112) were executed around 1611. Close to the exit hangs Mattia Preti's large *Concert* (s97).

on route

AROUND PIAZZA NAVONA

Campo dei Fiori

Campo dei Fiori occupies the platea of the ancient temple of Venus Victrix, which adjoined the Theatre of Pompey (55 BC). The cavea of the theatre later provided the foundations for houses in Via di Grottapinta. Transformed into a meadow by the 14c (hence its name: *fiori* means flowers), the Campo became one of the liveliest *piazze* of the Renaissance. In the centre, a monument commemorates the spot where the philosopher Giordano Bruno was burned as a heretic by the Inquisition in 1600. A colourful fruit and flower market is held here and numerous artisans' workshops populate the adjoining streets, which are named after their trades (eg Via de'Cappellari, once the hatmakers' street, etc).

Chiesa Nuova, Piazza della Chiesa Nuova (off Corso Vittorio Emanuele). The 'new church' was erected in 1575-1605, inspired by St Philip Neri, one of the central figures of the Counter-Reformation. The architecture, initially derivative of the Gesù (p 70), was transformed and completed by Martino Longhi the Elder in 1586-90. Inside, the vault, apse and dome were magnificently decorated by **Pietro da Cortona** between 1647 and 1664. In the presbytery are three paintings by **Peter Paul Rubens** who stayed in Rome in 1606-8. Daily 8.00-12.00, 16.30-19.30. Bus nos 40 and 64 from Termini to Vatican.

Adjoining the Chiesa Nuova is the **Oratorio dei Filippini** where St Philip Neri gave his sermons with interludes of polyphonic music. Known as *'oratori'*, they gave their name to a new form of musical composition. The complex was rebuilt by **Francesco Borromini** (1637-52), whose façade combines elements of chuch and palace design while skilfully disguising the spatial irregularities of the interior. The convent is largely occupied by the Vallicelliana Library. Mon-Thur 8.15-19.15, Fri-Sat 8.15-13.30; closed Sun.

Museo Barracco, Corso Vittorio Emanuele II 166. This elegant Renaissance palace houses the collection of ancient sculpture formed by Senator Giovanni Barracco (1829-1914). It includes a fine selection of Egyptian, Assyrian, Greek, Etruscan and Roman art. Closed for restoration, it should re-open in 2004, *T* 06 6880 6848. Bus nos 40 and 64 from Termini to Vatican.

Museo Mario Praz, Palazzo Primoli; entrance in Via Zanardelli. The top floor of the palace was the residence of the literature scholar and art critic Mario Praz (d. 1982) whose rich collection of Neoclassical art includes paintings, sculpture, miniatures, porcelain and furniture. Guided visits every hour 9.00-13.00; 14.30-18.30, closed Mon morning, *T* 06 686 1089. Bus nos 70, 81, 87, 186, 492.

Museo Napoleonico, located in Palazzo Primoli, 1 Piazza di Ponte Umberto I. The collection was donated to the city in 1927 by Count Giuseppe Primoli, son of Carlotta Bonaparte. It contains paintings, sculpture, furniture, costumes, jewels and various memorabilia related to Napoleon and his family. Tues-Sun 9.00-19.00, closed Mon, *T* 06 6880 6286.

Museo di Roma, Via di San Pantaleo (off Corso Vittorio Emanuele). The Neoclassical Palazzo Braschi, commissioned by Pius VI, was erected in 1791-6 by Cosimo Morelli and completed, after the French occupation of Rome (1798), by Giuseppe Valadier. The museum illustrates the history of Rome from the Renaissance to the modern age. Tues-Sun 9.00-18.00, closed Mon, *T* 06 6710 8312. Bus nos 40, 64 along Corso Vittorio Emanuele.

Oratorio dei Filippini See Chiesa Nuova, p 65.

Palazzo della Cancelleria This magnificent Renaissance palace can be found in the piazza of the same name. It was commissioned in 1485 by Cardinal Raffaele Riario, whose heraldic rose punctuates the architecture. Today it is the seat of the Tribunals of the Vatican. The beautiful courtyard, with double *loggie* and antique columns is ascribed to **Donato Bramante**. Upstairs, closed to the public, is the Salone dei Cento Giorni, frescoed by Vasari within 100 days and illustrating events from the pontificate of Paul III (1546).

The left side of Palazzo della Cancelleria overlooks the old Via Peregrinorum, once the pilgrims' route connecting the Lateran to St Peter's and today filled with interesting shops, some of which are housed in the arcades of the palace.

Palazzo Farnese Today the French Embassy, this is the finest

Renaissance palace in Rome. Commissioned by Alessandro Farnese, later Pope Paul III, it was begun in 1517 by **Antonio da Sangallo the Younger** and continued after 1546 by **Michelangelo**, who finished the upper storeys adding the central balcony and the splendid entablature with its Farnese lilies. The back of the building was completed by Vignola (d. 1573) and Giacomo della Porta (1589).

The gallery inside, which is not open to the public, has magnificent and influential frescoes of 1597-1604 by **Annibale** and **Agostino Carracci** and their pupils (Domenichino and Lanfranco). The piazza in front is adorned with two basins of Egyptian granite that were found in the Baths of Caracalla and adapted as fountains in 1626.

Palazzo Madama, Corso Rinascimento 11. It takes its name from the residence here of Madama Margherita of Austria, daughter of Charles V, widow of Alessandro de'Medici, remarried to Ottavio Farnese, and Regent of the Netherlands in 1559-67. The palace, which dates back to the 15c, was rebuilt at the beginning of the 16c for Giovanni de'Medici and owes its present façade to Paolo Marucelli (1637-42). It has been the seat of the Italian Senate since 1871.

Palazzo Massimo alle Colonne The plan and elevation of this palace, diagonally across the road from Sant'Andrea della Valle (p 69), show how Baldassare Peruzzi ingeniously solved the problem of a narrow and irregular site. It was commissioned by Pietro Massimo, a member of one of the oldest families in Rome, and built in 1532-6. The convex façade, unique at this date, follows the shape of the underlying Odeon of Domitian. The novel treatment of classical elements make the building one of the first examples of Mannerist architecture in Rome.

Palazzo Pamphilj, in Piazza Navona, was erected by Girolamo Rainaldi in 1644-50. It is now the Brazilian Embassy. The gallery inside was designed by Borromini and frescoed with the *Stories of Aeneas* by Pietro da Cortona (1651-4). Also by Borromini is the Sala Palestrina, a music room where Corelli's *Concerti Grossi* were first performed.

Next door, **Sant'Agnese** was built on the ruins of the stadium where, according to Christian tradition, St Agnes was exposed naked for refusing the advances of a praetor's son and was covered by the miraculous growth of her hair. Reconstruction began in 1652 under Girolamo and Carlo Rainaldi, and continued, with substantial changes, by Francesco Borromini (1653-7), who was also responsible for the façade.

Palazzo della Sapienza and Sant'Ivo alla Sapienza, Corso Rinascimento 40. Until 1935, this 16c palace was the seat of the University of Rome, founded in 1303 by Boniface VIII. It now houses the state archive. The inner court and church of Sant'Ivo were designed by **Francesco**

Sant' Ivo

Borromini, who worked here on and off from 1632 to 1660.

The church is entered from the court of Palazzo della Sapienza in Corso Rinascimento. It is Borromini's masterpiece and has a magnificent star-shaped interior enriched by the interplay of concave and convex curves. These are echoed outside in the lantern, which is set above a stepped dome and crowned by a famous spiral, of Gothic inspiration, compared by Romans to icing on a wedding cake. Daily 10.00-16.00, Sat 10.00-13.00, Sun 9.00-12.00.

Palazzo Spada Located in Piazza Capodiferro, the palace was built in 1548-50 for Cardinal Girolamo Capodiferro and decorated with elegant stuccoes by Giulio Mazzoni. In the 17c the palace was sold to Cardinal Bernardino Spada and renovated by **Francesco Borromini** whose perspective gallery (c 1653) is visible from the courtyard: in a narrow space measuring less than 9m the architect achieved the optical illusion of a 30m-long corridor. Since 1889 the palace has been the seat of the Supreme Court. A wing at the back houses the **Galleria Spada** of 17c-18c Italian paintings. Tues-Sun 9.00-18.00, closed Mon. *T* 06 683 2409.

Piazza Pasquino owes its name to a tailor who introduced the custom of pinning political satires to a statue that was placed here in 1501. The latter is a fragment of a marble group representing *Menelaus with the body of Patroclus* (after a Hellenistic original), which may have decorated the Stadium of Domitian.

Ponte Sisto This charming bridge was the only one built in Rome between the end of the Classical age and the 19c. It was erected during the time of Sixtus IV, c 1472, possibly by Baccio Pontelli, who incorporated an ancient Roman bridge that had collapsed in AD 589.

On the opposite bank is the popular quarter of **Trastevere**, packed with restaurants, pizzerias and wine bars, and centred around the splendid medieval church of **Santa Maria in Trastevere** (with mosaics by Pietro Cavallini, 1290, and earlier ones dating from 1145) and its piazza.

Sant'Agnese. See Palazzo Pamphilj, p 67.

Sant'Agostino Tucked away in the small piazza of the same name, this church was built in the 15c. Its austere Renaissance façade of 1483 was modelled on Santa Maria del Popolo and constructed with travertine taken from the Colosseum. The interior was rebuilt by Luigi Vanvitelli in 1756-61. By the entrance is the so-called *Madonna del Parto* (1521) by

Jacopo Sansovino; on the third pillar to the left is **Raphael**'s *Prophet Isaiah* (1512), strongly influenced by Michelangelo's prophets on the Sistine ceiling. Beneath is a *Madonna and Child with St Anne* (1512) by the sculptor Andrea Sansovino. In the first chapel to the left is **Caravaggio**'s famous *Madonna dei Pellegrini* of 1603-4. Daily 7.45-12.00 and 16.30-19.30.

Sant'Andrea della Valle, Corso Vittorio Emanuele. Begun at the end of the16c by Pietro Paolo Olivieri, it was continued from 1608 by Carlo Maderno, who added the dome, and finally completed by Carlo Rainaldi and Carlo Fontana whose façade dates to 1665. The interior follows the prototype of the Gesù and has no aisles. The fresco in the dome is by Lanfranco (1625-8), while his rival, Domenichino, painted the *Evangelists* in the pendentives below (1621-8). The latter also designed the presbytery and painted the scenes of the *Life of St Andrew* in the vault of the apse. The *Crucifixion*, *Martyrdom* and *Burial of St Andrew* on the walls below are by Mattia Preti (1650-1). Daily 7.30-12.00, 16.30-19.30.

Sant'Ivo alla Sapienza See Palazzo della Sapienza, p 67.

Santa Maria della Pace, Via Arco della Pace 5. The church was rebuilt in 1480-4, and restored for Alexander VII (1655-67) by Pietro da Cortona, who added the theatrical Baroque façade. Inside the church are **Raphael**'s frescoes of the *Sibyls*, executed in 1514 for the banker Agostino Chigi. The adjoining **cloister** is **Bramante**'s earliest work in Rome (1500-4); the two superimposed arcades reveal an admirable sense of classical balance. Tues-Fri 10.00-12.45, *T* 06 686 1156.

Via dei Coronari Once part of the ancient Via Recta, it was restored in the 15c by Sixtus IV and subsequently re-named after the vendors of rosaries (the 'sacred crowns') en route to St Peter's. It has interesting 15c-16c palaces, such as Palazzo Lancellotti, and is lined with antiques galleries.

Via Giulia Only partly altered by the demolitions of the early 20c Fascist era, Via Giulia retains its charm and has a number of interesting commercial galleries. It was laid out at the order of Julius II (1503-13) and was the most important street in 16c Rome, adorned with fine palaces and churches. Off the street, in Via di Sant'Eligio, is the goldsmiths' church designed by Raphael, in 1514, in the shape of a Greek cross. Entered from no. 1b Via della Scimia, is the **Oratorio del Gonfalone**, with late 16c frescoes (10.00-12.00 Mon, Tues, Thur, Fri).

Via del Governo Vecchio This street once formed part of the Via Papalis, an ancient route from the Lateran to St Peter's. Now filled with trendy clothes stores and restaurants, it has kept many traces of the early Renaissance.

AROUND THE PANTHEON

Collegio Romano Modelled on the Sorbonne in Paris, the Jesuit College was founded in 1551 by Ignatius of Loyola and was extremely influential in the Counter-Reformation when the Catholic church placed renewed emphasis on teaching. The building was erected in 1582-4 and included a substantial library (which formed the core of the National Library). It is still used as a school.

The Gesù, in Piazza del Gesù, off Corso Vittorio Emanuele. The principal church of the Jesuit order was erected between 1568 and 1575 and funded by Cardinal Alessandro Farnese. Both the building by Vignola and the façade by Giacomo della Porta provided the model for all subsequent Baroque churches in Rome and were adopted by Jesuits throughout Europe.

The original rigour of the architectural structure was subverted a century later by the overwhelming exuberance of the interior decoration and the ceiling frescoes painted by **Giovan Battista Gaulli**, called Baciccia (1674-9). The combination of stucco and fresco as well as the illusionist effects and dramatic intensity are typical of late Baroque art. Ignatius of Loyola (d. 1556), founder of the Jesuit order, lies buried in the left transept in an elaborate tomb (1696-1700) designed by Andrea Pozzo.

Largo Argentina In the centre of this square is an enceinte with four Republican temples dating from the early 3c to the end of the 2c BC. Their dedication is unknown. To the west is the **Teatro Argentina**, the most important theatre in 18c-19c Rome, which staged the first performances of Rossini's *Barber of Seville* (1816) and Verdi's *Rigoletto* (1851).

Palazzo Montecitorio To the north of the Pantheon is the seat of the Chamber of Deputies which, together with the Senate, has formed the Parliament of Italy since 1871. Bernini began the palace for the Ludovisi family in 1653, giving the façade its characteristic convex appearance. Transformed by Carlo Fontana into the Papal Tribunals in 1694, the building was adapted for the parliament in 1903-27 by Ernesto Basile who doubled its size and added an Art Nouveau façade at the back.

In the square is the ***obelisk of Psammetichus*** II (c 590 BC), which had been brought to Rome by Augustus to celebrate his victory over Cleopatra and set up in the Campus Martius (near the Ara Pacis) to serve as the gnomon of a huge sun-dial. It was found underground in the mid 18c.

Piazza Colonna takes its name from the *Column of Marcus Aurelius* standing in the centre. This was erected in AD 180-193 to celebrate the emperor's victories over the Germans and Sarmatians. The campaigns are illustrated in the continuous frieze which was inspired by Trajan's column, although stylistically less refined. At the top is a statue of

St Paul, placed there in 1589 by Sixtus V (as a pendant to the St Peter above Trajan's Column).

Piazza di Pietra Here are the remains of the huge **Temple of Hadrian**, one of the most impressive examples of the re-utilization of Classical antiquity in Rome. Built in AD 145 by Hadrian's adoptive son and successor Antoninus Pius, it was later transformed into a customs house and then a stock exchange. The right side of the peristyle survives, with 11 Corinthian columns and also the wall of the cella. This was originally covered with marble - you can see the holes that once held iron hooks to keep the marble slabs in place (the metal was extracted and melted down in the Middle Ages for tools and weapons).

Piazza di Sant'Ignazio Named after the church which rises at one end, the piazza is a Rococo masterpiece by Filippo Raguzzini (1727-8). Three buildings with curving façades close it off to the north, deliberately imitating a stage set, with the side streets becoming part of the theatrical scene.

Sant'Ignazio The church was begun in 1626 by Cardinal Ludovico Ludovisi, nephew of Gregory XV, to commemorate the canonization of St Ignatius of Loyola (1622). Supervised by Carlo Maderno and others, the Jesuit mathematician Orazio Grassi erected the building and the façade in imitation of the Gesù. Another Jesuit, **Andrea Pozzo**, was responsible for the remarkable frescoes (1691-4). They are masterpieces of trompe l'oeil perspective. Pozzo also painted a dome (never built because of lack of funds) on a huge canvas, which is best seen from a yellow disk in the pavement of the nave.

In the transepts are fine high-reliefs by Pierre Legros (*The Glory of St Louis Gonzaga*, on the right) and Filippo della Valle (*The Annunciation*, on the left). Daily 7.30-12.30, 16.00-19.00.

Santa Maria Sopra Minerva, Piazza Minerva, southeast of the Pantheon. In front of this church is a charming monument featuring an elephant, designed by Bernini (1667) to incorporate an Egyptian obelisk of the 6c BC that was unearthed nearby (on the site of the Temple of Isis).

The church was constructed over the ruins of the Temple of Minerva and remodelled in 1280 by the Dominicans. The simple façade dates to 1453 - notice the small plaques which indicate the level of the floods before the Tiber was walled in 1876-1900.

The interior was 'restored' in 1848-55 in neo-Gothic style. In the south transept is the Carafa Chapel, painted by **Filippino Lippi** in 1488-93. At the foot of the choir, on the left, is **Michelangelo**'s *Risen Christ* (1519-21),

Piazza Santa Maria sopra Minerva

finished by assistants. Under the 19c altar lies the body of St Catherine of Siena (d. 1380).

In the apse are the tombs of the Medici popes Leo X (d. 1521) and Clement VII (d. 1534), designed by Antonio da Sangallo. Off the north transept, in a passageway serving as an exit, is the pavement tomb of Fra Angelico by Isaia da Pisa. The Dominican painter from Florence died in 1455 in the adjoining monastery which, during the Counter-Reformation, housed the tribunal of the Inquisition and was the scene of Galileo's trial (1633).

commercial galleries

Many important galleries are in Trastevere on the other side of the river Tiber, a short walk across Ponte Sisto.

A.A.M., Via dei Banchi Vecchi 61, *T* 06 6830 7537. The initials stand for architecture and modern art. The only gallery of its kind in Rome, Carlo Aymonino was the subject of a recent exhibition. Other artists who have exhibited here include Mahi Binebine and Miguel Galanda.

Alice & Altri lavori in corso, Vicolo del Governo Vecchio 7 (Navona), *T* 06 686 1719, www.aliceealtrilavoriincorso.it. A very interesting and fairly recent gallery which shows contemporary work.

Alessandra Bonomo, Via del Gesù 62, *T* 06 6992 5858; closed Saturday and Sunday. Shows work by Schifano, Twombly, Tuttle, Nunzio, Sol LeWitt, as well as younger artists and photographers.

2RC Edizioni d'Arte, Via delle Mantellate 15a (Trastevere), *T* 06 686 8878. Recent exhibitions have featured the work of Grillo Demo, Janine Von Thungen, Mario Ceroli, Angele Etoundi Essamba.

Ugo Ferranti, Via dei Soldati 41 (Navona), *T* 06 6880 2146. One of the main galleries in town since its opening in 1974, showing the work of American Conceptual artists and their European contemporaries. Sol LeWitt, Christo, Kounellis, Twombly and the photographer Andrès Serrano have all exhibited here.

Galleria Giulia, Via Giulia 148t, *T* 06 6880 2061. Works by Italian and International artists of the early 20c (including German Expressionists). Among the latest events was the exhibition 'Blanca' by the Spanish neo-realist Pedro Cano.

L'Attico, Via del Paradiso 41 (Campo dei Fiori), *T* 06 686 9846. An historic gallery, at the centre of Rome's art scene in the 1960s (Schifano, Pascali, De Dominicis) and now featuring contemporary work.

Magazzino d'Arte Moderna, Via dei Prefetti 17 (Pantheon), *T* 06 687 5951, www.magazzinoartemoderna.com. Featured artists have included Massimo Bartolini, the Neapolitan duo Vedova-Mazzei, Atelier Van Lieshout, Carla Accardi, Alberto Garutti.

Il Ponte Contemporanea, Via di Montoro 10 (off Via di Monserrato), *T* 06 6880 1351, www.ilpontecontemporanea.it. The Macedonian artist Robert Gligorov has exhibited here, also Paul Ferman and Rocco Dubbini.

Gian Enzo Sperone, Via di Pallacorda 15 (Piazza del Parlamento), *T* 06 689 3525. The director, who was among the first to exhibit American Pop Art (Warhol, Lichtenstein), also runs a gallery in N.Y. and is an important promoter of contemporary and experimental art in Rome.

Stefania Miscetti, Via delle Mantellate 14 (Trastevere), *T* 06 6880 5880. One of the most interesting galleries in town. Among the artists who have exhibited here are Hermann Nitsch, Yoko Ono, Paolo Canevari, Luigi Cappelli, Enrico Corte, Claudia Peill.

Studio Lipoli e Lopez, Via della Penitenza 5 (Trastevere), *T* 06 5160 3618, www.studiolipolilopez.com. Claudio Abbate (photographs), Caroline Bachmann, Claudia Peill, Giuseppe Salvatori, Laura Palmieri.

Carlo Virgilio, Via della Lupa 10 (Piazza del Parlamento), *T* 06 687 1093, www.carlovirgilio.it. Founded 25 years ago, this gallery initially specialized in drawings from the 18c-20c and then widened its scope to include good contemporary painting and sculpture. It has an extensive photographic archive which is often consulted by art historians.

Volume!, Via San Francesco di Sales 86 (Trastevere), *T* 06 7030 1433, www.volumefnucci.it. This gallery has exhibited works by Marco Tirelli, Sol LeWitt, Mimmo Paladino, Jannis Kounellis, Paolo Canevari.

eating and drinking

RESTAURANTS

€ **Baffetto**, Via del Governo Vecchio, 114, *T* 06 686 1617; closed 15-30 August. A traditional favourite for thin crust pizza.

Cul de Sac, Piazza Pasquino, 73, *T* 06 6880 1094; never closed. The first wine bar in the capital (it opened 25 years ago) and still a favourite, with an extraordinary wine list and a good choice of cheeses, patés and simple dishes. The queues get long and the place is tiny, so get there early.

Da Ada e Alfredo, Via dei Banchi Nuovi 14, *T* 06 687 8842; closed Sunday. No sign or written menus. Home cooking in the traditional Roman way. Around €13 including wine.

Enoteca Corsi, Via del Gesù 87 (Largo Argentina), *T* 06 679 0821; open for lunch only; closed Sunday and August. An informal trattoria with very good food.

Er Pallaro, Largo del Pallaro 15 (Campo dei Fiori), *T* 06 6880 1488. A trattoria with typical Roman cooking.

La Bruschetteria degli Angeli, Piazza Cairoli 2a (Via Arenula), *T* 06 6880 5789; open lunchtime and 19.30-2.00; closed Saturday and Sunday lunchtime and 15-16 August. *Bruschette*, salads, pasta and beer.

Lilly, Via Tor di Nona 23 (Navona), *T* 06 686 1916; closed Sunday. A classic *trattoria* inside a 15c building.

Tonino, Via del Governo Vecchio 18. No telephone. No written menus. Closed Sunday. One of the last, original *osterie* of Rome: *pasta e fagioli* every day; *coda alla vaccinara* (ox tail) on Tuesday; *gnocchi* on Thursday; *baccalà* (cod) on Friday; tripe on Saturday. Around €13.

€€ **Albistrò**, Via dei Banchi Vecchi 140a, *T* 06 686 5274; evenings only; closed Wednesday and August. Good international cuisine.

Al Bric, Via del Pellegrino 51, *T* 06 687 9533; evenings only; closed Monday and 10-20 August. An encyclopedic wine list, excellent cheeses and inventive cuisine.

Boccon Divino, Via del Pavone 28, *T* 06 6813 5051. A tiny and charming place.

Fortunato al Pantheon, Via del Pantheon 55, *T* 06 679 2788; closed Sunday and 15-31 August. A classic, in every respect, and a favourite with the journalists and politicians working at the nearby Parliament.

Il Bacaro, Via degli Spagnoli 27 (Piazza delle Coppelle, Pantheon), *T* 06 686 4110; closed Sunday. Booking essential. Small and intimate for candlelit dinners. Tables outside. Beef carpaccio with truffles and a delicious chocolate dessert.

Il Fico, Piazza del Fico 24, *T* 06 687 5568; closed Monday lunchtime. A lovely setting (especially outside). Seafood and classics.

Mirò, Via dei Banchi Nuovi 8, *T* 06 6880 8527; closed Sunday lunchtime, Tuesday and August. A family business run with great enthusiasm and good food from Calabria. Limited wine list.

Monserrato, Via Monserrato 96, *T* 06 687 3386; closed Monday and August. Crowded and noisy, but good for seafood. Tables outside. Booking advisable.

Osteria dell'Ingegno, Piazza di Pietra 45, *T* 06 678 0662; closed Sunday and August. Located at the corner of one of Rome's prettiest piazze, this restaurant has a nice interior too. It gets crowded at lunchtime (offices and Parliament are nearby).

Taverna Giulia, Vicolo dell'Oro 23 (at the end of Via Giulia), *T* 06 686 9768. A charming, intimate place serving specialities from Liguria.

€€€ **Camponeschi**, Piazza Farnese 50, *T* 06 687 4927; evenings only; closed 10-24 August. The location and ambience are extraordinary, the high prices likewise. A long established restaurant favoured by celebrities, with a good but no longer exceptional cuisine.

Enoteca Capranica, Piazza Capranica 99, *T* 06 6994 0992; closed Saturday lunchtime and Sunday; in August open only in the evening. Good seafood and more.

Enoteca Ferrara, Via del Moro 1a (Trastevere), *T* 06 5833 3920; closed Sunday; open in August. Their experiments with food are certainly innovative if not always successful, while the huge Italian wine list is among the best in town. Beautiful setting.

Hostaria del Pesce, Via di Monserrato 32, *T* 06 686 5617; evenings only; closed Sunday and August. A very good choice of fresh seafood. Booking essential.

Il Bicchiere di Mastai, Via dei Banchi Nuovi 52, *T* 06 6819 2228; evenings only; closed Monday and August. A wine bar with a refined menu and a pleasant ambience.

Il Convivio, Vicolo dei Soldati 21 (Navona), *T* 06 686 9432; closed Monday lunchtime and Sunday. Excellent food and wines. One of the best restaurants in town.

La Rosetta, Via della Rosetta 8, *T* 06 686 1002; closed Sunday. For years this has been the best seafood restaurant in Rome. Can be noisy.

Montevecchio, Piazza Montevecchio 22a (Navona), *T* 06 686 1319; evenings only; closed Monday. Refined cuisine. Intimate atmosphere and tables outside.

Riccioli Café, Piazza delle Coppelle 10a, *T* 06 6821 0313; open 9.00-1.00. It started out as an oyster bar but now it's also popular for sushi, cocktails and breakfast.

COFFEE BARS

Antico Caffè della Pace, Via della Pace 3 (Navona), *T* 06 686 1216; open 9.00-3.00; closed Monday morning. From coffee in the morning to cocktails at night this coffee bar is always busy. Victorian interior and tables outside facing Santa Maria della Pace. A hot spot to see and be seen.

Caffè Farnese, at the corner of Via de'Baullari. A meeting place in one of the most beautiful squares of Rome.

Caffè Sant'Eustachio, Piazza Sant'Eustachio 82; open 8.30-1.00. Established in 1938 this is a cult bar for the best coffee in town. Fabulous creamy variations (try the *gran caffè speciale*) and any accessory that has to do with coffee.

Caffè Novecento, Via del Governo Vecchio 12, *T* 06 686 5242. A pleasant café with an Art Deco interior.

Tazza d'Oro, Via degli Orfani 84 (Pantheon). Great coffee and a superb *granita con panna*. Freshly ground coffee to buy.

ICE CREAM

Alberto Pica, Via della Seggiola 12 (Via Arenula), *T* 06 6880 6153. Inventiveness and taste are the rule for the innovative combinations on offer here.

Giolitti, Via Uffici del Vicario 40 (Parliament), *T* 06 699 1243. One of the oldest establishments in town producing 50 delicious varieties of ice cream each day.

Santa Barbara, Largo dei Librari 86 (Campo dei Fiori), *T* 06 6830 9324. Exceptional fruit *cremolati* and ice cream.

WINE BARS

Casa Bleve, Via del Teatro Valle 48-49, ☎ 06 686 5970. The name is a guarantee as the owners also run an excellent wine bar in the Ghetto. It is housed in the historic Palazzo Medici Lante della Rovere and the cellars have Roman remains.

Giulio passami l'olio, Via Monte Giordano 28 (Piazza dell'Orologio); open 18.30-2.00; closed 14-15 August.

Il Goccetto, Via dei Banchi Vecchi 14, ☎ 06 686 4268; open lunchtime and 17.00-23.30; closed Sunday. A long established favourite, with over 800 Italian wines.

Il Nolano, Piazza Campo dei Fiori 11-12, ☎ 06 687 9344; open 18.00-2.00. Set in a historic palace, this new winebar is often the venue of photo exhibitions and presentations of books.

La Bottiglieria, Via di Monte Giordano 49, ☎ 06 687 2231. A new place for an after-work glass of wine and good appetizers.

La Trinchetta, Via dei Banchi Nuovi 4, ☎ 06 6830 0133; open until 2.00; closed for holidays in July and August. Good wines, *grappe*, cheeses, patés, cakes, etc. Japanese dinner on Thursdays (booking essential) and Erithrean on Sundays.

Roscioli, Via dei Giubbonari 21, ☎ 06 687 5287; open until 1.00. The famous gourmet shop (see Food, p 82) has recently opened an excellent wine bar.

Vineria Reggio, Piazza Campo dei Fiori 15, ☎ 06 6880 3268. This is *the* winery in town. A favourite meeting place, it gets impossibly crowded on summer evenings. The wine, prices and location explain it all.

LATE-NIGHT BARS

Bar del Fico, Piazza del Fico 26-28 (Navona), ☎ 06 686 5205; open 8.00-2.00; closed Sunday morning. The milkshop of the neighbourhood is now a popular bar with tables in the little square.

Bloom, Via del Teatro Pace 30 (Navona), ☎ 06 6880 2029. Cocktails and drinks at the bar, sushi upstairs, salads and traditional food downstairs. Music from 23.00. Book for sushi.

Il Locale, Vicolo del Fico 3, ☎ 06 687 9075; open 22.00-4.00; closed Monday. A favourite for live music.

La Maison, Vicolo dei Granari 4, ☎ 06 683 3312; open 23.00-4.00; closed Monday. One of the trendiest clubs of the moment. Good DJs.

Le Bain Art Gallery, Via delle Botteghe Oscure 32a (Largo Argentina), *T* 06 686 5673; open 19.00-2.00; closed Monday. A stylish cocktail bar serving dinner too.

Supperclub, Via de'Nari 15 (Pantheon) *T* 06 686 4170. A stark white, post-modern look for a new restaurant where dinner is consumed reclining on comfortable sofas and watching interesting performances (actors, singers, artists, etc).

Trinity College, Via del Collegio Romano 6, *T* 06 678 6472; open until 3.00. There are pubs in Rome but they're just not the same. This is one exception. Besides the basic ales, there are salads for lunch and loud music for dinner.

Via Santa Maria dell'Anima (behind Piazza Navona) has a number of bars populated mainly by foreigners. The English favourites are **Anima** and **Bebamus**.

shopping

Most of the shops in this section are best reached on foot as they are tucked away in the narrow streets of the centre. To cover longer distances, the buses running along Corso Vittorio Emanuele (40, 46, 62, 64 etc) may come in handy.

ACCESSORIES

Baullà, Via dei Baullari 37. A small shop just off Campo dei Fiori with refined clothes and accessories.

Cappelleria Troncarelli, Via della Cuccagna 15 (off Piazza Navona), *T* 06 687 9320. All sorts of hats, from cylinders to Florentine straw hats and original Panamas.

Fabbrica Nuova, Via Monte Farina 50 (Campo dei Fiori), *T* 06 686 5859. Designer jewellery and more.

Josephine de Huertas. Bags by Hervè Chapelier and stylish shoes. See Clothes (p 80) for the address.

Le Tartarughe, Via Pie' di Marmo 33 (Pantheon), *T* 06 699 0874. Actually two shops facing each other selling bags, shoes, jewellery and clothes designed by the owners.

Manecchi, Via Campo Marzio 35 (Pantheon), *T* 06 687 1515. Fun shoes (by Camper) and leather accessories.

Yien, Via Campo Marzio 33 (Pantheon), *T* 06 687 1346. Fine leather goods and more.

ANTIQUES

Antiques galleries as well as artisans and restorers (marble sculptors, stucco workers, etc) concentrate around Via dei Coronari (near Piazza Navona), Via Giulia and Via dei Cappellari (off Campo dei Fiori).

Nardecchia, Piazza Navona 25, *T* 06 686 9318. Period prints.

ART SUPPLIES

Poggi, Via del Gesù 74-75, *T* 06 679 3674. All sorts of artists' materials. Wonderful papers and more next door.

BEAUTY

Casamaria, Via della Scrofa 71-72, *T* 06 6833 074l. Well stocked *profumeria* (soaps, lotions, creams, perfumes) with 30% discount on all items.

BOOKS

Altroquando, Via del Governo Vecchio 80, *T* 06 687 9825. This recently opened bookshop specializes in cinema.

Antica Libreria Cascianelli, Largo Febo 15 (Piazza Navona), *T* 06 6880 2806. The best address in Rome for rare books.

Babele, Via dei Banchi Vecchi 116, *T* 06 687 6628. The best gay bookshop in Rome.

Croce, Corso Vittorio Emanuele 158, *T* 06 6880 2269. An historic address for books.

Feltrinelli, LargoTorre Argentina 5a, *T* 06 6880 3248. One of the largest bookshops in town, it also has an international section.

La grotta del libro, Via del Pellegrino 172, *T* 06 687 7567. Art books, exhibition catalogues and more at discount prices.

Librars, Via Zanardelli 3 (Piazza Navona), *T* 06 687 5931. Fine art books and exhibition catalogues.

Libreria del Viaggiatore, Via del Pellegrino 78, *T* 06 6880 1048. The traveller's bookshop: anything from guidebooks to travel narratives and diaries, in various languages.

CHOCOLATE
Confetteria Moriondo e Gariglio, Via Piè di marmo 21-22, *T* 06 699 0856. No need for comment.

CLOTHES
Arsenale, Via del Governo Vecchio 64, *T* 06 686 1380. Trendy clothes and new designer labels.

Cenci, Via Campo Marzio 1-7, *T* 06 699 0681. Classical elegance for men and women (wonderful suits).

Degli Effetti, Piazza Capranica 79-93, *T* 06 679 1650. A small shop with a fine selection from the latest designer collections (Dolce & Gabbana, Robert Clergerie, etc).

Dulce Vidoza, Via dell'Orso 58 (near Palazzo Altemps), *T* 06 689 3007. A minimalist interior for essential clothes. Sandals and linen blouses for the blazing heat of the Roman summer.

EDO, Piazza del Paradiso 18 (close to Sant'Andrea della Valle), *T* 06 6819 2659. A Japanese shop and art gallery famous for its kimonos and original fabrics. Occasionally it organizes contemporary art exhibitions.

Fata Morgana, Via del Governo Vecchio 27, *T* 06 687 9995. A special shop for unusual clothes.

Jade e More, Via del Governo Vecchio 36, *T* 06 683 3936. Original clothes with precious fabrics designed by the owner. Shoes are sold as well.

Josephine de Huertas, Via di Parione 19-20, *T* 06 6830 0156; and Via del Governo Vecchio 68. Fine clothes and more.

Lei, Via dei Giubbonari 103, *T* 06 687 5432. Designer clothes (Alberto Biani, etc) and wonderful coats for young women.

LP 64, Via dei Prefetti 6, *T* 06 687 3646. Classic suits and shirts for gentlemen.

L'una e l'altra, Via del Governo Vecchio 105, *T* 06 6880 4995. Dries van Noten, Martin Margela and other designers.

Momento, Piazza Cairoli 9 (Via Arenula). From linen dresses to designer bags and other objects.

Nuyorica, Piazza della Pollarola 36-37 (Campo dei Fiori), *T* 06 6889 1243.

Minimalist style and unusual shoes for women.

SBU, Via di San Pantaleo 68, *T* 06 6880 2547. Innovative fashion by two young Roman designers.

Paola Vessarotti, Vicolo della Cuccagna 12 (Piazza Navona). Though not visible from the street, this is a special showroom producing beautiful knitwear - from sweaters and dresses in winter to delicate bathing suits in summer.

Wazoo, Via dei Giubbonari 27, *T* 06 686 9362. Stylish clothes and shoes by young French designers.

FLOWERS

Giardino segreto, Via di Panico 6 (opposite the bridge of Castel Sant'Angelo), *T* 06 683 3683. An art gallery of flowers. The owners treat every plant and composition as a unique work of art.

Ingegnoli, Via Arenula 22, *T* 06 687 2624. Anything from basil plants to sophisticated flower compositions (particularly over Christmas). Rare seeds and miraculous fertilizers.

Tulipani Bianchi, Via dei Bergamaschi 59 (Piazza di Pietra), *T* 06 678 5449. Floral design, compositions, vases and candles mixing Japanese minimalism with a Mitteleuropean twist (the owners are Swiss).

FOOD

Ai Monasteri, Corso Rinascimento 72, *T* 06 6880 2783. Established in 1892 by the Nardi family, it still collects the products of monasteries and abbeys throughout Italy: from honey, preserves and chocolate, to oil, wines and liqueurs, as well as soaps and creams.

Andreoli, Via del Pellegrino 116, *T* 06 6880 2121. A traditional *salsamenteria* (deli shop) with local cheeses (*caciotta, pecorino romano, ricotta*), *prosciutto* from Norcia and homemade sausages.

Antica Norcineria Viola, Campo dei Fiori 42, *T* 06 6880 6114. Since 1890 this shop has specialized in excellent cold meats.

Campo dei Fiori The market held here every morning (except Sundays) is the best place to get fresh fruit and vegetables.

Comptoir de France, Via Giulia 195, *T* 06 686 7762. French cheeses, patés, sauces, wines and champagne.

Ferrara, Piazza Trilussa 41 (Trastevere), *T* 06 5833 3920; never closed. The best chocolate brands, balsamic vinegar, olive oils, sun-dried tomatoes, coffees and more.

Fratelli Carilli, Via Torre Argentina 11 (Largo Argentina), *T* 06 6880 3789. One of the best charcuteries in town, with excellent varieties of prosciutto, homemade sausages and cold meats.

La Corte, Via della Gatta 1 (Pantheon), *T* 06 678 3842. A tiny shop selling caviar, smoked salmon and other fish delicacies.

Il Forno di Campo dei Fiori, Campo dei Fiori 22, *T* 06 6880 6662. Besides the classic breads, you can get an unbeatable *pizza rossa al taglio*: red pizza cut in squares, thin and crunchy as the Romans like it.

Roscioli, Via dei Giubbonari 21 (Campo dei Fiori), *T* 06 687 5287. This wonderful shop-cum-wine bar has about 300 different cheeses, fresh creamy butter, homemade pasta, *Jamon Iberico*, charcuterie of all sorts, wines, olive oils and whatever you wish. They also run a bakery at Via dei Chiavari 34, specializing in a continuous production of thin strips of pizza.

HOMES

D Cube, Via della Pace 38 (Piazza Navona), *T* 06 686 1218. Kitchen accessories from all over the world.

Giorgi e Febbi, Piazza della Rotonda 61, *T* 06 679 1649. Established over 200 years ago this shop is located on the ground floor of the historic Albergo del Sole, where famous guests from Ariosto to Mascagni spent their Roman days. The present owner keeps tradition alive with hand woven cottons in all designs and colours.

Ilaria miani, Via Monserrato 35, *T* 06 683 3160. Everything from furniture to picture frames in the owner's distinctive style.

Interno Rosso, Via del Pellegrino 15, *T* 06 686 7457. Symphony in red for homes and interiors (wonderful paper lamps).

Mastro Raphael, Piazza di Montecitorio 116, *T* 06 6920 0632. Famous fabrics and top quality linens for beds and tables.

Rob'art, Piazza di Pietra 32-33, *T* 06 6938 0484. Ceramics (Vietri, Grottaglie, etc) and artistic glass.

Sciam, Via del Pellegrino 56, *T* 06 6830 8957. Glass in all shapes and colours (dive into the boxes in the cellar). They also restore oriental carpets and serve delicious mint tea next door.

Spazio Sette, Via dei Barbieri 7, *T* 06 686 9747. Three floors of stylish ideas for homes, kitchens and tables. From the must-have classics to unusual pieces by avant-garde designers.

Stockmarket, Via dei Banchi Vecchi 51-52, *T* 06 686 4238. Fun objects and practical items for homes and gardens from all over the world. Good ideas for presents at bargain prices.

Tanca, Salita dei Crescenzi 10-12 (Pantheon), *T* 06 6880 3328. Period prints and more.

Tè e Teiere, Via del Pellegrino 85, *T* 06 686 8824. Everything you need for a proper tea ritual.

WA. BE 190 ZA, Via Monserrato 121a, *T* 06 687 8671. Interesting objects by young artists and designers.

What not Why not, Via Monserrato 35, *T* 06 683 3160. Designer objects.

JEWELLERY

Barbara Spinelli, Via dei Prefetti 25 (Pantheon), *T* 06 6830 1131. Ethnic creations with precious and semi-precious stones.

Danae, Via della Maddalena 40 (Pantheon), *T* 06 679 1881. Fine necklaces, bracelets and earrings from various countries.

Liliana Michilli, Via dei Banchi Vecchi 37, *T* 06 6839 2154. Copies of famous jewels from Cartier to Bulgari.

Massimiliano Arriga, Piazza Capranica 93a (Pantheon), *T* 06 678 4793. Unique pieces by great designers.

Via dei Pettinari A famous street filled with goldsmiths and jewellers selling new and secondhand pieces.

KIDS

Bertè, Piazza Navona 107-111, *T* 06 687 5011. An historic shop for wooden toys and more.

La Città del Sole, Via della Scrofa 65, *T* 06 6880 3805. A heaven for kids and adults alike: toys, models, books, etc.

Replay, Via della Rotonda 24, *T* 06 683 3073. Clothes for teenagers.

SHOES

AVC, Largo del Pallaro 1 (Campo dei Fiori). Adriana Campanile classics with a 50% discount.

Borini, Via dei Pettinari 86. Always crowded, this is a favourite with women of all ages.

Funke, Piazza della Maddalena 52, *T* 06 678 1183. Showroom in Via della

Rosetta 6. Shoes and leather goods for men.

Impronta, Via del Governo Vecchio 1, *T* 06 689 6947. Ladies' shoes from classic to extravagant.

Loco, Via dei Baullari 22, *T* 06 6880 8216. Extravagant shoes for young men and women.

Posto Italiano, Via dei Giubbonari 37a, *T* 06 686 9373. Trendy shoes for young men and women.

STATIONERY

Campo Marzio Design, Via Campo Marzio 41, *T* 06 6880 7877. Pens, paper and much more.

Gianfranceschi, Via della Rotonda 15, *T* 06 687 5313. Diaries, boxes, photo-albums, etc, in lovely Florentine paper.

Pagot, Via del Gesù 90, *T* 06 678 1137. Old stationery and postcards from the 1930s and 1940s.

Stilo Fetti, Via degli Orfani 82, *T* 06 678 9662. Wonderful fountain pens.

VINTAGE

Via del Governo Vecchio is your best bet. Along with the trendiest shops there are a number of places to brouse for vintage shirts, coats, gowns, bags and shoes.

WINE

Enoteca Corsi, Via del Gesù 87. Attached to the *trattoria* (see Restaurants, p 74) is a small wine shop.

Enoteca al Parlamento, Via dei Prefetti 15 (Parliament), *T* 06 6873 3446. One of the oldest and best stocked shops in town.

Mr Wine, Piazza del Parlamento 5, *T* 06 6813 4141.

TREVI SPAGNA

Fontana di Trevi

The symbol of Baroque Rome, the fountain derives its name from
'trivium' as it was erected at the junction of three streets. It takes
its waters from the Acqua Vergine, an underground aqueduct built
by Agrippa (19 BC) to supply his public baths near the Pantheon.
The conduits were restored in the 15c and 16c and still feed the
fountains of Piazza di Spagna, Piazza Navona and Piazza Farnese.

Various important architects, including Bernini, Ferdinando
Fuga and Luigi Vanvitelli, presented designs for a new, grander
fountain to replace a much simpler basin of 1453 by Leon Battista
Alberti. Clement XII held a competition in 1732 and chose the little
known Nicola Salvi whose monumental project was inspired by
Bernini's precedents, such as Piazza Navona, and featured, as a
theatrical backdrop, the façade of Palazzo Poli. The fountain was
completed in 1762, after Salvi's death, by Pietro Bracci who carved

Fontana di Trevi

the figures of **Neptune** and
the **Tritons**. To the sides are
the statues of **Health** and
Abundance by the Florentine
sculptor Filippo della Valle.
Above are two reliefs in
which a Virgin shows the
spring to Roman soldiers
and Agrippa approves the
plans of the aqueduct. The
four statues at the top
represent the **Seasons** and
higher still are the arms of
Clement XII Corsini. As a
traditional image of Rome
the fountain has featured

numerous films including Federico Fellini's La Dolce Vita (1959).
The well-known custom of throwing a coin into the waters is said
to ensure a return to the city.

Palazzo Colonna

OPEN	**Galleries** on the first floor open Sat 9.00-13.00
	Appartamento della Principessa Isabelle by appointment only and extra charge
CLOSED	August
CHARGES	7€; concessions €5.50
TELEPHONE	06 678 4350, 06 679 4362
WWW.	galleriacolonna.it
MAIN ENTRANCE	Via della Pilotta 17

Descendants of the powerful counts of Tuscolo, the Colonna are one of the oldest aristocratic families in Rome, their origins dating back to the 12c. Their first residence in Rome was a fortified tower built on the site of the Temple of Serapis. This was transformed into a palace by Oddone Colonna, who became Pope Martin V in 1417 and lived here from 1424 until his death in 1431. The palace was rebuilt and sumptuously decorated in the 17c and 18c. In 1654 Cardinal Girolamo I and his architect, Antonio del Grande, began the richly decorated gallery on the first floor. When Del Grande died in 1671 work continued under the direction of Girolamo Fontana and was concluded in 1730 by Nicola Michetti who added the façade on Piazza Santissimi Apostoli. A number of talented fresco painters, of Venetian inspiration, were employed in the gallery to illustrate one of the most important events in the family's history, the victory of Marcantonio II Colonna over the Turks in the naval battle of Lepanto (1571).

   (As the paintings in the collection are not labelled, their inventory numbers are included in the text.)

HIGHLIGHTS

Bronzino, *Venus, Cupid and Satyr*	Sala della Colonna Bellica
17c frescoes; **Salviati**, *Adam and Eve* **Cerrini**, *St Sebastian*	Gallery

Landscapes by Gaspard Dughet	Room of the Landscapes
Annibale Carracci, *Bean-eater* Veronese, *Portrait of a Man*	Room of the Apotheosis of Martin V

SALA DELLA COLONNA BELLICA The room is named after a column standing at the centre and is decorated with a ceiling fresco of the *Apotheosis of Marcantonio II Colonna* (1700) by Giuseppe Bartolomeo Chiari, a pupil of Carlo Maratta. The paintings include **Bronzino**'s *Venus, Cupid and Satyr* (32) and a *Madonna and Child with St Peter and a Donor* by Palma Vecchio (139). The side tables were designed by Giovanni Paolo Schor and are decorated with a siren and Turkish prisoners, both referring to the naval battle of Lepanto. The cannon ball on the steps leading to the gallery was shot from the Gianicolo, on the other side of the Tiber, during the French siege of Rome in the summer of 1849.

GALLERY The magnificent gallery is decorated with mirrors, chandeliers, paintings, frescoes and antique sculptures. The latter were found here on the site of the Temple of Serapis, which was demolished in 1625. The marbles were re-used in the construction of the palace while the sculptures, partially reconstructed by the sculptor Orfeo Boselli, became part of the family's collection. The frescoes on the ceiling were executed in 1675-8 by Giovanni Coli and Filippo Gherardi, two painters from Lucca whose work shows the influence of Veronese and Pietro da Cortona. The scenes depict the various episodes of the *Battle of Lepanto*.

The four Venetian mirrors on the walls have flower paintings by Mario de'Fiori and Giovanni Stanchi and putti by Carlo Maratta. The paintings include two versions of *St John the Baptist* (162-163) by Salvator Rosa, the fine *St Sebastian* (46) by Giovanni Domenico Cerrini, and Francesco Salviati's *Adam and Eve*, a replica of the fresco in the Chigi Chapel at Santa Maria del Popolo (1554).

ROOM OF THE LANDSCAPES Sixty-six landscapes used to hang in this room, which still displays a number of paintings by Gaspard Dughet (54-65) and J.F. van Bloemen (21-24). Also here are two fine desks. One is decorated with ivory bas-reliefs after works by Raphael and Michelangelo and was carved by Franz and Dominikus Steinhart from Augsburg; the other is adorned with semi-precious stones and bronze statuettes of Apollo and the Muses. The ceiling fresco of the *Battle of Lepanto* was painted in 1692 by the Venetian Sebastiano Ricci.

ROOM OF THE APOTHEOSIS OF MARTIN V This room is named after the painting by Benedetto Luti (c 1720) at the centre of the ceiling. On display here are important works of the 16c-17c, including the *Portrait of a Man* by **Veronese** (197) which in its handling of colours and painted surface anticipates El Greco; the *Portrait of Onofrio Panvinio* by Jacopo Tintoretto (190); the *Bean-eater* by **Annibale Carracci** (43), revolutionary in the realistic treatment of its theme, bringing to mind later Spanish painting or even Van Gogh's Potato Eaters. Also here are Salviati's *Raising of Lazarus* (169) and *Portrait of a Man* (170), Bronzino's *Virgin and Child with St Elisabeth and St John* (33), Lanfranco's *St Charles Borromeo* (97), and paintings by Guercino (83, 85, 86).

THRONE ROOM As in other princely houses, this was reserved for the pope. Here are portraits of *Martin V*, after a work by Pisanello, *Marcantonio II Colonna* and *Felice Colonna Orsini*, after paintings by Scipione Pulzone. The nautical chart and diploma were given to Marcantonio II by the senate and people of Rome after his victory at Lepanto.

ROOM OF THE PRIMITIVES The room is named after the late medieval and 15c paintings that were added to the collection in the 19c. Among these are the *Enthroned Madonna and Child* by Stefano da Zevio (179) and a *Crucifixion* by the Bolognese Iacopo Avanzi (early 15c). Also here is a *Madonna* by Bartolomeo Vivarini (198), one by Giuliano Bugiardini (35), and a small *Madonna and Child* by Bernardino Luini (107). Of special note are Simone Cantarini's fine *Holy Family* (38), Bernart van Orley's *Seven Sorrows* and *Seven Joys of the Virgin* (137-138), and the *Resurrection of Christ* (143) by the young Pietro da Cortona, showing members of the Colonna family.

APPARTAMENTO DELLA PRINCIPESSA ISABELLE (Open by appointment only.) The apartment includes frescoes of the 15c by Pinturicchio, of the 16c by Pomarancio and others, and of the 17c by Gaspard Dughet. There are paintings by Jan Bruegel the Elder and Gaspare Vanvitelli.

Palazzo Barberini

OPEN	Tues-Sun 9.00-19.00. Telephone in advance to see the apartments
CLOSED	Mon; 1/1, 1/5, 25/12
CHARGES	€5, booking fee €1.03
TELEPHONE	06 481 4591
MAIN ENTRANCE	Via Barberini 18

This magnificent palace was begun in 1624 by Carlo Maderno for the Barberini pope, Urban VIII. The initial block-like structure, which incorporated a pre-existing building, was soon transformed into an open-plan villa with two side wings, modelled on Peruzzi's Villa Farnesina. After his death, in 1629, Maderno was succeeded by Gianlorenzo Bernini who finished the palace in 1633 with the help of Francesco Borromini, Maderno's former assistant.

Pietro da Cortona painted the ceiling in the main hall with an impressive fresco illustrating *The Triumph of Divine Providence* and celebrating the glory of the Barberini (1633-9). The four allegorical scenes immediately below refer to the temporal work of the pope. On the walls are seven cartoons by the school of Pietro da Cortona showing scenes from the life of Urban VIII. They were designed for a set of tapestries woven in the Barberini workshop (active 1627-83) and now exhibited in the Vatican.

GALLERIA NAZIONALE D'ARTE ANTICA The palace houses a rich collection of 17c paintings, some good examples from the 15c-16c and a selection of foreign works. Highlights on the first floor include Filippo Lippi's **Madonna and Child** and **Annunciation**, a beautiful **Mary Magdalene** by Piero di Cosimo, a **Holy Family** by Andrea del Sarto, Raphael's famous portrait of a lady, arbitrarily identified with his mistress and called **La Fornarina** and Bronzino's portrait of **Stefano Colonna**. The second floor has 17c paintings by Annibale Carracci, Guido Reni, Domenichino, Guercino, Lanfranco, Gaulli, Sacchi, Caravaggio (**Narcissus**; **Judith with the Head of Holophernes**), Hans Holbein the Younger's **Portrait of Henry VIII** and Quentin Metsys' of **Erasmus**.

The 18c Barberini apartments, where the family lived until 1960, preserve their Rococo decoration and period furniture.

SAN CARLINO ALLE QUATTRO FONTANE

OPEN	Mon-Fri 9.30-12.30 and 16.00-18.00; Sat 8.00-12.00
CLOSED	Sat afternoon and Sun

On Via del Quirinale, not far from Palazzo Barberini, is another masterpiece of Baroque inventiveness, built by Francesco Borromini as his first independent commission and providing an interesting contrast with Bernini's Sant'Andrea. The cramped site on the corner of a narrow street prompted the unusual undulating façade (1665-8).

The interior, completed at a much earlier date (1638-41), anticipated the interplay of convex and concave expressed outside. Typical of Borromini's architecture is the use of geometric rather than arithmetic units to define volumes. The concept is more medieval than 17c and may have been inspired by his early training as a stonemason in Lombardy. The interior can be understood as an undulating Greek cross, inspired by the Piazza d'Oro of Hadrian's villa at Tivoli and obtained through a combination of triangles that are unified and governed by the oval dome above. The triangular unit, which refers to the Holy Trinity, recurred a few years later in Borromini's star-shaped Sant'Ivo alla Sapienza (1642-50; p 67).

Besides showing an extraordinary imagination, Borromini's

architecture is also marked by a strong sculptural quality, evident here in the massive columns and tight rhythm that articulates the façade and inner walls, and in the maze of deep geometrical coffers that decorate the dome. The adjoining cloister, octagonal in plan, and the crypt with its fantastical curves linked by a continuous cornice, were also designed by Borromini.

SANT'ANDREA AL QUIRINALE

OPEN	8.00-12.00 and 16.00-19.00
CLOSED	Tues

This beautiful small church, close to the Qurinal palace, was built by Gianlorenzo Bernini in 1658-70 for Cardinal Camillo Pamphilj. The unusual elliptical plan was ingeniously adapted to fit the narrow site. The elegant convex façade counteracts the embracing arms of the projecting side walls. The interior is articulated by niches that visually expand the oval space and are decorated with fine stuccoes and 17c altarpieces, including Baciccia's *St Francis Xavier* (first chapel to the right) and Carlo Maratta's *Virgin and Child with Stanislaus Kostka* (second chapel on the left). On the high altar is the *Crucifixion of St Andrew* by Borgognone, above which are stucco angels and cherubim, and the figure of St Andrew who rises to the sky through a concave opening in the pediment.

Piazza di Spagna

Piazza di Spagna is named after the Spanish Embassy to the Holy See, which has been located in the square since 1622. At that time, the French ambassador and British consul also had their offices here while foreign visitors and a thriving English community filled the hotels and *pensioni* of the area. Keats died in the pink house by the steps and the Brownings' residence was nearby. **Babington's Tea Rooms** (to the left of the steps) still caters for nostalgic 5 o'clock appetites and the English church is close at hand in Via del Babuino.

Today the piazza and the neighbouring streets are filled with elegant shops and fashion houses. At the centre is the *Fontana della Barcaccia*, commissioned in 1629 by Urban VIII from Pietro Bernini and his more illustrious son, Gianlorenzo. Shaped like a sunken ship, the fountain commemorates the flood of 1598 when the rising Tiber washed a boat here.

The **Spanish Steps** were built in 1723-6 by Francesco de Sanctis to connect the piazza with the church of Trinità dei Monti above. The theatrical design, curving in and out through a series of terraces, is a Rococo masterpiece. Opposite the steps runs the fashionable **Via Condotti**, the old Via Trinitatis, built in 1544 during the time of Paul III and re-named after the water conduits of the Aqua Vergine. At the beginning of the street is the **Caffè Greco**, established by Greek immigrants in 1760 and later frequented by artists, including Goethe, Gogol, Berlioz, Stendhal, Baudelaire and Wagner.

To the south of Piazza di Spagna is a tall Corinthian column dedicated to the Virgin Mary and erected in 1854 to celebrate the Dogma of the Immaculate Conception. Just opposite stands the **College of Propaganda Fide**, established in the 17c for the training of missionaries. The façade on Via di Propaganda and the chapel inside (1660-6) are among Borromini's most creative inventions.

MAUSOLEUM OF AUGUSTUS
OPEN   By appointment, **T 06 6710 3819** or **06 6710 2070**

West of Piazza di Spagna and Via del Corso, in Piazza Augusto Imperatore, are the remains of the huge tomb erected by Augustus for himself and the Julio-Claudian family (28 BC). The last emperor to be buried here was Nerva (AD 98); all subsequent emperors of the 2c AD, with the exception of Trajan, were entombed in the Mausoleum of Hadrian on the opposite bank of the Tiber (later transformed into the fortress of Castel Sant'Angelo, p 179).

Augustus' mausoleum followed Oriental models such as the 4c BC tomb of Mausolus, king of Caria, or the tomb of Alexander the Great, which the emperor had seen in Alexandria. The circular structure was faced with travertine and surmounted by a cylinder and a tumulus of earth. This was planted with cypresses and topped by a bronze statue of Augustus. At the sides of the entrance were two obelisks, later moved to Piazza del Quirinale and behind Santa Maria Maggiore. Close to the entrance was a series of bronze tablets inscribed with the autobiographical account of the emperor's deeds, *Res gestae Divi Augusti*. These were reproduced on the basement of the Ara Pacis (see below). In the Middle Ages the mausoleum was turned into a fortress for the Colonna family and then a quarry for travertine. The ruins were successively adapted as a garden, an arena (16c), a wooden amphitheatre (18c) and a concert hall (early 1900s).

ARA PACIS
OPEN   Reopening planned for 2004; for information, **T 06 6880 6848**

Between the mausoleum and the Tiber stands the monumental altar that was erected in 13 BC and dedicated four years later to the peace restored by Augustus after his victorious campaigns in Spain and Gaul. It was reconstructed in 1937-8 from scattered fragments and will eventually be displayed in a new exhibition space designed by Richard Meier.

The altar is one of the most remarkable examples of the art produced in the time of Augustus under the influence of Classical Greek sculpture. It consists of a square marble enclosure decorated with reliefs and a pattern of acanthus leaves and vines. At the sides of the north entrance are scenes referring to the origins of Rome. At the south entrance are the personifications of *Tellus*, Goddess of the Earth (left), and a much-damaged *Rome* (right). The panels on the sides depict the consecration ceremony of the altar, with the procession of Augustus, his family members, state officials and priests. They were intended to stress Augustus' piety and his attachment to tradition, and also to sanction his right to absolute power as successor of Romulus and Aeneas. The acanthus garlands represent prosperity, while the figure of 'Magna Mater' (holding babies and fruit and surrounded by lush plants and grazing animals) is connected to the idea of fertility and abundance supposedly introduced by Augustus' peace.

Piazza del Popolo

The piazza was redesigned in the 19c as the last great expression of papal Rome, but for centuries visitors from the north entered the city here via the **Porta del Popolo**, the ancient Porta Flaminia. The gate marked the beginning of the Via Flaminia (laid out by Caius Flaminius in 221-219 BC). The elevation overlooking the square was re-designed by Gianlorenzo Bernini for the triumphal entry of Christina of Sweden (23 December 1655), the queen who abdicated the throne, converted to Roman Catholicism and spent the rest of her life in Rome.

Piazza del Popolo

The square takes its name from the 15c church of Santa Maria del Popolo (p 96), and represents the grand culmination of an urban project that was begun in the 16c and found its final configuration more than three centuries later. The so-called Trident of streets which depart from the square took shape in the early 1500s when Via del Babuino and Via di Ripetta were added to the pre-existing Via del Corso. At the converging point of the three streets Sixtus V (1589) placed the *obelisk of Rameses* II (1200 BC), brought by Augustus from Egypt and originally set up in the Circus Maximus.

The twin churches of **Santa Maria in Montesanto** (designed by Bernini) and **Santa Maria dei Miracoli** (by Carlo Rainaldi and Carlo Fontana) were built in the second half of the 17c. The piazza was given its definitive appearance in the early 19c when Giuseppe Valadier designed the surrounding palaces and the ramps leading up to the Pincio, moved the obelisk to the centre and decorated its base with fountains and lions in the Egyptian style. In the hemicycles at the sides are two fountains shaped like giant seashells and surmounted by sculptures representing *Neptune with Tritons* and *Rome between the rivers Tiber and Anio* (1824).

Santa Maria del Popolo

OPEN   7.00-12.00 and 16.00-19.00. Sun and PH 8.00-13.30 and
              16.30-19.00

The church stands on the site of a chapel built in 1099 by Paschal II in thanksgiving for the liberation of Jerusalem and the end of the First Crusade. It was erected over the tomb where Nero had been buried and where demons were supposed to hide in the guise of black crows. The pope cut down the tree that sheltered them and commissioned the church at the expense of the Roman people (hence the name), dedicating it to the Virgin Mary. According to another tradition, the name derives from *populus*, or poplar tree, referring to a sacred wood of poplars that was here in ancient times.

The church was rebuilt in 1227 by Gregory IX and again under Sixtus IV (1472-7) Della Rovere. The façade, which dates from the 15c, is attributed to Andrea Bregno. Visible from the piazza are the octagonal dome (the first of its kind in Rome) and the bell-tower, unique for its conical top with terracotta scales and the four pinnacles of Lombard derivation (in 1472 the church had passed to a Congregation of Augustinians from Lombardy).

INTERIOR

The interior was changed in the early 16c when **Bramante** modified the choir and **Raphael** designed the Chigi Chapel, and even more in the mid 17c when **Bernini** transformed the interior with the addition of female saints and other decorations executed in stucco by Antonio Raggi.

The first chapel to the right has frescoes of 1485-9 by **Pinturicchio** and his assistant Tiberio d'Assisi, including a *Nativity* over the altar and a worn *Life of St Jerome* in the lunettes. The finely decorated screen and the *Tombs of the Cardinals Cristoforo* and *Domenico della Rovere*, nephews of Sixtus IV (to the right), are the work of Andrea Bregno and Mino da Fiesole (who carved the Madonna).

On the **high altar** is the venerated painting of the *Madonna del Popolo*, early 13c and in the Byzantine style. The choir behind is one of Bramante's earliest works in Rome, commissioned by Julius II Della Rovere and finely decorated in 1508-10 with ceiling frescoes by **Pinturicchio**. The splendid *Tombs of Cardinal Basso della Rovere* (1507) and *Cardinal Ascanio Sforza* (1505) are signed by **Andrea Sansovino** and are representative of the transition in style from the 15c to the High Renaissance.

In the left transept is the **Cerasi Chapel** with two masterpieces by **Caravaggio**, painted in 1600-1, contemporary with his paintings in San Luigi dei Francesi (p 55). The *Conversion of St Paul* is the second version of a rejected (and weaker) painting, now in the Odescalchi collection. The vertical format required by the site inspired the bold diagonal compositions of both canvases. In the *Crucifixion of St Peter* the entire picture plane is taken over by the essential elements of the story and the large scale figures, leaving no room for a descriptive setting. The lighting effects and sombre colours as well as the psychological realism of the faces and gestures enhance the emotional impact of the image. The intense drama expressed by Caravaggio contrasts strikingly with the *Assumption* above the altar by Annibale Carracci (1601), who also designed the frescoes in the vault. Monsignor Tiberio Cerasi evidently commissioned the paintings with the express intention of juxtaposing the work of the best artists of the day as representatives of two opposite trends: classicism versus naturalism.

The octagonal **Chigi Chapel** was commissioned from **Raphael** by the wealthy banker Agostino Chigi in 1513-6. Work came to a halt in 1520 with the deaths of both the patron and the artist, and was resumed after 1652 by Cardinal Fabio Chigi (the future Alexander VII) and Gianlorenzo Bernini.

Raphael designed the cartoons for the mosaics in the dome, while the frescoes of the *Creation* and *Fall* and the medallions of the *Seasons* are by Francesco Salviati (1552-4). The *Nativity of the Virgin*, over the altar, is by the Venetian Sebastiano del Piombo (1530-4), Michelangelo's most talented pupil. The prophets *Jonah*, with the whale, and *Elijah* were designed by Raphael and made by Lorenzetto. The statues of *Habakkuk*, with the angel, and *Daniel*, with the lion, were both sculpted by Bernini.

The former Augustinian convent adjoining the church was where Martin Luther stayed in 1511.

on route

AROUND FONTANA DI TREVI

Accademia Nazionale di San Luca In the piazza of the same name rises Palazzo Carpegna, ascribed to assistants of Giacomo della Porta and rebuilt by Francesco Borromini in 1643-7. This is the seat of the Painting Academy that was founded in 1577 by Girolamo Muziano of Brescia. The Galleria dell' Accademia di San Luca contains an interesting collection of paintings from the 17c to the 19c. Mon-Sat 10.00-12.30, *T* 06 679 8850; closed July and August.

Calcografia Nazionale In Via della Stamperia, behind the Trevi Fountain, is an important collection of some 23,000 engraving plates, including almost all of those by Piranesi. The Neoclassical building is by Luigi Valadier. Since 1975 the Calcografia has been united with the **Gabinetto Disegni e Stampe of the Villa Farnesina** (Via della Lungara), south of the river, which holds 21,000 drawings and 110,000 prints. Together they form the Istituto Nazionale per la Grafica. Mon-Sat 9.00-13.00, *T* 06 699 801.

Fontana del Tritone

Fontana del Tritone At the centre of busy Piazza Barberini, this scenic fountain was made by Gianlorenzo Bernini for Urban VIII (1642-3). A masterly Baroque invention, it combines naturalistic elements with mythological and allegorical motifs (e.g. the Barberini bees).

Galleria Comunale d'Arte Moderna, Via Francesco Crispi 22. Located in a former Carmelite convent, the gallery exhibits the art of some of the best 20c Italian artists, including Giacomo Manzù, Nino Costa, Aristide Sartorio, Vincenzo Gemito, Giacomo Balla, Duilio Cambellotti, Felice Casorati, Mario Sironi, Carlo Carrà, Filippo De Pisis and Alberto Savinio. Open 10.00-13.30 and 14.30-18.30, Sun and PH 9.30-13.00, closed Mon, *T* 06 474 2848.

Palazzo Pallavicini Rospigliosi, on Via Ventiquattro Maggio, occupies the site of the Baths of Constantine and was built for Scipione Borghese by Flaminio Ponzio and Carlo Maderno (1605-16). In 1704 it was acquired by the Pallavicini Rospigliosi. In the charming garden is the **Casino Pallavicini**, which was designed by Giovanni Vasanzio. The fresco decoration includes Guido Reni's *Aurora* of 1613-4. It is open on the first day of each month, except 1 Jan, 10.00-12.00 and 15.00-17.00, *T* 06 482 7224.

Palazzo Quirinale First built as a residence for the popes, it was transformed after 1870 into the palace of the kings of Italy and in 1948 into the official residence of the president of the Italian Republic. The building was begun in 1573 for Gregory XIII (Boncompagni) by Martino Longhi il Vecchio and Ottaviano Mascherino, who also laid out the gardens. The façade was designed by Domenico Fontana (1587) for Sixtus V. Flaminio Ponzio and Carlo Maderno, Paul V's architects, continued where Fontana left off (1605-21), then Bernini added the tower on the left of the entrance and worked on the long and monotonous front, the 'manica lunga' (the long sleeve) facing Via del Quirinale. Work was completed during the pontificate of Alexander VII Chigi (1655-67) who commissioned Pietro da Cortona to direct the interior decorations. *Sun 8.30-12.30; gardens only on 2 June; closed Aug and main public holidays.*

The Quirinal Hill is easily reached from the Trevi Fountain by Via di San Vincenzo and Via della Dataria. It acquired its name either from a Temple of Quirinus or from Cures, an ancient Sabine town northeast of Rome whose population came to settle on the hill before the foundation of Rome. During the late Republic and throughout the Empire the area was embellished with gardens and summer villas. Caracalla (AD 211-217) built a Temple of Serapis and Constantine (306-337) his Baths, where the colossal marble group of the *Dioscuri* (Castor and Pollux with their horses) was found. These Roman copies after Greek originals of the 5c BC became famous in the Middle Ages as one of *the* sights of Rome. In the late 16c, Domenico Fontana, Sixtus V's architect, placed the group at the centre of the piazza. The obelisk in the middle originally stood by the entrance of the Mausoleum of Augustus and was brought here by Pius VI in 1786.

Facing the square are the **Scuderie Pontificie**, the papal stables, built in 1722-30 by Alessandro Specchi and Ferdinando Fuga and restored in 2000 by Gae Aulenti as a major exhibition space. Fuga was also responsible for the **Palazzo della Consulta** (1732-4) opposite. Once the seat of the supreme court of the Papal State, it is now the Corte Costituzionale, the court for matters concerning the Constitution.

Sant'Andrea delle Fratte The peculiar name of this church (colloqially *'fratte'* means shrubs) indicates that it was originally located at the edge of the city. The church was rebuilt in the 17c by Gaspare Guerra from Modena and then, from 1653, by **Francesco Borromini**, who is the imaginative author of the apse, the dynamic campanile and the unfinished drum. Inside, to the left of the side door, is the epitaph of Angelica Kauffmann (1741-1807), the Swiss painter who became one of the most successful Neoclassical portraitists of her time and a good friend of Goethe. By the high altar are two *Angels* by Bernini, sculpted in 1668-9 for Ponte Sant'Angelo but replaced on the bridge by copies.

Santissimi Apostoli was first built by Pelagius I, c 560, and dedicated to the Apostles James and Philip (whose relics are preserved here). To the early 16c Renaissance portico Carlo Rainaldi added the balustrade with the *Apostles* (c 1665) and Giuseppe Valadier the Neoclassical façade (1827).

The interior was reconstructed by Carlo Fontana (1702-14) who destroyed most of Melozzo da Forlì's late 15c apse frescoes (fragments are preserved in the Quirinal and in the Vatican Pinacoteca). The ceiling fresco was painted by G.B. Gaulli (Baciccia) in 1707. The *Monument to*

Clement XIV, left of the apse, is Antonio Canova's first work in Rome (1789). His funerary stele for the engraver Giovanni Volpato (1807) is to the left of the portico. Daily 7.00-12.00 and 16.00-19.00.

Santa Maria della Vittoria stands on Via Venti Settembre, to the side of the fountain of Moses, designed by Domenico Fontana at the end of the 16c. The church was completed in 1620 for Cardinal Scipione Borghese, nephew of Paul V, and dedicated to the image of the Virgin (since destroyed) which had guided the victory of the Catholic Ferdinand II of Hapsburg over Protestant Prague (during the Thirty Years War).

   The architects were Carlo Maderno and G.B. Soria. The sumptuous interior is one of the best examples of Baroque decoration in Rome. The stuccowork, organ and cantoria are by Mattia de Rossi, a talented pupil of Bernini. Domenico Cerrini painted the ceiling frescoes (1675). The second chapel to the right has three paintings by Domenichino, his last works in Rome (1630). In the left transept is the **Cornaro Chapel**, a masterpiece by **Gianlorenzo Bernini** (1644-52) who used the shallow architectural space to create impressive illusionistic effects. In the centre is the magnificent *Ecstasy of St Teresa*; to the sides, seated in theatre-boxes and watching the scene as if looking at a mystery play, are the members of the Cornaro family from Venice.

AROUND PIAZZA DI SPAGNA

Biblioteca Hertziana The 16c artist Federico Zuccari built for himself the bizarre Palazzo Zuccari to the right of Trinità dei Monti (in the triangle between Via Gregoriana and Via Sistina). In the 18c the British artist Sir Joshua Reynolds lived here as did Johann Winckelmann, the German scholar. Today it is the seat of the Biblioteca Hertziana, the most important art history library in Rome. The entrance and windows in Via Gregoriana are shaped like monsters.

Casa di Goethe, Via del Corso 18. The German poet Johann Wolfgang Goethe, together with his painter friend Johann Heinrich Tischbein, lodged on the upper floor of this house between 1786 and 1788. Goethe spent his time in Rome sightseeing and writing. His *Italian Journey*, published in 1828, is one of the most beautiful accounts of Italy of its time. Goethe's circle of friends in Rome included the painter Angelica Kauffmann and the archaeologist-scholar Johann Winckelmann. Displayed here are mementoes of the poet's travels in Italy, copies of some of his drawings, and charming portrait-sketches by Tischbein. Open 10.00-18.00, closed Tues, *T* 06 3265 0412.

Casa Museo di Giorgio de Chirico, Piazza di Spagna 31. The apartment on the fifth floor was the home and studio of Giorgio de Chirico (1888-1978), the Metaphysical painter, who lived here from 1947 until his death. The 50 works exhibited in the museum, mostly from his last two decades, were chosen and hung by the artist himself. Visits by appointment Tues-Sat 10.00-13.00, closed Aug, *T* 06 679 6546.

Keats and Shelley Memorial House, Piazza di Spagna 26. To the right of the Spanish Steps, on the second floor of an 18c building, is the apartment where John Keats spent the last three months of his life. The house was a small *pensione* in 1820 when Keats arrived to spend the winter in Rome. He died from tuberculosis on 23 February 1821, at the age of 25, and was buried in the Protestant Cemetery. The house is now a museum. It also has a library containing over 9000 volumes and numerous autograph letters and manuscripts. Mon-Fri 9.00-13.00 and 15.00-18.00, Sat 11.00-14.00 and 15.00-18.00, closed Sun, *T* 06 678 4235.

The Pincio Named after the Pinci family who owned the hill in the 4c, it was designed as a park by Giuseppe Valadier in the early 19c. Together with the adjoining Villa Borghese, it forms the largest garden in the centre of Rome. The avenues are lined with magnificent trees, including giant ilexes, umbrella pines and oaks. The views from the terraces are spectacular.

San Lorenzo in Lucina on the square by the same name, off Via del Corso, rises the church that was first built by Sixtus III (432-440). It was rebuilt at the beginning of the 12c (from this time date the bell-tower, portico and doorway) and again in 1650 by the architect Cosimo Fanzago. The 19c restoration destroyed much of the Baroque decorations in the nave.

   The first chapel to the right contains part of the gridiron on which St Lawrence is said to have been martyred. By the third pillar is the tomb of Nicolas Poussin (1594-1665). Bernini designed the fourth chapel to the right for the family of *Gabriele Fonseca*, the doctor of Innocent X, whose lively bust, also by Bernini, is to the left of the altar (1668-73). On the high altar, designed by Carlo Rainaldi, is Guido Reni's all too famous *Crucifixion* (early 17c).

   Excavations beneath the church have brought to light remains of the titulus Lucinae, a house of the mid 1c AD, and a fragment of the Horologium Augusti, Augustus' sun-dial of 10 BC. The excavations are open at 16.30 on the last Saturday of the month.

Trinità dei Monti The church above the Spanish Steps, attached to a French convent, rose above the ruins of the Villa of Lucullus. It was begun in 1502 by Louis XII and restored in 1816 by Louis XVIII.

   Inside the church are two important 16c paintings by Daniele da Volterra representing the *Deposition* (second chapel to the left) and the

Assumption (third chapel to the right) which includes a portrait of Michelangelo. Other Mannerist painters were active here, including Perin del Vaga, Giulio Romano, Taddeo and Federico Zuccari.

Via del Babuino Opened in 1525 as part of the Trident (see Piazza del Popolo, p 95), it is famous for its antiques galleries and elegant shops. The street takes its present name from one of the 'talking statues' used in ancient times for pinning up slogans against the government. The 'Baboon' is in fact a very worn Roman sculpture of a reclining Silenus which decorates a fountain here.

Via del Corso This long street running from Porta del Popolo to Piazza Venezia has been an important thoroughfare since Roman times when it was known as the Via Lata. Its present name derives from the riderless horse races (*corse*) inaugurated here by Paul II in 1466 and held at Carnival time until their suppression in 1882. Since then, the Corso has given its name to the main street of countless Italian cities.

Via Margutta This charming 16c street, which runs parallel to Via del Babuino, has been for centuries the favourite residence of artists. Street fairs selling paintings are held in autumn and spring; in May there is a famous exhibition of children's art.

Via Sistina Sixtus V built the road which runs from the top of the Spanish Steps all the way to Santa Maria Maggiore, and from there, on a straight line, to the Lateran. Most of the artists residing in Rome in the 18c-19c lodged in Via Sistina. The **obelisk**, with hieroglyphs imitating those of the obelisk in Piazza del Popolo, was brought here in 1789 from the Gardens of Sallust where it had been set up in the 2c or 3c AD.

Villa Medici Viale Trinità dei Monti leads to Villa Medici, built in 1564-74 by Nanni di Baccio Bigio and Annibale Lippi for Cardinal Ricci da Montepulciano, and acquired in 1576 by Cardinal Ferdinando de'Medici, later the Grand-Duke of Tuscany (1587). The palace and garden were decorated with a famous collection of Classical sculpture, a great part of which was transferred to Florence in 1775. The villa was bought by Napoleon in 1801 and became the seat of the French Academy. It is only open for special exhibitions. For guided tours of the gardens, *T* 06 67611.

Villa Medici

commercial galleries

Anna D'Ascanio, Via del Babuino 29, *T* 06 3600 1804, 06 3600 1876. Well established gallery for modern and contemporary art.

De Crescenzo & Viesti, Via del Corso 42, *T* 06 3600 2414, www.decrescenzoviesti.com. Italian names such as Afro, Capogrossi, Leoncillo, but also Chagall, Lichtenstein, and contemporaries like Pistoletto and Perilli.

Del Cortile, Via del Babuino 51, *T* 06 323 4475. It has shown work by Mochetti, Innocenza Odescalchi, Bettina Werner; photographic exhibitions (L.E. Badessi, W. Daan); and works by Tano Festa and Sante Monachesi.

Il Gabbiano, Via della Frezza 51, *T* 06 322 7049. Long established gallery founded by the publisher Alberto Mondadori, with a branch in New York. Italian names have included Morandi, Pirandello, Mafai, Guttuso; on the international scene, Balthus, Rauschenberg, Valdes.

Il Segno, Via Capo le Case 4, *T* 06 679 1387. Prints and drawings by Perilli, Novelli, D'Orazio, as well as Miró, Chagall, Braque, Ernst, Picasso.

L'Archimede, Via del Vantaggio 28, *T* 06 321 5688, www.larchimede.com. Barcelò, Botero, Casorati, Christo, Cucchi, Guttuso and more.

La Nuova Pesa, Via del Corso 530, *T* 06 361 0892. It started out showing works by Guttuso, Attardi, Mafai, Donghi, Licini, Cagli, Manzù; now it has turned to the young and famous: Salvatori, Di Stasio, Salvo, Pirri, Mochetti, Kounellis, Horn.

eating and drinking

RESTAURANTS

€ **Antica Birreria Peroni**, Via di San Marcello 19 (Trevi), *T* 06 679 5310; closed Sunday and 15 August. It's been here for nearly a century, serving good beer and simple dishes.

Fiaschetteria Beltramme, Via della Croce 39. No phone. An historic *osteria* and an absolute favourite for Roman food.

Gina, Via San Sebastianello 7a (Piazza di Spagna), *T* 06 678 0251. Variations of white for the modern interior, light food to eat in or readymade picnic baskets to take up to Villa Borghese.

Il Leoncino, Via del Leoncino 28, *T* 06 687 6306; closed Wednesday. Good Roman pizza (thin crust).

€€ **Gusto**, Piazza Augusto imperatore 9, *T* 06 322 6273. Open throughout the year for brunch, lunch and dinner. Includes a restaurant with an inventive cuisine, a wine bar, pizzeria and shop. One of the hot spots in Rome.

Il Margutta, Via Margutta 118, *T* 06 3265 0577. A trendy vegetarian restaurant.

Matricianella, Via del Leone 2, *T* 06 683 2100; closed Sunday and August. Among the favourite places in town for traditional Roman dishes, it serves the best *bucatini all'amatriciana* (with tomato sauce and bacon) that you'll ever have. Tables outside in summer.

Nino, Via Borgognona 11, *T* 06 679 5676; closed Sunday and August. A long established restaurant with a Tuscan flavour.

Osteria Margutta, Via Margutta 82, *T* 06 323 1025; closed Sunday and August. A charming restaurant and the food is good too (especially the meat dishes).

Ripashà, Via di Ripetta 242, *T* 06 323 0179; closed Sunday. Trendy minimalism, good pizzas, abundant charcoal-grilled meats and more.

€€€ **Dal Bolognese**, Piazza del Popolo 1, *T* 06 361 1426; closed Tuesday lunchtime, Monday, August, and over Christmas. A great classic and one of the best choices in town both for ambience and quality.

Federico I, Via della Colonna Antonina 48, *T* 06 678 3717; closed Sunday. Fine and quiet setting (tables outside in summer) and excellent seafood. Very expensive.

La Penna d'Oca, Via della Penna 53, *T* 06 320 2898; evenings only; closed Sunday and August. Small but good.

Reef, Piazza Augusto Imperatore 47, *T* 06 6821 7532; evenings only; closed Monday and 5-25 August. A trendy place with a minimalist interior.

CAFÉS & COCKTAIL BARS

Babington's Tea Rooms, Piazza di Spagna 23, *T* 06 678 6027. The English tea room par excellence.

Bar de l'Hotel d'Inghilterra, Via Bocca di Leone 14, *T* 06 69981. An elegant option for a coffee, an aperitif or a cocktail.

Caffè Greco, Via Condotti 86, *T* 06 679 1700. Founded in 1760, it was the meeting place of writers, artists and foreigners populating the area. Although it maintains its 19c atmosphere the service and quality are disappointing. It's expensive too.

Casina Valadier Housed in a lodge built by Valadier at the top of the Pincio, this charming café-restaurant has undergone extensive restorations and is due to re-open soon.

Ciampini, Piazza San Lorenzo in Lucina 29, *T* 06 687 6606. Tables outside in the charming square. Excellent coffee, sandwiches and aperitifs. Also at Via della Fontanella Borghese 59, *T* 06 6813 5108 and Viale Trinità dei Monti 1, *T* 06 678 5678 (closed Wednesday).

Gran Caffè La Caffetteria, Via Margutta 61a, *T* 06 321 3344. A charming café serving Neapolitan coffee and *sfogliatelle* as well as savoury specialities from Campania. Also at Piazza di Pietra 65, *T* 06 679 8147. This second branch is scenically located in front of the Temple of Hadrian.

Rosati, Piazza del Popolo 5a, *T* 06 322 0424. An historic address with Art Nouveau decorations. Splendid view over the piazza. Expensive.

Stravinskij, Bar de l'Hotel de Russie, Via del Babuino 9, *T* 06 3288 8874; open 10.00-1.00. The trendiest place for aperitifs in Rome.

ICE CREAM

Il Gelato di San Crispino, Via della Panetteria 42 (Trevi), *T* 06 679 3924; closed Tuesday. Entirely natural, homemade ice cream (no colourings or additvtes). An absolute must for serious *gelato* lovers.

WINE BARS

L'Enoteca Antica, Via della Croce 76b, *T* 06 679 0896; open 10.00-1.00. It is also a restaurant and coffee bar.

Shaki, Via Mario de'Fiori 29a, *T* 06 679 1694; open 10.00-24.00. A refined wine bar in a Japanese-minimalist style.

Vineria Buccone, Via di Ripetta 19-20, *T* 06 361 2154; open Mon-Thur

9.00-20.30, Fri-Sat 9.00-0.30; closed Sunday. A good selection of wines and food. Not many tables.

Vineria Il Chianti, Via del Lavatore 81 (Trevi), *T* 06 678 7550; open until late; closed Sunday and August. Tuscan wines and food.

LATE-NIGHT BARS

Baja Lungotevere Arnaldo da Brescia (Ponte Margherita), *T* 06 3260 0118; closed Monday. A boat on the Tiber with a restaurant upstairs and a cocktail bar below. Bossa and lounge music over dinner and dub, ethno or house afterwards (until 3.00).

Gilda, Via Mario de'Fiori 97, *T* 06 678 4838; open 23.30-5.00. A long established club, popular with VIPs. The music could be better but the place is a must if you want to see and be seen.

Green Rose Pub, Passeggiata di Ripetta 33, *T* 06 321 5548; open 9.00-2.00; closed Saturday morning and Sunday evening. An Irish pub at the back of the Accademia delle Belle Arti, so it is populated by artists and students who go there for a coffee, lunch or a drink.

Gregory's, Via Gregoriana 54d, *T* 06 679 6386. Jazz club with frequent jam sessions and 75 brands of whisky.

shopping

ACCESSORIES

Cappelleria Radiconcini, Via del Corso 139, *T* 06 679 1807. Since 1932 the best known hat shop in Rome.

Cravatterie Nazionali, Via Vittoria 62, *T* 06 6992 2143. Ties.

Dotti, Via Belsiana 26, *T* 06 6992 0456. Crocodile bags and more.

FFI, Via Vittoria 53. Bags and suitcases.

Furla, Via Condotti 55-56, Piazza di Spagna 22, Via del Corso 481. Elegant bags, watches, jewellery and other accessories.

Louis Vuitton, Piazza San Lorenzo in Lucina 36, *T* 06 6880 9520, and at Via Condotti 15. A classic for bags and suitcases.

Mandarina Duck, Via Borgognona 42b, Via di Propaganda 1. Functional bags with innovative designs.

Marina G, Via Sistina 58, *T* 06 678 0971. Everything from jewellery to clothes and elegant tableware.

Perrone, Piazza di Spagna 92, *T* 06 678 3101. Gloves and hosiery.

Sermoneta, Piazza di Spagna 61. Gloves.

Thè verde, Via Vittoria 23, *T* 06 3211 0174. Oriental clothes, shoes and home accessories.

ANTIQUES

Most of these galleries have period furniture and old master paintings.

Di Castro Alberto, Piazza di Spagna 5, *T* 06 679 2269.

Di Castro Nicola & C., Via del Babuino 92, *T* 06 679 0210.

Gasparrini, Via Fontanella Borghese 46, *T* 06 678 5820.

Lampronti Giulio, Via del Babuino 67, *T* 06 323 0100.

Lilia Leoni, Via Belsiana 86, *T* 06 678 3210. Furniture only.

1900, Via Vittoria 37, *T* 06 3600 2201.

Sestieri Antichità, Via Alibert 18, *T* 06 678 5766.

Simotti Rocchi, Largo Fontanella Borghese 76, *T* 06 687 6656. Archaeological items and more.

BEAUTY & PERFUMES

Castelli, Via Frattina 52, *T* 06 678 0066, and at Via Condotti 22 and 61, *T* 06 679 5918.

L'Olfattorio, Via di Ripetta 34. Come here to find your ideal perfume.

Mac Store, Via del Babuino 124, *T* 06 679 2492. Makeup.

Materozzoli, Piazza San Lorenzo in Lucina 5, *T* 06 6889 2686. The most elegant address in town. Artisan perfumerie and luxurious creams.

BOOKS

Al Ferro di Cavallo, Via di Ripetta 67, *T* 06 322 7303. Art, architecture, design, fashion, photography.

Anglo American Book Co, Via della Vite 102, *T* 06 679 5222. Books in English.

Feltrinelli, Via del Babuino 39-40, *T* 06 3600 1842. A good bookshop with an international section.

F.M. Ricci, Via del Babuino 49. Magnificent art editions.

Fratelli Alinari, Via Alibert 16a/b, *T* 06 679 2923. Photograph bookshop and archives.

Godel, Via Poli 1 (Trevi fountain), *T* 06 679 0264. Literature, philosophy, architecture and publications on Rome.

Libreria Borghese, Via Fontanella Borghese 64, *T* 06 687 6403. Architecture and more.

Mel Giannino Stoppani, Piazza Santi Apostoli 59a-65, *T* 06 6994 1045. A wonderful store for children, including books in English.

Rappaport, Via Sistina 23, *T* 06 483 826. A fine antiquarian bookshop.

Spazio Corto Maltese, Via Margutta 96, *T* 06 3265 0515. A tiny bookshop specializing in comics.

The English Bookshop, Via di Ripetta 248, *T* 06 320 3301.

The Lion's Bookshop, Via dei Greci 36, *T* 06 3265 0437. An English bookshop and café.

CASHMERE & KNITWEAR
Choses de Cachemere, Via del Babuino 105, *T* 06 679 8488. All things cashmere.

Choses- St Tropez, Via Belsiana 32, *T* 06 679 7250. Cashmere woollens and more for men and women.

Malo, Via Borgognona 4m, *T* 06 679 1331. One of the most famous brands for cashmere clothing.

CHOCOLATE
Chocolate & Pralines, Vicolo della Torretta 5, *T* 06 687 1023.

Fellus, Via Belsiana 70b, *T* 06 679 2352. Fine chocolates and sweet wines.

Quetzalcoatl Chocolatier, Via delle Carrozze 26, *T* 06 6920 2191.

CLOTHES FOR WOMEN
Alan Journo, Via Fontanella Borghese 59a, *T* 06 6830 1540. Stylish clothes.

Bang, Via della Penna 67, *T* 06 3612343. Clothes and accessories.

Bomba, Via dell'Oca 39, *T* 06 361 2881. A tiny shop with great ideas.

DA Dress Agency, Via del Vantaggio 1b, *T* 06 321 0898. Designer clothes at half the price.

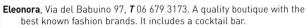

Du-du, Via della Croce 78 and Via delle Carrozze 45. A lot of black and other basics for boys and girls.

Eco Wear, Via del Vantaggio 26, *T* 06 322 2404. Clothes and more in ecological fabrics (cottons, wools, raw hemp, silks).

Eleonora, Via del Babuino 97, *T* 06 679 3173. A quality boutique with the best known fashion brands. It includes a cocktail bar.

Gente, Via del Babuino 80-82. Trendy clothes and fashion labels.

Il Baco da Seta, Via Vittoria 75, *T* 06 679 3907. Luxurius Shantung silk dresses.

Le Tableau, Via Belsiana 96a, *T* 06 678 5031. Elegant clothes.

Nia & Co, Via Vittoria 30-31, *T* 06 322 7421. A long established favourite.

Scapa, Via Vittoria 58-59, *T* 06 678 9368. Hats, shoes and wonderful clothes.

Strada, Via del Corso 443, *T* 06 687 8423. A great place for the trendiest designer clothes.

CLOTHES FOR MEN

Aspesi Uomo, Via Mario de'Fiori 62, *T* 06 6791066. A well known designer.

Battistoni, Via Condotti 61a, *T* 06 6976 1126. A classic address.

Brioni, Via Condotti, *T* 06 678 3635. High quality fashion.

Caleffi, Via Colonna Antonina 53, *T* 06 679 3773. Established in 1911, this is one of the finest addresses for men's shirts.

Comandini, Via Frattina 83. Fabrics for suits.

Ermenegildo Zegna, Via Borgognona 7e, *T* 06 678 9143. A classic.

Polidori, Via Borgognona 4a, *T* 06 678 4843. Classic suits and sportswear for men.

Testa, Via Frattina 42-43 and Via Borgognona 13. Fashion for men.

DESIGNER FASHION

Most designer shops are in the streets off Piazza di Spagna. Here are the addresses of the most important ones.

Bottega Veneta, Piazza San Lorenzo in Lucina 7-13, *T* 06 6821 0024.

Costume National, Via del Babuino 106, *T* 06 678 5829.

Dolce & Gabbana, Piazza di Spagna 93, *T* 06 6938 0870.

Emporio Armani, Via del Babuino 140, *T* 06 322 1581.

Etro, Via del Babuino 102, *T* 06 678 8257.

Fendi, Via Borgognona 36-40, *T* 06 696 661.

Gianfranco Ferrè, Via Borgognona 5-6, *T* 06 679 7445.

Giorgio Armani, Via Condotti 77, *T* 06 699 1460.

Gucci, Via Condotti 8, *T* 06 679 0405.

Laura Biagiotti, Via Borgognona 43-44, *T* 06 679 1205.

Loro Piana, Via Borgognona 31, *T* 06 6992 4906.

Mariella Burani, Via Bocca di Leone 28, *T* 06 6790630.

Max Mara, Via Frattina 28, *T* 06 679 4246, and at Via Condotti 17-19 .

Missoni, Piazza di Spagna 7, *T* 06 679 2555.

Prada, Via Condotti 92, *T* 06 679 0897, and Via del Babuino 91,
    T 06 3600 4884.

Trussardi, Via Condotti 49-50, *T* 06 678 0280.

Valentino, Piazza Mignanelli 22, *T* 06 67391 (Alta Moda); Boutique at Via
    Condotti 13, *T* 06 7679 5862, and at Via del Babuino 61,
    T 06 3600 1906.

Versace, Via Bocca di Leone 26-27, *T* 06 678 0521.

FOOD

Cambi, Via del Leoncino 30, *T* 06 687 8081. Open 8.00-20.30 for
    delicious cheeses, cured meats, bread, pizza and wine.

Fior fiore, Via della Croce 17-18, *T* 06 679 1386. Delicious *pizza a taglio*
    (by the slice).

Focacci, Via della Croce 43, *T* 06 679 1228; open 8.00-20.00. Bread, etc.

Fratelli Fabbi, Via della Croce 27, *T* 06 679 0612. Since 1939 it has
    specialized in gourmet food, ranging from buffalo mozzarella and
    gorgonzola to truffles, fine charcuterie and takeaways.

Giovanni Riposati, Via delle Muratte 8 (Trevi), *T* 06 679 2866. Good bread
    and sandwiches.

Il Salumiere di G. Ciavatta, Via del Lavatore 31 (Trevi), *T* 06 679 2935.
    A small shop with great cheeses and charcuterie.

Teichner, Piazza San Lorenzo in Lucina 17, *T* 06 687 1449. The finest
    prosciutto, parmigiano, pecorino, aceto balsamico, pasta, wild boar
    sausages, truffles and other delicatessen.

Vini e Oli Sant'Andrea, Via Sant'Andrea delle Fratte 13. The tastes of Italy.

HOMES

Cesari, Via del Babuino 195, *T* 06 361 3451. Fine towels and linens for beds and tables.

C.u.c.i.n.a., Via Mario de'Fiori 65, *T* 06 679 1275. Kitchen accessories and more.

Culti, Via F. Crispi 45-47, *T* 06 679 0272. Ideas for the home.

D 3 - D Cube, Piazza Mignanelli 24, *T* 06 678 9054, and Via de'Crociferi 38, *T* 06 6920 0911.

Decò, Vicolo della Torretta 2, *T* 06 689 7061. Furniture and objects for the home.

Entroterra, Via della Vite 35, *T* 06 6992 5224. Simply beautiful objects (vases, etc).

Gusto, Piazza Augusto Imperatore 9, *T* 06 323 6363. As well as a restaurant and wine bar, Gusto also has a shop selling gourmet specialities, wine, accessories and books.

Non Solo Bianco, Via della Fontanella Borghese 38, *T* 06 687 6657. 'Not only white' home linens and tableware with unusual fabrics, colours and designs.

Roberto Cavalli, Via delle Carrozze 67, *T* 06 679 1527. A line for interiors by the well known fashion designer.

Shaki, Piazza di Spagna 65, *T* 06 678 6605. Gourmet food and Japanese inspired accessories for the table.

T.A.D., Via del Babuino 155, *T* 06 326 9511. The trendiest concept store for modern furniture, china, household accessories, fabrics, table and bed linens, etc. It also has a bar.

Urushi, Via Margutta 21-22, *T* 06 3211 0358. Japanese Zen in the home.

Venier Colombo, Via Frattina, *T* 06 679 2979. Fine fabrics (including Swiss muslin and Irish linen) as well as lace, embroidered linens and beautiful tablecloths.

Zappia, Via Mario de'Fiori, *T* 06 678 3205. Wonderful handmade picture frames.

JEWELLERY

Ansuini, Via del Babuino 150d, *T* 06 3600 2219.

Bulgari, Via Condotti 10, *T* 06 696 261.

Cartier, Via Condotti 82-83, *T* 06 678 2580.

Damiani, Via Condotti 84, *T* 06 6920 0477.

Pomellato, Via del Babuino 63, *T* 06 324 1623.

Tiffany & Co, Via del Babuino 118, *T* 06 679 0717.

Zendrini, Via Borgognona 41, *T* 06 67 0209.

KIDS

Benetton, Via del Corso 426; Via Condotti 9 and 59; Piazza di Trevi 91-94 (0-12 years).

Bonpoint, Piazza San Lorenzo in Lucina 25, *T* 06 687 1548. Fine clothes for little ones.

Calico Lion, Via della Vite 80, *T* 06 678 4626. For 0-8-year-olds.

Confetti, Via Vittoria 74, *T* 06 679 4626. Fun baby clothes.

Diesel, Via del Corso 186, *T* 06 678 3933. For teenagers.

Faire Dodo, Via Tomacelli 128. Maternity gear.

Kids Subdued, Via Tomacelli 13-14, *T* 06 683 3711. T-shirts, jeans.

La Cicogna, Via Frattina 138, *T* 06 678 6959. Clothes and accessories for babies and kids.

Mettimi Giù, Via Due Macelli 59e, *T* 06 678 9761. Beautiful clothes for babies and children.

Nicol Caramel, Via di Ripetta 261, *T* 06 361 2059. Maternity clothes.

Pure Sermoneta, Via Frattina 11, *T* 06 679 4555. Ages 0-14.

Silvana del Plato, Via della Vite 75, *T* 06 678 6596. Clothes and accessories for 0-12-year-olds.

LINGERIE

Emy Funaro, Piazza di Spagna 79, *T* 06 6992 2267.

La Perla, Via Condotti 79, *T* 06 6994 1934.

Marisa Padovan, Via delle Carrozze 81, *T* 06 679 3946. *The* address for ladies' swimsuits.

MUSIC

Messaggerie Musicali, Via del Corso 472, *T* 06 684 401. CDs of all musical styles.

Ricordi, Via del Corso 506, *T* 06 361 2370 and at 120, Via C. Battisti

(Piazza Venezia), *T* 06 679 8022. The latter branch also sells fine instruments.

SHOES

Avc Adriana Campanile, Piazza di Spagna 88-89 and at Via Vittoria 19, *T* 06 678 0095, 06 361 3691.

Brugnoli, Via del Babuino 57, *T* 06 3600 1889. Classics for both sexes.

Bruno Magli, Via del Gambero 1, *T* 06 679 3802. A long established brand.

Campanile, Via Condotti 58, 06 678 3041. Fine shoes for men.

Dal Cò, Via Vittoria 65, *T* 06 678 6536. Fine shoes for women.

Fabrizio Bulkaen, Via del Babuino 158, *T* 06 322 2343. Interesting shoes.

Fausto Santini, Via Frattina 120. A well known address.

Ferragamo Donna, Via Condotti 73-74, *T* 06 679 1565.

Ferragamo Uomo, Via Condotti 66, *T* 06 678 1130.

Fragiacomo, Via delle Carrozze 28, *T* 06 679 8780. Classics.

Rossetti, Via Borgognona 5a and at Via del Babuino 59a, *T* 06 678 2676. Another classic.

Sergio Rossi, Piazza di Spagna 97-100, *T* 06 678 3245. For spiky heels.

Tanino Crisci, Via Borgognona 4h/i, *T* 06 679 5461. A favourite with men.

Testoni, Via Condotti 80, *T* 06 678 8944. Great shoes for men.

STATIONERY

Pineider, Via Fontanella Borghese 22, *T* 06 6830 8014. Elegant pens, desktop accessories, writing paper, leather briefcases, etc.

Vertecchi, Via della Croce 72, *T* 06 679 0155. Great stationery and more.

WATCHES

Antonio Senzacqua, Via della Vite 14a, *T* 06 678 9437. Repairs antiquarian and modern watches.

Bedetti, Piazza San Silvestro 11, *T* 06 679 7941. Rolexes and more.

Hausmann, Via Condotti 28, *T* 06 679 1558 and at Via del Corso 406, *T* 06 687 1501.

VILLA
BORGHESE

The park of Villa Borghese is the green lung of the city of Rome
and takes its name from the Borghese family whose property it
was until 1902. Re-designed in the late 18c as a Romantic garden
with distant vistas and magnificent trees, it extends from the
terraces of the Pincio (a fashionable promenade in the 19c) to the
elegant Via Veneto (the focus of *la dolce vita* in the 1950s). Viale
delle Belle Arti, at the other end, was created for the
International Exhibition of 1911 and is marked by the presence of
cultural institutes, the Etruscan Museum and the National
Gallery of Modern Art. These and the Galleria Borghese are best
reached by taking a stroll through the park.

Galleria Borghese

OPEN	Tues-Sun 9.00-19.00. Entrance allowed every two hours (9.00, 11.00, etc). Ticket office open from 8.30. **It is essential to book in advance**
CLOSED	Mon; 1/1, 25/12
CHARGES	€6.50 + €2 booking fee
	€3.25 + €2 booking fee for EU citizens aged 18-25
	€2 booking fee only for EU citizens under 18 and over 65 years of age, and for students of art history, architecture and archaeology
TELEPHONE	**06 841 7645; 06 32818** (for booking)
WWW.	**galleriaborghese.it**; **www.ticketeria.it** for booking
MAIN ENTRANCE	Piazza Scipione Borghese 5
BUS	Buses 95 and 116 from city centre to Via Veneto

*There are guided tours in English at 9.00 and 11.00, €5, otherwise audio guides
are available. There is access for disabled visitors. The café and shop are on the
ground floor*

Among the finest museums in Rome, the Galleria Borghese
contains a precious collection of paintings and sculptures begun
in the early 17c by Cardinal Scipione Borghese, nephew of Paul V,

and continued in the 18c and 19c by Prince Marcantonio IV and his son Camillo Borghese.

A passionate art lover, Cardinal Scipione was a great patron of churches and an obsessive collector with infallible taste and intuition. He assembled works by the finest talents of his day, discovered Bernini and used every possible means at his disposal to pursue his ambitions. He confiscated 107 paintings owned by the artist Cavalier d'Arpino (including a number of Caravaggios) had Raphael's *Entombment* stolen from Perugia, and Domenichino's *Hunt of Diana* taken from the artist's studio. He also collected antique art and employed sculptors like Bernini to restore the fragmentary pieces.

His passion was continued by his successors: Prince Marcantonio IV employed a team of fresco painters to re-decorate the villa, while Camillo Borghese commissioned Canova to make a sculpture of his wife in 1805. Two years later Camillo was forced to surrender 344 pieces from the collection of antiquities to Napoleon, while the best paintings had already made their way to Paris with the Treaty of Tolentino (1797). These were recovered after the Congress of Vienna (1815), and Camillo continued to add to his collection: he found Correggio's *Danaë* in Paris, in 1827. In the late 19c the Borghese family were forced to sell up, and in 1902 the Italian state acquired the park, villa and entire collection for a ridiculous 3,600,000 Lire (about €1800).

THE BUILDING

Villa Borghese was created as a pleasure villa surrounded by a park and gardens 'filled with the most delightful statues, fountains, fishponds', rare plants and exotic birds. While the family palace was inside the city (near the Tiber), the villa served as a retreat where the arts were cultivated and guests received with great magnificence. It was begun by the architect Flaminio Ponzio, and continued after his death in 1613 by the Flemish Jan van Santen, known in Italy as Giovanni Vasanzio (later he worked at Palazzo Doria Pamphilj).

The idea of the *villa suburbana* derived from Peruzzi's Villa

Farnesina built a century earlier on the Trastevere side of the Tiber.

The exterior façades are filled with busts and reliefs in the style of ancient Roman villas. Even the stark white colour, recently restored and obtained by mixing ground marble with white plaster, was designed to bring to mind the glory of ancient Rome.

The same principle inspired the decoration of the interior space: Scipione's Classical statues were set against a light background of leather tapestries in pale blue and gold. The architectural elements were all in white marble. The coloured marble decoration and richly painted ceilings we see today were executed in 1770-1800. Most of the paintings, originally housed in Palazzo Borghese, were brought here in 1891.

HIGHLIGHTS

Bernini, *Truth*	Salone
Canova, *Paolina Borghese*	Room 1
Bernini, *David*	Room 2
Bernini, *Apollo and Daphnis*	Room 3
Bernini, *Pluto and Proserpina*	Room 4
Caravaggio, *Madonna dei Palafrenieri* **and other paintings**	Room 8
Raphael, *Deposition*	Room 9
Correggio, *Danaë*	Room 10
Bernini, portrait busts of *Paul V* **and** *Self-portraits*	Room 14
Domenichino, *Hunt of Diana*	Room 19
Titian, *Sacred and Profane Love*	Room 20

GROUND FLOOR

PORTICO Here are displays of antique sculpture, including fragments of a triumphal frieze of Trajan (set in the short walls).

SALONE The salone has a fine fresco of the *Apotheosis of Romulus*, painted in 1778 by Mariano Rossi, a late Baroque painter from Sicily. There are large fragments of a mosaic (AD 320) illustrating gladiators and wild beasts in combat. Among the statues exhibited here are a fine *Bacchus* of the 2c AD imitating a prototype by Praxiteles, and a *Satyr* (AD 120) after a bronze original of the Hellenistic age, with the head restored by Pietro and Gianlorenzo Bernini.

Also here are a statue of *Augustus* as Pontifex Maximus (AD 10-70) and four colossal heads of the 2c AD representing *Hadrian*, *Antoninus Pius*, *Juno* and a female goddess restored as *Isis*. The busts of the 12 *Caesars* in the higher niches were made in the 16c by G.B. della Porta. The fine statue of *Truth* was begun by **Bernini** in 1645 for the vestibule of his house in Via del Corso, but left incomplete. The sculpture was originally conceived as Time unveiling Truth and was begun at a difficult time in Bernini's career. His main patron, Urban VIII, had died and he had fallen out of favour with the new pope (Innocent X), particularly after his new bell-tower at the side of St Peter's developed structural problems (it was demolished in 1646). *Truth* remained in Bernini's house until 1924 when it was brought to the Gallery.

ROOM 1 In the centre lies the statue of *Paolina Borghese*, the sister of Napoleon, who married Prince Camillo Borghese in 1805 and is here depicted as Venus Victrix holding the golden apple of the Hesperides given to her by Paris. The theme of the Judgement of Paris, with the victory of Venus, goddess of love, over Juno (power) and Minerva (wisdom) was painted on the ceiling by Domenico de Angelis in 1779. The statue, exceptional in its time for portraying a contemporary personality of high rank in the nude, was carved by **Antonio Canova** between 1805 and 1808 and is justly considered an absolute masterpiece of Neoclassicism. It is polished to the highest degree of perfection through the use of special waxes that give the surface a smooth and shimmering texture. Contemporary accounts describe how the statue was shown at night lit by candles and slowly rotating by means of a mechanism hidden inside the wooden day-bed.

On the opposite wall stands another Neoclassical masterpiece, the *Herm of Bacchus*, by Luigi Valadier, in bronze and a rare pink alabaster (1773). Also here is the lively portrait of *Clement XII* by Pietro Bracci (1735), revealing the influence of Bernini's portraits of earlier popes (including the two versions of Paul V exhibited upstairs). An interesting sarcophagus of *Apollo and the Muses* was cut in two and placed on the walls in the 18c to create a symmetrical arrangement. The lace-like quality of the drill work seems to indicate that it was produced in Asia Minor around AD 220.

ROOM 2 The statue of *David*, in the centre of the room, was commissioned by Cardinal Scipione from Gianlorenzo Bernini in 1623-4 (the face is a self-portrait). As opposed to earlier examples (such as Michelangelo's) which showed the young hero in repose after his victory over Goliath, Bernini chose to represent the most dramatic moment, when David is about to throw the stone with his sling. The statue is meant to be seen from multiple viewpoints (another innovation on Renaissance precedents) offering a different aspect of the action from each side. On the walls are a painting of the same subject by Battistello Caracciolo (1612), Annibale Carracci's *Samson in Prison* (1595) and a cut sarcophagus with the *Labours of Hercules* (AD 160).

ROOM 3 At the age of 23 **Bernini** created for his mentor an unprecedented work of art, transposing to marble a subject previously only treated in literature or painting. In his *Metamorphoses*, Ovid narrates the story of *Apollo and Daphnis* describing how the nymph chased by Apollo is transformed into a laurel tree. Again, Bernini chose to capture the climax of the drama, illustrating the very moment of the nymph's transformation. Just when Apollo is about to seize her, her hands turn into leaves, her feet into roots and her soft body into a coarse tree trunk. The fact that every detail (from the leaves to the hair and drapery) is crisply defined without breaks leaves one wondering at the astounding inventiveness and technical ability already achieved by the young artist.

The ceiling frescoes by Pietro Angeletti (1780-5) complete the

Bernini *Apollo and Daphnis* (1621; detail)

scene, while the theme of the Metamorphoses recurs in the fine paintings on the side walls. Dosso Dossi's *Apollo* presents us with the god's desolation after the loss of Daphnis (1522), while the mysterious witch Circe is seen transforming human beings into little creatures tied to a tree (1520).

CHAPEL Here are frescoes by Claude Deruet (1617-8), a silver altarpiece by Matthias Wallbaum, a talented goldsmith from Augsburg (late 16c), and a large *Pietà* by Federico Zuccari (1567) after a painting by his brother Taddeo.

ROOM 4 Like the rest of the ground floor, the overall decorative scheme of the room, filled with precious marbles, stuccoes and frescoes, was devised by the architect Antonio Asprucci in the late 18c. The hexagonal tables with porphyry tops are by Luigi Valadier (1773), the vases decorated with the Seasons by Maximilian

Laboureur (1785), while the busts of Roman emperors, in porphyry and alabaster, date from the early 17c.

Exhibited here is **Bernini**'s *Pluto and Proserpina* (1621-2), with the god of the underworld abducting the daughter of Gea, goddess of the earth. The spiral composition of the figures, reminiscent of Mannerist sculptures, enhances the contrast between Pluto's muscular force and the nymph's delicate softness. Walking around the group, different moments are revealed, from Pluto's powerful stride and the moment of capture, to Proserpina's tears and vain defence; from Pluto's hands delving into her skin to the three-headed dog Cerberus, guardian of hell.

The bronze **Neptune** was cast by Bernini in 1628 as a study for a fountain now in the Victoria and Albert Museum in London. The small *Farnese Bull* is a bronze copy by Antonio Susini (1613) of the monumental group found in the Baths of Caracalla and now exhibited in the Archaeological Museum in Naples.

ROOM 5 The *Sleeping Hermaphrodite* is 1c copy of an original by Polykles of the 2c BC. Other antique sculptures displayed here include a portrait of *Agrippina Maggiore* (AD 37-41), a statue of *Ceres* (1c AD) and a head of *Aphrodite* (AD 100). Above the doors are late 16c landscapes by Paul Bril.

ROOM 6 The marble group of *Aeneas and Anchises* was carved by **Bernini** in 1619 when he was 21 years old. He was helped by his father Pietro and the work still follows the Mannerist 'tower' compositions of the late 16c. Aeneas, with his father Anchises and his son Ascanius, is fleeing from Troy, carrying away the sacred fire and the images of the household gods (Penates). The theme also provided an excuse for the effective description of the three ages of man. The ceiling fresco by Laurent Pecheux (a follower of Mengs' Neoclassicism) illustrates the discussion on the Trojan War in the *Council of the Gods* (1783). On the side walls are late Mannerist paintings by Jacopo Zucchi (*Cupid and Psyche*, 1589) and Lavinia Fontana (*The Toilet of Minerva*, 1613).

ROOM 7 The room was re-designed in the 18c to house the Egyptian pieces of the Borghese collection. The ceiling fresco by Tommaso Conca illustrates the *Nile and his Children* (the Floods) and the *Goddesses of Ancient Egypt*, while the frieze below has stories of *Antony and Cleopatra*. In the centre is a sculpture of a *Satyr riding a Dolphin*, a 1c copy after a Hellenistic original inspired by Lysippos. The head was taken from an antique statue and added in the 16c. The great statue of *Isis* in black marble is shown running in search of her deceased husband Osiris. It was carved in the mid 2c AD and integrated with a marble head, hands and feet.

ROOM 8 The *Dancing Satyr* in the centre of the room is a 2c copy inspired by Lysippos and found in 1824 at Monte Cavo to the south of Rome. Originally shown playing the flute, the satyr was arbitrarily restored by the sculptor Bertel Thorvaldsen at the end of the 18c. An analogous theme reappears in Tommaso Conca's ceiling fresco of the *Sacrifice to Silenus* (1778).

Exhibited here are six of the twelve **Caravaggios** collected by Cardinal Scipione (they included the *Supper of Emmaus* now in the National Gallery, London). The *Boy with the Fruit Basket* and the *Sick Bacchus*, executed around 1592, belong to Caravaggio's first years in Rome - he came from Lombardy and was employed as a painter of still lifes in the studio of Cavalier d'Arpino.

His famous use of chiaroscuro appeared slightly later in works such as the *Madonna dei Palafrenieri*, painted in 1606 for an altar in St Peter's and soon rejected for lack of 'decorum'. The painting, which was immediately acquired by Scipione Borghese, represents St Anne with the Virgin and Child (treading on the snake, symbol of evil) as peasants. Around the same time he painted *St Jerome*, while *St John the Baptist*, a variation on the Capitoline and Corsini versions, was made in 1609-10.

In 1606 the artist was accused of murder and fled from Rome. He went to Naples, Sicily and Malta and pleaded for grace, sending the pope his self-portrait as the beheaded Goliath. Forgiveness came, but too late for he died on the shores of Porto Ercole, in Tuscany (1610).

FIRST FLOOR

On the landing are portraits of *Paul V* (1621) and *Cardinal Scipione* (1618) as Orpheus (charming the animals including the Borghese dragon). They were both executed in micro-mosaic by Marcello Provenzale. Also here is an interesting work in tempera on paper by J.W. Baur which depicts the villa in 1636.

ROOM 9 has tondi (named after their round shape) by 15c masters including Botticelli (1488), with his workshop, and Fra Bartolomeo (1495), as well as fine paintings by Perugino (Raphael's master) and Pinturicchio. On the wall opposite the entrance is **Raphael**'s *Deposition*, painted in 1507 for Atalanta Baglioni to commemorate the death of his son Grifonetto in the civil wars of Perugia. The painting was stolen one night from the family's chapel for Scipione Borghese. The perfectly balanced composition, inspired by Classical sarcophagi, also shows the influence of Michelangelo (e.g. the Pietà in St Peter's and the Tondo Doni in the Uffizi).

Also by Raphael are the *Portrait of a Lady with a Unicorn* (1506), possibly of Maddalena Strozzi, and the *Portrait of a Man* (1502). Other paintings include Andrea del Sarto's fine *Virgin and Child with the Infant St John the Baptist* (1517) and Bronzino's *St John the Baptist* (1527). Both exemplify Florentine Mannerism with their contrived poses and sophisticated compositions, but whilst Del Sarto dissolves his line and colours, Bronzino traces the contours and applies the colours with an extreme (almost cold) precision.

ROOM 10 Exhibited here is **Correggio**'s *Danaë* of 1531, one of the four paintings representing the Loves of Jupiter commissioned by Federico II Gonzaga, Duke of Mantua, as a present for Charles V. **Cranach**'s ethereal *Venus* of 1531 provides an interesting comparison with Andrea Brescianino's version of 1525. The two fantastical landscapes by Girolamo da Carpi and Niccolò dell'Abate show the development of Mannerism in the area around Bologna and the influence of northern art (e.g. Bosch). In the centre of the room stands an antique statue in black marble which Nicolas Cordier restored as a *Gypsy Girl* (1612).

ROOMS 11-13 display more early 16c art from Venice, Ferrara, Bologna, Siena and Florence.

ROOM 14 The large gallery, formerly an open loggia, has a ceiling fresco of the *Council of the Gods* by Giovanni Lanfranco (1624). Exhibited here are the works of masters active in Rome in the 1620s, from the classical Guercino, Guido Reni and Francesco Albani, who were inspired by the art of Annibale Carracci, to the followers of Caravaggio.

   Also here are several works by **Bernini**, including the early *Goat Amaltea* (carved before 1615) and the busts of *Paul V* (1618), executed twice because the first version developed a break in the pope's forehead. Above the busts are two *Self-portraits* by Bernini, painted in 1623 and 1630-5, as well as a *Portrait of a Boy* (1638). The terracotta study for an equestrian monument of Louis XIV dates from 1669-70, towards the end of Bernini's long career (he was 72). The final sculpture was carried out by assistants but found no favour at the French court and was transformed into a *Marcus Curtius*, now exhibited in the Louvre. In the centre of the room is Alessandro Algardi's splendid *Allegory of Sleep*, carved in black marble in 1635.

ROOM 15 Paintings by 16c artists from Brescia, Ferrara and Venice: Giovanni Gerolamo Savoldo, Dosso Dossi, Jacopo Bassano.

ROOMS 16-18 contain paintings by 16c Mannerists following Michelangelo (Jacopo Zucchi, Pellegrino Tibaldi, Giorgio Vasari), as well as Gaspare Landi's double portrait of himself and his friend Antonio Canova (1806), Rubens's *Deposition* (1602), and Pietro da Cortona's fine *Portrait of Marcello Sacchetti* (1626).

ROOM 19 Displayed in the room are masterpieces of the early 17c including **Domenichino**'s *Hunt of Diana* (1616-7) and the *Sibyl* of the same period. The large painting of *Norandino and Lucina surprised by the Giant* was commissioned in 1624 from Domenichino's rival Lanfranco for the Borghese villa at Frascati. It illustrates an episode from Ariosto's epic poem *Orlando Furioso* and is treated with sweeping brushstrokes quite unlike Domenichino's sleek precision. Also here are *Aeneas' Flight from Troy* (1598) by Federico Barocci and the fine portrait of a *Laughing Boy* painted with great immediacy by Annibale Carracci (1583).

ROOM 20 The last room is devoted to Venetian Renaissance painting. The *Portrait of a Man* (1475) is the work of Antonello da Messina, the artist who introduced the technique of oil painting to Venice after his trip to Flanders. A northern influence, mediated by Dürer's prints and presence in Venice, is also evident in Lorenzo Lotto's *Holy Family with Saints* (1508). Giovanni Bellini's *Madonna and Child* was painted in 1510 when the master was 84 years old. From the same period are the *Two Singers* attributed to Giorgione.

   Titian's *Sacred and Profane Love* ranks among the absolute masterpieces of the Borghese collection. As suggested by the coat of arms on the sarcophagus, it was painted in 1514 for the wedding of Niccolò Aurelio and Laura Bagarotto. The arbitrary title was given in the 18c when the painting was misinterpreted. It was intended to celebrate love in all its forms: earthly love and beauty, symbolized by the clothed spouse close to Cupid; eternal love, embodied in the celestial Venus holding the perpetual flame; and life after death as suggested by the sarcophagus filled with water. Such Neoplatonic interpretation was very common in aristocratic and intellectual circles of the time and seems to be particularly appropriate for a wedding present. On the opposite wall hangs Titian's *Venus blinding Cupid*, painted in 1565 and a good example of the dissolution of form typical of his late style.

Galleria Nazionale d'Arte Moderna

OPEN	Tues-Sun 8.30-19.30
CLOSED	Mon; 1/1, 1/5, 25/12
CHARGES	€6.50. €3.25 for citizens of the EU between 18 and 25 years of age. Free admission for EU citizens under 18 and over 65 or students of art, architecture and archaeology
TELEPHONE	06 322 981
WWW.	gnam.arti.beniculturali.it/gnamco.htm
MAIN ENTRANCE	Viale delle Belle Arti 131
BUS	Tram lines 3 (Via Colosseum and a long detour) and 19 (from Piazza Risorgimento)

Access for disabled visitors is at Via Gramsci 71. The museum has a popular café-restaurant.

The National Gallery of Modern Art was founded in 1883 with the initial aim of preserving and documenting the artistic masterpieces produced in recently unified Italy. It is housed in the Palazzo delle Belle Arti, erected by Cesare Bazzani for the International Exhibition held in Rome in 1911, and later extended. The collection, which today comprises 4400 paintings and sculptures and 13,000 prints and drawings, forms the most complete overview of 19c and early 20c Italian art in the world.

The museum is divided into four areas. The left wing has works dating from the Napoleonic age to 1883; the right wing covers the period 1883 to 1910. The displays continue in the upper right wing with works from the early to mid 20c, while the upper left wing shows art of the 1950s and '60s. A new museum is being built by Zaha M. Hadid in the Flaminio district to house works from the 1960s onwards and contemporary art.

HIGHLIGHTS

	Left wing
Works by the Tuscan 'Macchiaioli'	Room 2
Antonio Canova, *Hercules and Lyca*	Room 4
	Right wing
Giovanni Fattori, *Battle of Custoza*	Room 4
Courbet, *Hunters in the Snow*	Room 5
Van Gogh, *The Gardener* and *L'Arlesienne*	
Giovanni Boldini, *Portrait of Giuseppe Verdi*	
	Upper right wing
Klimt, *The Three Ages*	Room 2
Early works by Giacomo Balla	Room 3
Futurist works by Giacomo Balla and Umberto Boccioni, Amedeo Modigliani	Room 5
Mario Sironi, *Solitude*, Carlo Carrà, *Horses* Felice Casorati, *Portraits*	Room 9
	Upper left wing
Jackson Pollock, Alberto Giacometti	Room 2
Alberto Burri	Room 3
Lucio Fontana, Enzo Cucchi	Room 4

LEFT WING, 1880-1883

SALA DELLA PSICHE *Room 1* Artists active in Rome between the end of the 18c and the beginning of the 19c, including the Neoclassical Gaspare Landi, Andrea Appiani (*Portrait of Vincenzo Monti*, 1809), Vincenzo Camuccini and Filippo Agricola (*Portrait of Costanza Monti Perticari*, 1821), as well as the Purists Tommaso Minardi (inspired by 15c art) and Pietro Tenerani, whose sculpture of *Psyche* (1822) gives her name to the room. Also here are a number of views of Rome by artists of the Roman school and a study by Canova for a monument to *Vittorio Alfieri* (1807).

SALA DELLA SAFFO *Room 2* Works of the Tuscan school, ranging from sculptures by the Purists Giovanni Dupré (*Sappho*) and Lorenzo Bartolini to paintings by the **'Macchiaioli'**, a group of artists active in the 1850s and 60s who were interested in realism and anticipated some of the ideas of Impressionism. The group included Odoardo Borrani, Raffaello Sernesi, Antonio Puccinelli (*Portrait of Nerina Badioli*, 1865), Giovanni Fattori, Silvestro Lega (*The Visit*), Nino Costa, Vincenzo Cabianca.

SALA DELLO JENNER *Room 3* Paintings by the Romantic schools of northern Italy, including Giovanni Carnovali (called Il Piccio), Tranquillo Cremona, and Domenico Induno as well as Antonio Fontanesi, one of the greatest landscape painters of 19c Italy.

SALA DELL'ERCOLE *Room 4* The large central hall is named after the colossal statue of *Hercules and Lyca* by **Antonio Canova** (1815). Also here are a number of late Neoclassical sculptures from the Torlonia collection and historical paintings, including the *Sicilian Vespers* (1846) by Francesco Hayez, one of the most famous works of the period.

SALE PALIZZI, MORELLI AND CLEOPATRA *Rooms 5-7* The three rooms to the right of the central hall are dedicated to the Neapolitan school. The Sala Palizzi has paintings donated by the Neapolitan painter Filippo Palizzi (1818-99), including the *Forest of Fontainebleau* (1874) by his brother Giuseppe and views of Naples by Anton Sminck Pitloo (*Castel dell'Ovo*, 1820) and Giacinto Gigante. The adjoining Sala Morelli has paintings donated by Domenico Morelli, including the *Temptations of St Anthony* (1878) and *Torquato Tasso reading his poem to Eleonora d'Este*. The Sala della Cleopatra, named after a sculpture by Alfonso Balzico, has works by representatives of 'Verism' (Realism), including the paintings of Gioacchino Toma and Antonio Mancini reflecting the reality of working class life.

RIGHT WING, 1883–1910

ROOMS 1-3 feature the work of artists of different parts of Italy: the south (Room 1) – F.P. Michetti, Antonio Mancini, Vincenzo Gemito, Teofilo Patini – Tuscany (Room 2), Venice (Room 3).

SALA DI GIORDANO BRUNO *Room 4* In the centre is the plaster model for Ettore Ferrari's bronze statue of *Giordano Bruno* in Campo dei Fiori. Several of the sculptures and paintings celebrate Italy's Risorgimento (struggle for Independence) and include battle scenes by **Giovanni Fattori** (*Battle of Custoza*, 1880) and Michele Cammarano (*San Martino*, 1883), and busts of *Alessandro Manzoni* and *Giuseppe Garibaldi* (1875) by Ercole Rosa. Other works such as the bronze sculpture *Proximus tuus* by Achille d'Orsi (1880) or *The Emigrants* by Angelo Tommasi (1896) reflect the social reality of Italy at the end of the 19c.

SALA DEL GIARDINIERE *Room 5* The overall theme here is art in Paris in the late 19c, from **Courbet**'s *Hunters in the Snow* (1867) to works by Cézanne, Monet and Degas, as well as **Van Gogh**'s paintings of *L'Arlesienne* and *The Gardener* (which gives its name to the room). Among the Italians working in the French capital were Giuseppe de Nittis, Vittorio Corcos and **Giovanni Boldini**, who became one of the favourite portraitists of the fin de siècle high society and whose *Portrait of Giuseppe Verdi* (1886) recalls Whistler in its use of black and grey tones.

SALA DELLA STANGA *Room 6* The name of the room, which exhibits works by north Italian artists, derives from the large painting by Giovanni Segantini *Alla Stanga* (1886).

SALA PREVIATI *Rooms 7-10* The first room is dedicated to Gaetano Previati (1852-1920) and Italian Divisionism (Vittore Grubicy de Dragon) and includes wax sculptures by Medardo Rosso (1858-1928). The last three rooms contain sculptures by Ettore Ximenes, Domenico Trentacoste and Arturo Dazzi. Paintings by Giulio Aristide Sartorio move from academic classicism to Symbolism: *The Gorgon and the Heroes* (1899), *Diana of Ephesus and the Slaves*, and his powerful and desolate *Malaria*, which illustrates a reality that was, sadly, widespread in Italy at the end of the 19th century.

UPPER RIGHT WING, 1911-50

ROOMS 1-2 contain Secessionist art and the work of Italian artists represented at the International Exhibition of 1911. The first room has sculptures by Auguste Rodin. In the second room are two masterpieces: *The Three Ages* (1905) by **Gustav Klimt** and *Old Women* (1909) by **Felice Casorati**.

ROOM 3 has early works by Umberto Boccioni and **Giacomo Balla**, including the latter's Divisionist paintings such as *Villa Borghese, Parco dei Daini* of 1910.

ROOM 4 Portraits of the bourgeoisie by Giovanni Boldini (paintings) and Paolo Troubetzkoy (bronzes). Also here is De Chirico's *Portrait of his Mother* (1911). More art from 1910-20 is exhibited in the adjoining room, including Fortunato Depero's large tapestry of *Guerra-Festa* and pieces from the DADA collection of Arturo Schwarz, such as Marcel Duchamp's *Bicycle Wheel* (1913) and *Porte-bouteilles* (1914).

ROOM 5 The Futurists **Giacomo Balla** and **Umberto Boccioni** (whose portrait of *Maestro Busoni*, of 1916, reflects the influence of Cubism mediated by Cézanne); and works by **Amedeo Modigliani**, Kees van Dongen (*Woman in White*, 1911), Giorgio Morandi's still lifes, Carlo Carrà, Piet Mondrian, Laszlo Moholy Nagy.

ROOMS 6 & 7 The first room features art inspired by rural Italy in the 1920s and 1930s. Room 7 has paintings by Virgilio Guidi (*In the Tram*, 1923) and Felice Casorati (still lifes).

ROOM 8 Works by **Giorgio de Chirico**, creator of Metaphysical art (*Hector and Andromaca*, 1924), his brother Alberto Savinio, and Filippo de Pisis, all three active in Paris in the mid 1920s.

ROOM 9 The large hall contains the Futurist 'Regime' paintings of Gerardo Dottori (*Fascist Polyptych*, 1934) and the Surrealist Futurism of Enrico Prampolini. There are also early figurative works by Giuseppe Capogrossi (*Il Temporale*, 1933) and Massimo Campigli's *The Brides of the Sailors* of 1934; and works by the Roman school of the late 1920s and '30s.

Important paintings by **Mario Sironi** (*Solitude*, of 1926, and the cartoon of *The Constructor* executed a decade later), **Carlo Carrà**'s *Horses* (1927) and **Felice Casorati**'s *Portraits* (1934). In the centre of the last section is Arturo Martini's terracotta sculpture of *The Sisters* (1934) and *The Bather* by Marino Marini (1934).

ROOM 10 has paintings by Renato Guttuso (*Crucifixion*, 1941) and sculptures by Giacomo Manzù, including *La Grande Pietà* (a bronze composition of 1943), *The Cardinal* of 1938 and the *Crucifixion*, a series of bronze reliefs made between 1939 and 1942.

ROOMS 11-12 contain post-war art including Neo-Realism and Neo-Cubism. A sculpture gallery leads to the last wing.

UPPER LEFT WING, 1950S AND 1960S

This part of the collection features (Room 2) Abstract Expressionism and beyond, with works by **Jackson Pollock**, Karel Appel, Hans Hartung and Antoni Tapiès, and sculptures by **Alberto Giacometti** and Alexander Calder. Room 3 has **Alberto Burri** and his Informal-Materic art. Room 4 includes **Lucio Fontana**, Cy Twombly and **Enzo Cucchi**, and sculptures by Pietro Consagra, Arnaldo and Giò Pomodoro. Rooms 5 and 6 have works of the 1960s, while Conceptual art is the theme in Room 7.

Beyond a corridor with Kinetic art, steps lead to the mezzanine floor and the collection of Palma Bucarelli (director of the museum in 1935-75).

Museo Etrusco di Villa Giulia

OPEN	Tues-Sun 8.30-19.30
CLOSED	Mon; 1/1, 1/5, 25/12
CHARGES	€4
TELELEPHONE	**06 320 1951**
MAIN ENTRANCE	Piazza di Villa Giulia 9
BUS	Tram, lines 3 (via Colosseum and a long detour) and 19 (from Piazza Risorgimento)

There is a café in the orangerie

The Etruscan Museum was founded in 1889 to house pre-Roman art from Lazio, Umbria and southern Etruria. It contains works of the Etruscan and Faliscan civilizations, as well as examples of Greek art from the 7c-5c BC. The initial holdings were substantially enlarged by the donation in 1908 of the Barberini collection and subsequent acquisitions (such as the Castellani collection).

THE BUILDING

Built in 1551-5 for Pope Julius III by Giorgio Vasari, Bartolomeo Ammannati and Jacopo Barozzi (Vignola), and decorated with frescoes by Prospero Fontana and Taddeo Zuccari, the villa reflects the taste and culture of the mid 16c and is among the best examples of Mannerist secular architecture in Rome. Conceived as a suburban pleasure villa on the model of the early 16c Villa Farnesina, its design featured gardens embellished with fountains and statues.

Beyond the two-storeyed façade of the main wing, an atrium leads to a round portico decorated with a fictive pergola. This is followed by a succession of courtyards interrupted by a loggia and a nymphaeum that were designed by Ammannati. The fountain here took its waters from the conduits of the Acqua Vergine (see p 86). The garden to the right of the first courtyard has a hypothetical 19c reconstruction of the Temple of Aletrium (Alatri) of the 3c-2c BC. The long side wings flanking the gardens were added in the 1910s. A further extension is due to open in Villa Poniatowski (built by Vignola in the late 16c and modified by Valadier in the early 19c) where objects currently exhibited in rooms 32-35 will be relocated.

HIGHLIGHTS

Terracotta sculptures from the sanctuary of Portonaccio at Veio	Room 7
Sarcophagus with a reclining husband and wife	Room 9
Cista Ficoroni	Room 12
Olpe Chigi	Room 17
The Castellani collection of Greek vases and jewellery	Rooms 19-20
Finds from Pyrgi	Rooms 21-22
Bust of Apollo	Room 30
Furnishings from the Barberini and Bernardini tombs at Praeneste	Room 34

GROUND FLOOR, LEFT WING

VULCI *Rooms 1-5* are dedicated to Vulci, an Etruscan town that flourished in southern Etruria between the 9c and 5c BC. Excavations conducted in the territory since the 18c have revealed about 15,000 tombs whose furnishings are exhibited here. Room 1 has sculptures of a **Man Astride a Sea-horse** and a **Centaur** dating from the 6c and influenced by Greek art. The objects exhibited in Room 2 belong to the early Iron Age (9c to end of 8c BC) and testify to the custom of cremating the deceased (progressively abandoned in the 6c BC). The ashes were kept in bronze urns shaped like miniature huts and interred with votive objects. Interesting bronze statuettes, such as the **Warrior with a Pointed Helmet**, a shield and plaited hair, were influenced by the Nuragic cultures of Sardinia.

Rooms 3-4 exhibit black-figure vases imported from Greece and local Etruscan-Corinthian ceramics. Room 5 has a Hellenistic sarcophagus with a *Battle of the Amazons* and a number of votive offerings (terracotta heads, figurines of children, models of buildings, etc) that were dedicated to deities associated with health and fertility. Stairs lead down to a reconstructed tomb from the necropolis at Cerveteri, the ancient Caere, containing beds and the belongings of the deceased.

BISENZIO *Room 6* Tomb furniture from the Villanovan and Etruscan tombs of Bisenzio (Vesentium), including a bronze incense burner mounted on wheels and a situla with figurines dancing around a chained animal (both date from the late 8c BC).

VEIO *Room 7* displays important finds from the sanctuary of Portonaccio at Veio, the great enemy of Rome (17km further north) which controlled the right bank of the Tiber and was finally defeated after a ten-year siege by Furius Camillus (396 BC). Veio was the first Etruscan town to fall under Roman rule. The statues of *Apollo* and *Herakles* from the Temple of Apollo (c 510 BC) show a high degree of workmanship and can be ascribed to Vulca, a famous sculptor who was also summoned to decorate the Temple of Jupiter on the Capitoline Hill. The sculptures will soon be relocated to Rooms 32-35.

CERVETERI *Rooms 8-10* display finds from the necropolis at Cerveteri (Caere), the main Etruscan centre for maritime commerce, which flourished in the 7c-5c BC and also owned the nearby port of Pyrgi. The town declined after the defeat of the Etruscans at Cuma (474 BC) and the sack of Pyrgi by the Syracusans (384 BC). It was finally conquered by the Romans in the 3c BC.

The tombs of the necropolis at Cerveteri are of the tumulus type derived from models of the Near East. The finds exhibited here illustrate the introduction and influence of eastern artefacts (bronzes, jewellery and ivory) and vases from Greece.

In Room 9 is a famous *sarcophagus with a reclining husband and wife* which housed the ashes of the couple (c 520). The two figures are represented with the characteristic 'archaic' smile.

Room 10 has a fine collection of **Greek and Etruscan vases** dating from the 7c to 2c BC. Two important hydriai of Greek inspiration and local production illustrate respectively the blinding of Polyphemus and the Apotheosis of Herakles (c 520 BC). Other fine examples include a red-figure cup by Oltos decorated with the deeds of Herakles (c 520 BC), vases by Hermonax, and a krater (large vase for mixing wine and water) by the Berlin Painter (480 BC).

UPPER FLOOR, LEFT WING

ROOMS 11-18 Beyond a collection of inscriptions (Room 11) are objects from the Antiquarium founded in 1651 by Father Athanasius Kircher in the Jesuit College (Collegio Romano).

The most celebrated piece here is the *Cista Ficoroni* (Room 12), named after its first owner who donated it to the Antiquarium in 1738. Cistae were cylindrical toilet boxes holding mirrors, strigils and whatever else was needed for the care of the body. They were largely produced at **Praeneste** (Palestrina) and were decorated with incised motifs often derived from Greek compositions. This one shows a fight between Pollux and King Amykos for the use of a fountain. The inscription on the lid identifies the artist as Novios Plautios and the commissioner as Dindia Macolnia who gave the cista to her daughter, possibly as a wedding present.

Room 13 has bronze figurines, used as votive offerings, including a *Ploughman* found at Arezzo (late 5c BC). Room 15 has a series of bronze mirrors with finely incised decoration on the back. Among the ceramics displayed in Rooms 16-17 is the famous *Olpe Chigi*, a late Protocorinthian vase (c 630 BC) of refined taste and workmanship. It was found at Formello, near Veio, and was probably destined for a person of high rank. Villanovan and archaic vases (8c-6c BC) are exhibited in Room 18.

CASTELLANI COLLECTION *Rooms 19-20* Stairs lead up to Rooms 19 (the hemicycle) and 20 housing the substantial Castellani collection of ceramics, bronzes and jewellery. It was formed in the

19c by Augusto Castellani, from a family of goldsmiths.

The **ceramics** are organized chronologically from the 8c BC to the Roman period and begin with red on white examples of eastern taste (late 8c-early 6c BC), Etruscan bucchero ware (7c-6c BC) and Corinthian vases. Among the Attic red-figure vases (520-440 BC) are fine examples by Kleophrades and the Berlin Painter.

The southern part of the hemicycle is dedicated to Etruscan **bronzes**, ranging from banqueting implements to ornaments and toilet ware. Of special note are the shield and two vases of the early 7c BC which were found in a tomb at Praeneste. An impressive bronze chalice with caryatids was found at Caere and dates from the late 7c BC, while the refined statuette of *Alexander Hunting* can be ascribed to a Greek workshop (early 3c BC).

In the centre of the hemicycle is the entrance to Room 20 displaying the Castellani collection of antique **jewellery**, one of the finest in existence, including Greek, Etruscan, Roman and Oriental examples as well as copies made by the Castellani jewellers.

PYRGI *Rooms 21-22* These two rooms exhibit very important finds from a sanctuary at Pyrgi, one of the three Etruscan ports of Cerveteri, sacked in 384 by the Siracusans. Excavations revealed a sacred precinct, or temenos, with the remains of two temples built around 500-450 BC by Thefarie Velianas, King of Caere (Cerveteri). The impressive terracotta relief with the myth of the *Seven against Thebes* formerly decorated the rear tympanum of temple 'A'. This was dedicated to the goddess *Leucotea* whose lively terracotta head, of later date, ranks among the finest pieces surviving from the site.

The adjoining room contains three **gold plaques** with the earliest known historical inscriptions of pre-Roman Italy. Two of them are written in Etruscan, the third in Phoenician and they relate how Thefarie Velianas dedicated a statue and a temple to a goddess called Astarte in Phoenician and Uni in Etruscan. The mention of such a goddess, who was assimilated into the Etruscan Leucotea, testifies to the influence of foreign cultures encountered by the Etruscans along their trade routes.

HISTORY OF THE VILLA *Rooms 23-25* (on the other side of Room 20) illustrate the history of the museum and the villa, which in the 17c housed guests of the papal court, including Queen Christina of Sweden, and was later turned into a hospital, a veterinary school, military quarters and a storage depot.

UPPER FLOOR, RIGHT WING

AGER FALISCUS *Rooms 26-31* are dedicated to finds from the Ager Faliscus, an area between Lake Bracciano and the right bank of the Tiber that was inhabited by two people: the Falisci, related to the Latins, and the Capenati, or Sabines, from Capena (south of Monte Soratte).

In Room 26 are finds from Capena, including a dish decorated with a war elephant and her baby, which belonged to a series created after the victory over Pyrrhus and his elephants in 275 BC.

Room 27 has finds from Narce, possibly the ancient Fescennium, which flourished between the 8c and 7c BC as the main centre of the southern Ager Faliscus. The refined tomb furnishings of the local aristocracy included Greek and Etruscan vases, precious jewellery, bronze shields, chariots and more.

FALERII *Rooms 28-29* Here are artefacts from Falerii (modern Civita Castellana), the capital of the Faliscan territory built on a high tufa mound. Although its origins date to the late Bronze Age, it fully developed between the 8c BC and the mid 3c BC. Praised for its architectural terracottas and votive bronzes, the town reached its maximum splendour in the 4c BC when Greek immigrants made it a centre of ceramic production.

Falerii was completely destroyed by the Romans in 241 BC and the surviving inhabitants settled in the valley below, where they founded Falerii Novi. Important pieces exhibited here include a bronze cinerary urn in the shape of a hut (7c BC) and a drinking horn (rhyton) shaped like a dog's head attributed to Brygos (first half of the 5c BC).

FALERII VETERES *Room 30-31* display terracotta sculptures used for the decoration of temples near Falerii Veteres. Downstairs are a fine bust of *Apollo* and a head of *Mercury*, showing a strong Greek influence, which once decorated the front of a temple dedicated to Apollo at Scasato (end of the 4c BC).

GROUND FLOOR, RIGHT WING

LATIUM *Rooms 32-34* exhibit material from the first systematic excavations conducted in Latium at the end of the 19c.

The small-scale objects and figurines in Room 32, such as the model of an archaic temple from Velletri, were offerings to deities. Among the architectural terracottas is a female head from the Temple of Juno at Lanuvium (c 500 BC). Also here is the funerary equipment of an aristocrat from Gabii, including his coffin carved from the trunk of an oak tree (early 7c BC).

In Room 33 are finds from **Satricum**, in the territory of the Volsci (southwest of Rome), where a settlement of about 30 huts developed on the acropolis between the 9c and 6c BC. The vital centre was the sanctuary of Mater Matuta, initially just a large oval hut and later a shrine and a temple decorated with terracotta reliefs of the *Battle of the Amazons*. From the Tomba delle Ambre, excavated in the necropolis of Satricum, came an exceptional quantity of ambers as well as the fine bronze furnishings and table.

Room 34 has works from **Praeneste** (Palestrina), an important and wealthy centre southeast of Rome that flourished from the end of the 8c BC along the trade routes of the Latins and Sabines.

In the 19c, the discovery of the 'princely' tombs **Barberini**, **Bernardini**, Castellani and Galeassi yielded impressive objects in gold and silver, bronze and ivory of the so-called Oriental period (7c BC). The influence of Greek, Egyptian and Assyrian art was assimilated by the Italic and Etruscan civilizations and gave rise to a distinctive local production and the extensive importation of goods from the East.

The decoration of the silver-gilt cauldron and libation dishes (phialai) from the Bernardini tomb is particularly fine and represents horsemen, foot-soldiers, hunting scenes and triumphs that seem to identify the deceased as a warrior. It can be dated to 680-650 BC.

UMBRIA *Room 35* contains works from centres in Umbria. Among the finest exhibits are a bronze helmet from Todi inlaid with silver and decorated with battle scenes (late 5c BC), a mirror incised with the *Judgement of Paris*, and banquet furnishings in bronze (3c BC).

on route

EXPLORA, Via Flaminia 82. Apart from the zoo (a rather sad place, close to the Galleria Borghese), EXPLORA is the best centre for children in Rome. Here they are invited to explore the functions and activities of a real city, child's size. Entrance at set times only: 9.30, 11.30, 15.00, 17.00; Sat, Sun and PH 10.00, 12.00, 15.00, 17.00; August 15.00, 17.00, 19.00; closed Mon. Adults €5, children €6, 0-3s free. *T* 06 361 3741. *M* A to Flaminio

Park of Villa Borghese Once the property of the Borghese family, the park is the largest in the centre of Rome. Laid out in the early 17c for Cardinal Scipione Borghese, it was re-designed in the late 18c by Prince Marcantonio IV Borghese and Jacob More of Edinburgh. With the acquisition of the Giustiniani gardens it was enlarged all the way to Piazza del Popolo and re-organized with monumental entrances, structures and avenues designed for Camillo Borghese by the architect Luigi Canina (1822).

Santa Maria della Concezione, Via Veneto. The church was founded in 1626 by Cardinal Antonio Barberini and decorated by major artists of the Baroque age, from Guido Reni, Domenichino and Lanfranco to Pietro da Cortona and Andrea Sacchi. The adjoining crypt has five chapels filled with the bones and skeletons of 4000 Capuchin monks.

Via Veneto Opened in 1886-9, this large street soon filled with

fashionable hotels, cafés and luxury shops, becoming the theatre of
Rome's 'Dolce Vita' in the 1950s and '60s.

It occupies part of the site of Villa Ludovisi, built in 1621-3, over the
Gardens of Sallust, by Cardinal Ludovico Ludovisi (nephew of Gregory
XV). In the early 19c the property was acquired by the Boncompagni
Rospigliosi, who enlarged it further and then sold it as building ground to
the Italian state (1883). The only reminder of the original magnificence is
the **Casino dell' Aurora** (Via Lombardia 46), a garden house with a fine
ceiling painting of *Aurora* (1621) by Guercino.

Halfway down the road is the large **Palazzo Margherita**, built by
Gaetano Koch (1886-90), the residence of Queen Margherita after the
death of Umberto I (1900). It is now the US Embassy.

eating and drinking

AT THE MUSEUMS
GALLERIA NAZIONALE D'ARTE MODERNA
Caffè delle Arti, Via Gramsci 73, *T* 06 3265 1236. This café-
restaurant has become a favourite, particularly for its pleasant
ambience both inside and outdoors.

VILLA GIULIA
Caffè degli Aranci, the orangerie in the garden of Villa Giulia, has
been turned into a pleasant café.

RESTAURANTS
€   **Gaudì**, Via R. Giovannelli 8, *T* 06 884 5451. Not too far from the
Borghese Gallery, this is a good place for salads, pasta, grilled
meats and pizza. Closed for lunch over the weekends.

Il Regno di Napoli, Via Romagna 20, *T* 06 474 5025; closed Saturday
and Sunday lunchtime. Neapolitan pizzeria.

Jasmine, Via Sicilia 45, *T* 06 4288 4983; closed Tuesday. One of the
best restaurants in town for authentic Chinese food.

La Villa di Pizza Ré, Via Lucullo 22, *T* 06 4201 3075. Neapolitan (thick crust) pizza and other Campanian specialities.

€€ **Buca Vino**, Via Ofanto 35, *T* 06 841 2803 and at Via Po 45a, *T* 06 884 8873; closed Sunday and August. Not too far from the Borghese Gallery, these *trattorie* are a good option for a light lunch or dinner.

Girarrosto Fiorentino, Via Sicilia 46, *T* 06 4288 0660; never closed. A long established and impeccable Tuscan restaurant.

Trattoria Cadorna dal 1947, Via R. Cadorna 12, *T* 06 482 7061; closed Saturday and Sunday lunchtime, and August. Huge servings of traditional food.

Vivienne, Via Ofanto 8, *T* 06 6854 6705; closed Sunday, feast days and 14-31 August. Not far from the Borghese Gallery. A small and comfortable restaurant with good food and a menu for children (a rarity in Rome).

€€€ **Asador Caffè Veneto** (at the Café Veneto), Via Vittorio Veneto 118, *T* 06 4827 107; closed Monday. Specialities from the grill.

Cucina Italiana, Via Aurora 19, *T* 06 4890 5880. Good seafood.

Harry's Bar, Via Vittorio Veneto 150, *T* 06 484 643; closed Sunday. The scene of the 'Dolce Vita' in the 1960s has turned even more international both in terms of clientele and cuisine. A piano and a singer provide background music.

La Terrazza de l'Hotel Eden, Via Ludovisi 49, *T* 06 478 121. Justly famous for its roof terrace, less for its food.

Mirabelle de l'Hotel Splendide Royal, Via Porta Pinciana 14, *T* 06 4216 8838; never closed. With magnificent views over domes and rooftops, this is one of the most beautiful dining locations in Rome. Excellent cuisine and good wines.

NYCE (New York City Express), Via Lucullo 9, *T* 06 4202 0434. The name says it all about the style and food of this restaurant. High-tech look and international dishes.

Papà Baccus, Via Toscana 36, *T* 06 4274 2808; closed Saturday lunchtime and Sunday. Quality cuisine, service and ambience. According to many this is the best Tuscan restaurant in town.

Vivendo del St Regis Grand, Via Vittorio Emanuele Orlando 3, *T* 06 4709 2736; evenings only; closed Monday and August. A sumptuous interior for a light and balanced cuisine.

COFFEE BARS

Café de Paris, Via Veneto 90, *T* 06 488 5284. Established in 1956, this was the main stage of the 'Dolce Vita'.

Caffè Strega, Via Vittorio Veneto 173.

Doney, Via Vittorio Veneto 145, *T* 06 4708 2805. Completely re-styled, this café remains one of the highlights of Via Veneto.

LATE-NIGHT BARS & CLUBS

Siena Art Café, Viale del Galoppatoio 33, *T* 06 3600 6578. Set in an open space beneath the park of Villa Borghese, this is the largest disco-club of central and northern Rome as well as one of the trendiest places in the capital.

shopping

BOOKS
La Strada, Via Veneto 42, *T* 06 482 4151.

CLOTHES
Albertina, Via Lazio 20, *T* 06 488 586. Fine knitwear and more.

Aston, Via Boncompagni 27, *T* 06 4282 6647. Haute couture fabrics.

Brioni, Via Barberini 79-81, *T* 06 4845 1706; Via Condotti 21a, *T* 06 6783 635; Via Vittorio Veneto 129. High quality fashion for gentlemen (ready- or tailor-made) and some for ladies.

Chez Garage, Via Pinciana 53, *T* 06 8535 5971. A wonderful luxury bazaar with multi-ethnic clothes, shoes and objects.

DEPARTMENT STORES
La Rinascente, Piazza Fiume 1, *T* 06 6884 1231.

FOOD

Alberto Pasquali Biologico, Via Marche 21, *T* 06 474 3344. Organic produce including fruit and vegetables.

Casabianca, Via Piemonte 123, *T* 06 4201 3190; open 8.30-19.30; closed Saturday afternoon and August. Good sandwiches.

Gargani, Via Lombardia 15, *T* 06 4740 865; open 7.00-20.00. Wines, cheeses, cold meats and readymade dishes to eat in or take away.

Golosa Mente, Via Sicilia 144, *T* 06 488 3747; open 9.00-20.00. The best Campanian products, from pasta and fresh buffalo mozzarella to sun-dried tomatoes in olive oil, bread, etc. Sandwiches and pizza available too.

Mediterraneo, Via Lazio 15, *T* 06 4201 3297. Excellent pizza by the slice.

Palombi, Via Veneto 114, *T* 06 488 5817. Established in 1913, this high-class bakery has fine breads as well as good croissants and sweets to accompany your coffee at the bar.

Vincenzo Pasquali, Via Sardegna 20, *T* 06 482 1937; open 7.30-20.00. Gourmet food since 1928 and readymade dishes to take away.

HOMES

Driade, Via Po 1h, *T* 06 855 3210. Contemporary objects and furnishings.

Loto Design, Via Gramsci 54 (above the Modern Art Gallery), *T* 06 3600 6879. Interior design and contemporary furniture.

JEWELLERY

Capuano, Via Vittorio Veneto 102, *T* 06 488 4998.

De Pascalis, Via Vittorio Veneto 187, *T* 06 482 1908.

SHOES

Albanese, Via Lazio 21, *T* 06 4201 0114. Shoes for men and women.

Bruno Magli, Via Vittorio Veneto 70a; also at Via del Gambero 1.

Mencucci, Via Piemonte 55-57, *T* 06 4274 13 64. Shoes and a great variety of sandals in summer.

R & Co., Via Vittorio Veneto 104, *T* 06 420 10264.

Shop, Via Vittorio Veneto 195, *T* 06 420 14867.

VATICAN
ST PETER'S

In the 1c AD, the area that is now the Vatican formed part of the Trans Tiberim district outside the city proper. Gradually the emperors turned it into a pleasure ground with villas and large gardens that included a stadium for naval contests, a hippodrome, and a circus where innumerable Christians were martyred. Among the victims of Nero was St Peter, whose burial site was consecrated almost three centuries later by Constantine, the first Christian emperor, who founded a basilica there in 324. During the Middle Ages a new quarter developed around it, populated mainly by foreign pilgrims, while the popes themselves continued to live in the Lateran Palace at the opposite end of town.

During the exile of the popes to Avignon (1305-77), and the subsequent Western Schism (1378-1417), the Lateran Palace fell into disrepair. Upon their return to Rome, the popes took up residence in the Vatican, building new palaces and decorating their apartments with frescoes by the most celebrated artists of the day. They also tore down the old basilica and built a much larger one, as an expression of the grandeur of vision that

St Peter's from the river Tiber

characterized the city of Rome in the High Renaissance and Baroque periods.

The Vatican has been an independent state ever since the Lateran Pacts of 1929 granted the Pope a separate rule within the city of Rome. The boundaries are marked by St Peter's and walls built in the 16c-17c; the total area is about 44 hectares.

The Vatican has about 900 inhabitants and 1300 non-resident employees. Some 3 million visitors crowd the museums each year. It also has its own jurisdiction, military organization (the 300 Swiss Guards), currency, newspaper, postage stamps, television and radio stations.

The Vatican Museums

OPEN	Mon-Fri; March-Oct 8.45-15.20 (exit 16.45); Nov-28 Feb 8.45-12.20 (exit 13.45); Sat and the last Sun of the month 8.45-12.20 (exit 13.45)
CLOSED	Sun; 1/1, 6/1, 11/2 (anniversary of the Lateran Pacts), 19/3, Easter Sun-Mon, 1/5, Ascension Day (the 6th Thursday after Easter), Corpus Christi (9th Thursday after Easter), 29/6, 14-15/8, 1/11, 8/12, 25-26/12
CHARGES	€10, €7 for students with ID up to 26 years of age and pilgrim groups with a letter from their diocese. Free for disabled visitors and children under 6 years old Free for all on the last Sunday of each month
TELEPHONE	**39 06 6988 4947**. Recorded info **39 06 6988 3333**
WWW.	**vatican.va**
MAIN ENTRANCE	Viale Vaticano
METRO/BUS	Line A to Ottaviano (the closest station) or Cipro. Bus nos 64 and 40 Express from Termini Station, 46 from Piazza Venezia. All run through the city centre (Corso Vittorio Emanuele)

Audio-guides €5.50, also guided tours (ask at the entrance). Disabled visitors can reserve wheelchairs in advance (F 06 6988 5433) or request one at the entrance. To arrange visits for the visually impaired, F 06 6988 1573. The museum has several bookstalls, a self-service restaurant, a currency exchange office, post office, telephones and three first-aid stations.

The Vatican houses the largest collection of ancient sculpture in the world as well as important masterpieces such as the Sistine Chapel and the *Stanze* painted by Raphael. The collections have their origins in the sculpture garden of Julius II, set up in 1506 to display his antiquities. The museums, housed in the papal palaces, were created during the second half of the 18c and the beginning of the 19c, a time marked by the Enlightenment and the great archaeological discoveries.

THE BUILDINGS

The first pope to build in the area was Symmachus, who was driven out of the Lateran during the Laurentian Schism (501-506). He erected two temporary residences at the sides of St Peter's.

A new fortified structure (around the Cortile dei Pappagalli) was begun by Nicholas III (1277-80) and finished by Nicholas V (1447-55) after the move of the papal court to the Vatican.

Sixtus IV (1471-84) added the Sistine Chapel and had it decorated by the best Florentine artists of the early Renaissance. Innocent VIII (1484-92) erected the Belvedere Pavilion at the top of the Vatican hill. Alexander VI (1492-1503) employed Pinturicchio for the frescoes in his apartments, and Julius II (1503-13) had Raphael and Michelangelo decorate his rooms and private chapel (the Sistine). He also commissioned Donato Bramante to link the palace of Nicholas V to the Belvedere Pavilion, where his sculpture garden had been installed. By constructing two long corridors Bramante created the great Belvedere courtyard. This was later cut in two by the transversal wing of the new library, which Domenico Fontana built for Sixtus V (1585-90). Fontana was also responsible for the construction of the block overlooking St Peter's Square, where the pope has his private quarters today. The Belvedere Pavilion and the courtyard were further transformed in the 18c and 19c to provide room for the new museums of Classical antiquity.

HIGHLIGHTS

Classical sculpture: *Augustus of Prima Porta, Doryphoros, Athena Giustiniani*, the *Nile*	Braccio Nuovo
Classical sculpture: *Apoxyomenos, Apollo Belvedere, Laocoön, Torso Belvedere* and porphyry sarcophagi of Saints Costantia and Helena	Museo Pio-Clementino
Regolini-Galassi tomb finds, *Mars of Todi* gold jewellery, collection of Attic vases	Etruscan Museum
16c frescoes of Italy	Gallery of Maps
Raphael's frescoes for Julius II	Stanze di Raffaello
Michelangelo's ceiling and *Last Judgement*	Sistine Chapel
Giotto's *Stefaneschi triptych*	Pinacoteca Vaticana

Raphael, *Transfiguration* **and tapestries** **Leonardo da Vinci,** *St Jerome* **Caravaggio,** *Deposition*	Pinacoteca Vaticana
Stele of a Youth, Chiaramonti Niobid *Cancelleria reliefs, Tomb of the Haterii*	Gregorian Museum
Sarcophagi, statue of the *Good Shepherd*	Pio-Christian Museum

Beyond the Neoclassical Atrium of the Quattro Cancelli (Four Gates), which has signposts to the various galleries, lies the **Cortile della Pigna**. It takes its name from the 4m-high pine cone that was found near the Baths of Agrippa, behind the Pantheon. It was made of bronze in the 1c AD and served as a fountain - see the tiny holes on its scales.

The Cortile della Pigna is at the north end of the Belvedere courtyard. In the centre is a sculpture by Arnaldo Pomodoro (1990).

EGYPTIAN MUSEUM

The museum was founded by Gregory XVI in 1839.

Rooms 1 and 2 contain funerary objects which date from the Old Kingdom to the Christian era (c 2600 BC-600 AD). There are funerary stelae and tomb reliefs, painted mummy cases (1000 BC) and mummies, canopic jars (1500-500 BC) for the preservation of entrails, jewellery and *ushabtis* (statuettes of servants who accompanied the deceased in the afterlife). Room 2 also has also a painted shroud of the 3c AD from Antinoupolis.

Room 3 houses a reconstruction of the *Serapeum of the Canopus* built by Hadrian in his villa at Tivoli after his journey to Egypt (AD 130-131). The sculptures include *Serapis*, a colossal bust of *Isis*, and *Antinous* (Hadrian's favourite) as the Egyptian god Osiris.

There are significant examples of Egyptian art in Room 5, including a sandstone head of *Mentuhotep II*, from the 11th dynasty (c 2050 BC) and a black granite statue of the lion goddess *Sekhmet* (c 1350 BC). There are colossal statues of *Queen Tuya*, mother of

VATICAN MUSEUMS
Lower Floor

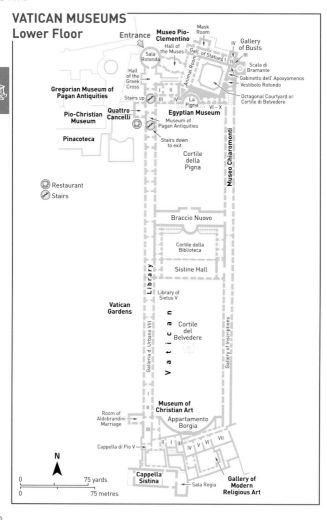

Entrance

Museo Pio-Clementino

Hall of the Muses

Mask Room

IV Gallery of Busts

III

Sala Rotonda

Gall. of Statues I

Scala di Bramante

Hall of the Greek Cross

Animal Room

Gabinetto dell' Apoxyomenos

Vestibolo Rotondo

Gregorian Museum of Pagan Antiquities

Stairs up

III

IV

La Pigna

VI – X

Octagonal Courtyard or Cortile di Belvedere

Quattro Cancelli

Pio-Christian Museum

Egyptian Museum

Museum of Pagan Antiquities

Pinacoteca

Stairs down to exit

Cortile della Pigna

Museo Chiaromonti

Restaurant

Stairs

Braccio Nuovo

Cortile della Biblioteca

Sistine Hall

Library of Sixtus V

Vatican Gardens

Library

Cortile del Belvedere

Galleria d. Urbano VIII

V a t i c a n

Gallery of Inscriptions

I

II

Museum of Christian Art

Room of Aldobrandini Marriage

Appartamento Borgia

III

Cappella di Pio V

II   I III

IV V VI

VII

N

0   75 yards

0   75 metres

Cappella Sistina

Sala Regia

Gallery of Modern Religious Art

VATICAN MUSEUMS
Upper Floor

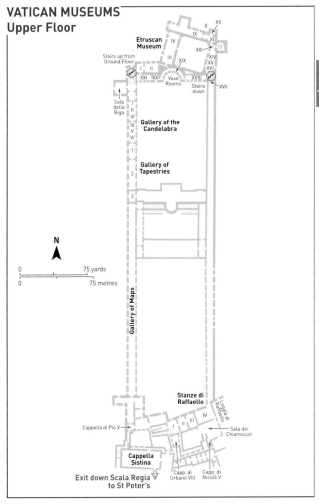

Etruscan
Museum

Stairs up from
Ground Floor

Sala
della
Biga

Vase
Rooms

Stairs
down

**Gallery of the
Candelabra**

**Gallery of
Tapestries**

N

0 ——————— 75 yards
0 ——————— 75 metres

Gallery of Maps

**Stanze di
Raffaello**

Loggia di
Raffaello

Cappella di Pio V →

← Sala dei
Chiaroscuri

**Cappella
Sistina**

**Exit down Scala Regia
to St Peter's**

Capp. di
Urbano VIII

Capp. di
Nicolò V

Rameses II (c 1250 BC), **Ptolemy Philadelphos**, the Greek king of Egypt (284-46 BC), and his wife **Arsinoë**. These were imported from Egypt and placed in the Sallustian gardens by Caligula (AD 37-41) who likened himself to a pharaoh and who, like Ptolemy Philadelphus, married his own sister, Drusilla (who is represented in the fourth colossal statue as Arsinoë).

Next is the Grassi collection of small bronzes and terracotta statuettes, vases and ceramics, as well as seals and tablets with cuneiform inscriptions from Mesopotamia (3000-1000 BC). Room 9 has Assyrian reliefs (8c-7c BC) from the royal palaces of Nineveh. Some bear the traces of the fire that destroyed the city in 612 BC.

CHIARAMONTI MUSEUM

Located in Bramante's east corridor, the gallery was named after its founder, Pius VII (1800-23), and was arranged by the sculptor Antonio Canova (1807-10). Nearly 1000 pieces of sculpture are exhibited here: statues of gods (mostly copies of Greek originals), portraits (fine examples include **Augustus** and **Tiberius**), architectural decoration and sarcophagi.

Beyond is the **Gallery of Inscriptions**, open only to scholars. It contains more than 3000 pagan and Christian inscriptions from cemeteries and catacombs. To the right is the Braccio Nuovo.

BRACCIO NUOVO

(This gallery is sometimes closed.) Built in 1817-22 for Pius VII, it has fine examples of Roman sculpture. The floor is inlaid with 2c mosaics representing the adventures of Ulysses.

To the right of the entrance is the famous **Augustus of Prima Porta**, found in 1863 in the villa of his wife Livia on the Via Flaminia, north of Rome. Augustus is identified by his standard portrait (a youthful image), and is represented as a victorious general addressing his soldiers. The decorations on the cuirass refer to an event that took place in 20 BC, depicting a Parthian king returning the Roman insignia lost by Crassus in 53 BC in northern

Mesopotamia. The statue, copied many times, is a replica of a bronze original whose character and pose are influenced by the statue of the Spear-bearer exhibited on the opposite wall.

The *Spear-bearer* is a Roman copy after the celebrated *Doryphoros* by Polykleitos (440 BC). It reveals the artist's close study of proportions and demonstrates the contrapposto pose for which he became famous: one leg carries the weight while the other is at rest; one arm is in action while the other is relaxed.

Further on, along the same wall, is the *Resting Satyr*, one of the many replicas of the famous statue by Praxiteles (the Vatican owns a number of them). The *Athena Giustiniani*, named after its first owner, is the best existing copy of an original in bronze by Kephisodotos or Euphranor (4c BC). Athena is identified by her snake, shield and helmet as the goddess of the intellect and of arms.

In the hemicycle halfway through the gallery is the colossal statue of the *Nile*, found in 1513 on the site of the Temple of Serapis (close to the Pantheon). The river god is identified by sphinxes and crocodiles and is surrounded by 16 children (symbolizing the floods). It is a Roman work of the 1c AD, based on a Hellenistic original.

Opposite is a fine bust of *Julius Caesar* and two **bronze peacocks** (copies of which are in the Cortile della Pigna) from Hadrian's mausoleum (Castel Sant'Angelo), where they stood as a symbol of immortality.

At the end of the gallery is the bust of *Pius VII* by Antonio Canova.

MUSEO PIO-CLEMENTINO

The museum was begun by Clement XIV (1769-74) and enlarged by Pius VI (1775-99). It has its origins in the sculpture garden of Julius II, housed in the Belvedere Pavilion, which the Neoclassical architect Michelangelo Simonetti adapted as a museum. The galleries contain some of the finest Classical pieces of the Vatican museums.

The *Apoxyomenos* is an athlete who has returned from a race and is scraping the oil, sweat and dust from his body with a strigil.

Found in Trastevere in 1849, it is a 1c AD copy of the bronze masterpiece by Lysippos (320 BC). Working at the court of Alexander the Great, Lysippos' sculpture exemplified the new quest for realism that inspired Greek art of the period. He may have been influenced by Aristotle (teacher of Alexander), whose idea of good portraiture was to render 'the motions of the mind'. Pliny the Elder said of Lysippos that he sought to portray men not as they are but as they appear to be in the truth of each fleeting moment. The Apoxyomenos is shown not in the moment of glory, but afterwards, tired and dirty, performing a trivial action. The frontal approach of earlier sculpture has been discarded: this was one of the first examples to be conceived in the round. Such sculptures changed the spirit of Classical art and its idealization of the human figure, as it had been codified in the 5c BC, and paved the way for the Hellenistic style.

The small room beyond gives access to the **spiral staircase** built by Bramante in the early 16c. At each turn the style of the columns changes from Tuscan, to Ionic and Corinthian, in imitation of the superimposed orders of the Colosseum.

OCTAGONAL COURT This was once the sculpture garden of Julius II. To the left is the *Apollo Belvedere*, a Roman copy (2c AD) of a bronze original attributed to Leochares (330 BC), which was described by Pausanias in the Agora of Athens. The sculpture, known since the 14c, came into the hands of Julius II who brought it to the Vatican in 1503. The god, shown in an elegant, almost dancing pose, has just shot an arrow. He once held a bow in his raised left hand.

Across the courtyard is the famous *Laocoön* group, illustrating the story related by Virgil in the *Aeneid*. Laocoön, priest of Apollo, had warned his fellow Trojans against the wooden horse left by the Greeks 'as an offering to Athena'. As punishment, the outraged goddess sent two enormous serpents to kill him and his sons. In his *Natural History*, Pliny the Elder ascribed the group to the sculptors Agesander, Polydoros and Athenodoros (c 1c AD). He also wrote that he saw it in the palace of the Emperor Titus. It was discovered in 1506 on the Esquiline Hill, near the Domus Aurea and the Baths of Titus, and immediately recognized as the piece described by Pliny. It was bought by Julius II and greatly admired by the artists of the day, including Michelangelo. Combining realism with a sense of drama, force and movement, this masterpiece of Hellenistic art anticipates Baroque sculpture.

The recess to the right of the entrance has three Neoclassical sculptures by Canova (1800): *Perseus*, clearly inspired by the Apollo Belvedere, and the Nemean boxers *Kreugas* and *Damoxenes*.

ROOM OF THE ANIMALS The sculptures displayed here were either restored, integrated or (the majority) entirely made up by Antonio Franzoni (1734-1818).

GALLERY OF STATUES This gallery is often closed. It was once an open loggia in the Belvedere Pavilion, built in the 15c for Innocent VIII. Traces of frescoes by Pinturicchio and his school are still visible on the walls. The *Mattei Amazon* is after a bronze by Phidias (430 BC). According to Pliny, a series of Amazons had been created in a competition between Polykleitos, Phidias, Kresilas and Phradmon, and set up in the Temple of Artemis at Ephesus. Also here is a copy after Praxiteles' *Apollo Sauroctonos* (350 BC).

GALLERY OF BUSTS Here are portraits of emperors and gods, including the enthroned *Jupiter Verospi*, a restored 3c AD replica after Apollonius' gold and ivory original (after 85 BC) in the Temple of Jupiter on the Capitoline Hill.

ROOM OF THE MASKS (Usually closed to the public.) It contains mosaics of theatrical masks from Hadrian's villa at Tivoli (2c AD) as well as a fine copy after Praxiteles' *Venus of Cnidus* (360 BC).

HALL OF THE MUSES It takes its name from the statues of the muses, philosophers and poets exhibited along the walls. In the centre is the *Torso Belvedere*, a Neo-Attic work of the 1c BC. The muscular male figure sits on a rock which bears the inscription 'made by Apollonios the Athenian, son of Nesto'. Signatures on antique sculptures are extremely rare. Given the presence of a lion skin, the figure has been associated with Hercules, but other identifications have been suggested. Found in the 15c, it was first kept in the palace of the Colonna family, and then moved here at the time of Clement VII (1523-34). Renaissance artists, including Michelangelo, studied it closely for its understanding of anatomy and movement.

CIRCULAR HALL This was designed by Simonetti (1780) and modelled on the Pantheon. On the floor is a late antique mosaic showing battles between Greeks and centaurs, tritons and nereids. In the centre is a huge **monolithic basin** (13m in circumference) found in the Domus Aurea. It is made of porphyry, a very hard stone extracted in Egypt and used almost exclusively for imperial commissions.

Among the colossal sculptures in this room are, to the right of the entrance, a head of *Hadrian* (117-138), from his mausoleum at Castel Sant'Angelo; a *Hercules* in gilded bronze, found in 1864 near the Theatre of Pompey (Campo dei Fiori); and a head of *Antinous*, the young favourite of Hadrian who drowned in the Nile in AD 130 and was subsequently deified by the emperor.

HALL OF THE GREEK CROSS The room contains two splendid **porphyry sarcophagi**. The one on the right, found beside the church of Santa Costanza on the Via Nomentana, belongs to Constantia, daughter of the Emperor Constantine (c 360 AD). It is decorated with motifs translated from a Classical vocabulary into a Christian language: acanthus scrolls have become vine branches, putti are now angels, and the grapes allude to the blood of Christ. The peacocks are associated with eternity and the ram with sacrifice.

The other sarcophagus comes from the Tomb of St Helena, mother of Constantine, on the Via Labicana. It is slightly earlier in date and is decorated with high-relief images of Roman soldiers on horseback and prostrate or chained barbarians. Though the Christian overtone is less obvious (the triumph of good over evil) the decoration does reflect a transitional phase from late Antique to early Christian art. Because of its military character, the sarcophagus has been associated with Helena's husband, Constantius Chlorus.

ROOM OF THE BIGA The staircase built by Michelangelo Simonetti ascends to the Gallery of Candelabra and the Room of the Biga (to the right) which takes its name from the two-horsed chariot reconstructed by Antonio Franzoni from antique fragments (1786-94). Only part of the far side horse and the body of the chariot are original (1c AD). The *biga* had been used as a bishop's throne in the church of San Marco. The staircase ascends one more floor to the Etruscan Museum.

ETRUSCAN MUSEUM

(This museum closes at 12.30.) It was founded in 1837 by Gregory XVI to house one of the most important collections of Etruscan art, which came mainly from excavations in southern Etruria. It was enlarged in 1989 by the acquisition of the Guglielmi collection of finds from Vulci. It also includes a substantial display of Greek and Italic vases.

ROOM 2 Finds from chamber tombs of the 7c BC unearthed in 1836 in a necropolis south of Cerveteri, including the *Regolini-Galassi tomb*, named after its discoverers. The tomb was the burial place of a princess called Larthia, a warrior of high rank, and a king or priest who was cremated (which explains the presence of the cinerary urn). To the woman belong the remains of a bronze throne, a number of jewels and precious objects of fine workmanship. The warrior lay on a bed and was accompanied by a bronze *biga* and a funeral carriage.

ROOM 3 In the centre is the famous *Mars of Todi*, a bronze sculpture of the early 4c BC showing the influence of 5c Greek art. Two particularly fine examples of **engraved mirrors** depict the stories of Herakles and Atlas, and of Chalcas, the soothsayer. They show how Greek mythology was adopted in the Etruscan world.

ROOM 4 has funerary inscriptions of the 4c-3c BC: particularly interesting is one from Todi with a bilingual text in Latin and Celtic.

ROOMS 5-13 include architectural decoration and votive offerings in terracotta, fine gold jewellery (Rooms 7-8), the Guglielmi collection of Attic and Corinthian vases as well as bucchero ware (Etruscan black ceramics) and alabaster urns.

ROOMS 14-16 house the **Antiquarium Romanum**, with bronzes, silverware, glass and other objects from the Roman period and earlier. In Room 15 are three terracotta reliefs of the *Labours of Hercules*.

ROOMS 17-22 contain Greek, Italic and Etruscan vases from the tombs of southern Etruria, and vases from Vulci and Cerveteri (6c BC), and from Magna Graecia. Room 19 is the Hemicycle with an impressive collection of Attic vases, including the black-figure amphora signed by Exekias with Achilles and Ajax playing dice, and, on the other side, Castor and Pollux being welcomed by their parents (530-520 BC). In the last case is a kylix (a shallow two-handled cup) by Duris depicting Oedipus trying to solve the riddle of the Sphinx (490-480 BC).

GALLERY OF CANDELABRA

This is the first of a series of galleries housed in Bramante's west corridor. It is named after the pairs of **marble candelabra**, of the Roman Imperial period, placed at the sides of the arches that divide the room into six sections. The display includes some fine Hellenistic works featuring charming and trivial scenes from mythology and daily life. In size, character and treatment they are far removed from the idealized grandeur of 5c-4c BC representations of divinities or athletes.

SECTION 2 On the left: *Ganymede abducted by the Eagle*, a Roman copy of a bronze original by Leochares (mid 4c BC), described by Pliny. Opposite is a statue representing the many-breasted *Diana* *of Ephesus*, goddess of fertility, from Hadrian's villa at Tivoli.

SECTION 4 On the right: sarcophagus with *Bacchus and Ariadne* (2c AD); on the left: sarcophagus with the *Massacre of the Niobids*, with Apollo and Diana firing their arrows at the 14 children of Niobe - she had boasted that she was more fertile than their mother Leto (2c AD). The *Boy with a Goose* is from a bronze original by Boethus of Chalcedon (180 BC).

SECTION 5 On the right: statue of a girl running in a race, known as *Atalanta*, after a bronze of the 5c BC. On the left: statuette of a *Persian soldier*, after a bronze original from an altar given by Attalos I of Pergamon to the city of Athens and placed on the Acropolis (2c BC).

GALLERY OF TAPESTRIES

Exhibited here are tapestries depicting the *Life of Christ*, designed by Raphael's pupils (some after drawings by their master). They are called the 'New School' series to distinguish them from the 'Old School' tapestries designed by Raphael himself and exhibited in the Pinacoteca. Both series were woven in the Brussels workshop of Pieter van Aelst. On the opposite wall are tapestries of the *Life of Urban VIII* made in Rome in the 17c.

GALLERY OF MAPS

It takes its name from the 40 maps painted in 1580-3 for Gregory XIII from cartoons by Ignazio Danti, one of the greatest cosmographers of his time.

The maps feature the Italian peninsula, with the regions washed by the Ligurian and Tyrrhenian seas painted on the left, and the Alpine and Adriatic regions represented on the right. At the far end are two general maps of Italy, one at the time of Augustus (*Italia Antiqua*), and the other of Italy in the 16c (*Italia Nova*).

The barrel vault is decorated with contemporary stuccoes and frescoes illustrating 80 episodes from the history of the church and the lives of saints related to the regions represented below.

Beyond the gallery of maps is the former Apartment of St Pius V (1566-72) which now houses a series of Flemish tapestries. A particularly fine example, woven in Tournai in the late 15c, illustrates episodes from the *Passion* in a style that looks back to the late Middle Ages.

THE STANZE DI RAFFAELLO

The Stanze di Raffaello are located on the second floor of the palace which was built for Nicholas V (1447-55) and decorated by Piero della Francesca and Andrea del Castagno. Half a century later Julius II (1503-13) employed Perugino and Signorelli, as well as Sodoma, Lorenzo Lotto and Baldassarre Peruzzi to continue the work. Then Julius' court architect, Donato Bramante, suggested Raffaello Sanzio, a fellow citizen from Urbino and pupil of Perugino, who arrived in Rome in 1508. The young artist's talent was immediately revealed in the first room he painted (the Stanza della Segnatura) and the Pope dismissed all the other artists, ordering their work to be destroyed to make way for Raphael's frescoes. In their harmonious compositions, the classicism of the figures, and the perfect balance of colour and line, they epitomize the ideals of High Renaissance painting. Raphael worked on and off in the Stanze until his death in 1520, the last room (Sala di Costantino) being completed by his assistants in 1524. It is this last room that you see first as you enter via a covered passage running above the Belvedere courtyard.

SALA DI COSTANTINO This room was used for official receptions and was decorated in 1517-24 by Giulio Romano and Francesco Penni. The walls depict events from the life of Constantine, the first Christian emperor. On the left is the *Vision of the Cross*, by Giulio Romano. Before the battle against his rival Maxentius, the emperor had a miraculous vision of the Cross and heard the words *in hoc signo vinces* (by this sign you shall win). The next fresco, also by Giulio Romano, depicts the *Victory of Constantine* in the battle on the Milvian Bridge. Both scenes are greatly indebted to the antique, with traceable references to the reliefs on Trajan's Column and the Arch of Constantine.

To the right is the *Baptism of Constantine*, attributed to Francesco Penni. The event is set in the Lateran Baptistery and Pope Sylvester has the features of Clement VII, the pope at the time. The last fresco, also by Francesco Penni, illustrates *Constantine's Donation of Rome to Pope Sylvester*. Although the 'Constitutum Constantini' was a medieval forgery, for centuries it provided the legal foundation for the right to temporal possession of the Church, hence its depiction in a room where diplomats, princes and sovereigns would wait to be received by the pope.

STANZA DEI CHIAROSCURI The grisaille (grey) figures of the *Apostles* and *Saints* (particularly fine are Saints Peter and Paul) were executed by the school of Raphael and extensively restored in 1560 by Taddeo and Federico Zuccari. The ceiling featuring the Medici arms was carved at the time of Leo X de' Medici (1513-21).

CHAPEL OF NICHOLAS V Frescoed by the Florentine artist **Fra Angelico** between 1447 and 1451, the scenes depict events from the lives of St Stephen (above) and St Lawrence (below). The four Evangelists are shown on the vault and the Doctors of the Church on the pilasters.

STANZA DI ELIODORO Raphael painted this room in 1512-4, after the Segnatura. The general theme is the miraculous intervention of God to protect the threatened Church. On the right wall is the *Expulsion of Heliodorus* from the Temple of Jerusalem where he had been sent by the King of Syria to steal the treasures. His action was hindered by a horseman and two angels armed with whips, an allusion to the pope's success in freeing the State of the Church from foreign powers; the message is underlined by the presence of Julius II who is portrayed seated on the left. Raphael also portrayed himself (at the back) and his engraver friend Marcantonio Raimondi as the chairbearers.

To the right is the **Mass of Bolsena**, depicting a miracle that took place in 1263. A Bohemian priest who had doubts about the presence of Christ in the Eucharist was convinced when he saw blood dropping from the Host while he was celebrating mass in Bolsena. Julius II is shown kneeling opposite the priest.

Next is the fresco showing **Leo I Repulsing Attila**. The event, which took place near Mantua, is set in the vicinity of Rome, recognizable in the background. Attila and his Huns are struck with terror at the vision of Saints Peter and Paul. Leo I is given the features of Leo X, who had become pope in 1513 and is also shown as a cardinal in the foreground. The fresco is an obvious reference to the Battle of Ravenna of 1512 in which the French were expelled from Italy.

On the fourth wall, in three episodes, is the **Liberation of St Peter from Prison**. First an angel wakes the apostle (centre), and leads him out of prison (right), while a soldier with a torch calls the sleeping guards (left). The event takes place at night allowing the artist to create remarkable lighting effects. On the ceiling are representations of God's miraculous apparitions in the Old Testament.

STANZA DELLA SEGNATURA This was Julius' library, where he also signed bulls and briefs (hence the name 'segnatura'). It was the first room that Raphael painted (1508-11) and the complex programme was undoubtedly devised by a court theologian. The iconography relates to the three highest categories of the human spirit according to Neo-Platonic philosophy: the true, the good, and the beautiful. Supernatural truth (Theology) is represented in the **Dispute over the Holy Sacrament**. The composition is divided into two parts: above is the Triumphant Church, with saints and Old Testament figures seated at the sides of the Trinity, the Virgin, and St John; below is the Militant Church, with doctors and theologians discussing the Eucharist which is placed on an altar in the centre. Some of the figures can be identified as portraits: Dante with a laurel wreath on the right, Fra Angelico in black Dominican habit on the left, and Bramante leaning over the balustrade in the foreground.

The fresco on the opposite wall depicts rational Truth as personified by the philosophers of the *School of Athens*. The setting is a basilica similar to that planned by Bramante for the new St Peter's. In the centre are Plato (possibly a portrait of Leonardo da Vinci) pointing upwards to the world of ideas, and Aristotle stretching his hand towards the ground to indicate the principles of Logic. Close to Plato, dressed in olive green, bald-headed and recognizable by his characteristic profile, is Socrates; in front of him is Alexander the Great, clad in armour. To the far left, crowned with vine-leaves, is Epicurus. Beside him, writing out his harmonic tables, is Pythagoras, with Averroës looking over his shoulder. In the foreground is the isolated figure of Heraclitus, the melancholic philosopher thought to represent Michelangelo writing his sonnets (he was painting at the same time as Raphael, one floor down in the Sistine Chapel). Diogenes, the Cynic philosopher, reclines on the steps. On the right is Euclid (a portrait of Bramante) tracing figures with a compass on a blackboard. Behind him are the geographer Ptolemy (seen from the back) with the terrestrial globe, and the astronomer Zoroaster holding the celestial globe. At the far right are portraits of Raphael (in a black cap) and Sodoma (dressed in white).

On the short wall by the doors is the *Parnassus*, illustrating Beauty as personified by the nine Muses and Apollo, who is shown in the centre playing the lyre. To his right are the epic poets Dante, Virgil and the blind Homer. Seated below are the lyric poets led by Sappho in the foreground. Among the figures on the right are famous Italian poets and writers: Ariosto, Boccaccio, and Sannazaro.

In the lunette opposite are the *Cardinal* and *Theological Virtues* shown respectively as female figures and angels. Below is the *Institution of Canonical Law* and the *Institution of Civil Law*. Both these frescoes were executed by assistants, like the monochrome paintings on the dado which were painted by Perin del Vaga. The decoration of the ceiling precedes Raphael and is attributed to Sodoma.

STANZA DELL'INCENDIO This was the last room painted by Raphael (1514-7), who left much of the frescoes to his assistants.

In the 16c it served as a dining room, with the kitchen located in the adjoining service area. The paintings are an allegory of the political ambitions of Leo X through episodes from the lives of his namesakes, Leo III and Leo IV.

Left of the entrance is the *Victory of Leo IV over the Saracens at Ostia* (849), alluding to the crusade against the Turks proclaimed by Leo X (who is depicted with his retinue). The battle takes place in the background, in front of the fortified castle built at Ostia under Julius II. The foreground is dominated by Roman soldiers (inspired by antique reliefs) receiving their prisoners and tying them up in a variety of contrived poses. Though Raphael made numerous preparatory drawings, the fresco seems to be by his workshop.

The *Incendio di Borgo* illustrates the fire that broke out in Rome in 847 which was miraculously extinguished when Leo IV made the sign of the Cross from the loggia of St Peter's. It alludes to Leo X's diplomatic ability in restoring peace to Italy. The background is dominated by the façade of Old St Peter's. On the left is the fire of Troy, with Aeneas fleeing with his son and father; to the right is a feminine figure seen from the back that would be admired and copied for years to come.

The *Coronation of Charlemagne*, which took place in St Peter's in 800, is an obvious reference to the agreement between France and the Church reached in Bologna in 1515. Hence Leo III has the features of Leo X, while Charlemagne is portrayed as Francis I. It was executed by Raphael's workshop.

The last fresco, also by Raphael's assistants, depicts the *Oath of Leo III*. It alludes to the principle decreed by the Lateran Council (1516) that the pope must answer for his actions to God alone. The Egyptian telamones depicted on the dado are those found at Tivoli and now in the Pio-Clementine Museum. The vault decorations are by Perugino and represent the *Glorification of the Trinity*.

Beyond is the small **Chapel of Urban VIII**, decorated with stuccoes and paintings by Pietro da Cortona and exhibiting terracotta models by Antonio Canova.

At this point you can either proceed directly to the Sistine Chapel (left) or go down to the Borgia Rooms and the Museum of Modern Religious Art, and then enter the Sistine.

THE BORGIA ROOMS

The apartment of Pope Alexander VI Borgia was decorated in 1492-5 by Pinturicchio with *grottesche* imitating the recently discovered ornaments of the Domus Aurea, and frescoes of various subjects. The Rooms of the Sibyls, the Creed and the Liberal Arts come first, but it is the **Room of the Saints** that is Pinturicchio's masterpiece. It depicts events from the lives of Saints Sebastian, Susannah, Barbara, Catherine of Alexandria, Anthony Abbot and Paul the hermit. Particularly fine is the *Disputation of St Catherine of Alexandria and Maximian*, with the Arch of Constantine in the background.

The Room of the Mysteries was executed almost entirely by Pinturicchio's assistants, while the Room of the Popes, originally decorated with portraits, was painted by Perin del Vaga and Giovanni da Udine.

GALLERY OF MODERN RELIGIOUS ART

Inaugurated in 1973, it comprises a vast array of paintings, drawings and sculptures which were presented to Pope Paul VI (1963-78) by invited artists, collectors and donors. Stairs lead up from the last room to the Sistine Chapel.

THE SISTINE CHAPEL

The Chapel is named after Sixtus IV della Rovere who employed the best Florentine artists to decorate it in 1481-3. It was both a defensive structure (evident from its shape and thick walls) and a private chapel. The conclave for the election of the popes is held here.

The artists painting on the side walls included Perugino, Botticelli, Ghirlandaio, Cosimo Rosselli and Signorelli, assisted by their pupils Pinturicchio and Piero di Cosimo. The frescoes depict parallel events from the lives of Christ and Moses, the latter being the Old Testament pre-figuration and forerunner of the Saviour in his role as priest, legislator, and leader of his people. The complex iconography was suggested by court theologians and is filled with political overtones. Each fresco has a hidden or obvious thematic link with the one on the opposite wall.

The most important scene is *The Giving of the Keys* by Perugino, as Christ's charge to Peter marks the institution of the papacy. Opposite is Botticelli's punishment of those who dared question the authority of their leaders. The cycles began on the altar wall, but the first two frescoes were later destroyed to make way for Michelangelo's *Last Judgement*. Various episodes are condensed into one scene (a medieval device), while the protagonist is made recognizable by the recurring colours of his dress.

LEFT WALL In the **first fresco** (by Perugino and Pinturicchio) is Moses taking leave of his father-in-law before returning to Egypt; Moses and Zipporah (his wife in Egypt) and the circumcision of their son. The **second fresco** is by Botticelli: Moses kills the Egyptian who mistreated an Israelite and escapes from Egypt; he defends Jethro's daughters at the well, kneels in front of the burning bush and leads the Jewish people out of Egypt. The **third** and **fourth** are by Cosimo Rosselli: Crossing of the Red Sea and Moses receives the tablets of the Law, while his people worship the golden calf. Botticelli painted the **fifth**: Punishment of Korah, Datan and Abiram who were swallowed up by the earth for rebelling against their leaders (to the right is the attempted stoning of Moses); in the background is the Arch of Constantine and the Septizodium from ancient Rome. The **sixth**, by Signorelli: the Testament of Moses; Moses gives his rod to Joshua; Death of Moses.

RIGHT WALL The **first** is by Perugino and Pinturicchio: Baptism of Christ; the **second** by Botticelli: Temptations of Christ and the purification of the leper; the **third** by Ghirlandaio: Calling of the first Apostles; the **fourth** by Cosimo Rosselli and Piero di Cosimo: the Sermon on the Mount; the **fifth** is by Perugino: the Giving of the Keys and, in the background, the payment of the tribute money and the attempted stoning of Christ (matching the same subject of the fresco opposite); and the **sixth** by Cosimo Rosselli: the Last Supper. The last two frescoes on the east wall were painted over in the 16c.

On the upper register, at the sides of the windows, are representations of the first 28 popes, painted by the artists responsible for the scenes below. To the same period belong the choir screen (by Mino da Fiesole and Andrea Bregno), the pulpit and the pavement in *opus alexandrinum*.

THE CEILING Twenty-five years after the walls of the chapel were frescoed, Julius II, nephew of Sixtus IV, entrusted **Michelangelo** with repainting the ceiling (up to that point a starry blue sky). The reluctant artist, who considered himself a sculptor rather than a painter, completed the vault between 1508 and 1512. It illustrates the history of mankind before the coming of Christ.

Beginning over the altar the scenes show: the *Separation of Light and Darkness*; the *Creation of the Sun, the Moon and Plant Life on Earth* (two days are summarized into one field, which is why God appears once from the front and once from the back with an incredible foreshortening); the *Separation of Land and Sea*; the *Creation of Adam*; the *Creation of Eve*; the *Fall and Expulsion from Paradise*; the *Sacrifice of Noah* (chronologically this scene takes place after the Flood, but was placed here because it requires less space); the *Flood*; the *Drunkenness of Noah*.

The scenes are set in a painted architectural framework on which nude figures (the famous *ignudi*) are sitting. These are clearly inspired by the *Torso Belvedere*, and might be intended to symbolize the geniuses of the Golden Age (inaugurated once more by Julius II). They hold bronze medallions with Old Testament stories from the Book of Kings. Immediately below are five *Sibyls* and seven *Prophets*, respectively the Pagan and Hebrew harbingers of the coming of the Messiah.

The **spandrels** and **lunettes** above the windows contain the *Ancestors of Christ*. In the four corner spandrels are scenes of the miraculous salvation of Israel (*Moses and the Brazen Serpent*; the *Death of Haman*; *Judith and Holophernes*; *David and Goliath*), anticipating the sacrifice of Christ and the renewed salvation of mankind.

Michelangelo *Delphic Sybil* (1508-12)

Michelangelo started painting from the end of the story, above the original entrance to the chapel. As yet unfamiliar with the fresco technique, his first scenes were executed with the help of assistants and are characterized by a multitude of small figures. He gradually became more confident and continued working alone. The first half of the ceiling was unveiled in 1510 when the impatient Julius ordered the scaffolding to be taken down. Michelangelo realized that he had to increase the scale of the figures, so the prophet Jonah, sitting above the altar as a pre-figuration of the death and Resurrection of Christ, is enormous and exceeds by far the architectural framework. By comparison, Zachariah, the first prophet to be painted (directly over the entrance), is much smaller and contained by his surroundings.

The frescoes were restored in 1980-94 to reveal an unexpectedly bright colour scheme, which had been darkened by centuries of candle smoke. It also became clear from the restoration that Michelangelo painted directly on to the surface of the wet plaster (without cartoons or under-drawings).

THE LAST JUDGEMENT More than 20 years later, Pope Paul III urged Michelangelo, who was in his sixties, to paint the *Last Judgement* (1536-41). The overall composition, with figures arranged on two levels, recalls earlier illustrations of the subject, although the dramatic quality of Michelangelo's scene is unprecedented and enhanced by a strong circular movement.

On the left, the blessed are seen rising to the heavens; on the right, the damned are hurled down into hell. High above is the vengeful Christ (untraditional in his youthful, naked and beardless appearance, which recalls a Classical statue). At his sides are the figures of Mary (recoiling in fear, instead of interceding for the souls) and crowds of saints and martyrs who are identified by their symbols or the instrument of their martyrdom. Clearly recognizable at the feet of Christ are St Lawrence with his gridiron, and St Bartholomew with his flayed skin, which is thought to be a distorted self-portrait of the artist. In the centre are the trumpeting angels (unusually, all naked), while others are shown at the top carrying the symbols of the Passion (the crown of thorns, the cross and the column to which Christ was tied and whipped).

The central group, with an angel lifting up two souls by means of a rosary, refers to the Counter-Reformation and is a clear statement about the role of faith and prayer. At the bottom, to the left, are the resurrecting bodies. To the right are two figures borrowed from Dante: Charon shipping the souls across the river Styx; and Minos with donkey ears, possibly a portrait of Biagio da

Cesena, the master of ceremonies at the time who had objected to the nudity of the figures. In fact these were soon covered up with loin-cloths painted by Daniele da Volterra. The restoration carried out in 1990-4 removed many of these additions.

At this point you can leave the museums by the exit on the right, which leads directly into the portico of St Peter's (it is closed on Wednesdays). Alternatively you can continue the tour and return, via the doorway on the left and the Vatican library, to the main entrance on Viale Vaticano. The following rooms, and the Vatican library, are located on the lower floor of Bramante's west corridor.

CHAPEL OF PIUS V (1566-72) It is decorated with Mannerist frescoes (Vasari and Jacopo Zucchi) and displays reliquaries and treasures from the Sancta Sanctorum (the private chapel of the pope in the Lateran).

ROOM OF THE ADDRESSES Named after the congratulatory documents that were kept here, it contains Roman glass and liturgical objects in ivory, enamel and precious metals.

ROOM OF THE ALDOBRANDINI WEDDING The room was built in 1611 for Paul V and decorated by Guido Reni. It contains a large fresco of the Augustan age (27 BC-14 AD), known as the *Aldobrandini Marriage* after its first owner.

SISTINE ROOMS AND VATICAN LIBRARY The rooms are decorated with frescoes by Cesare Nebbia and other artists glorifying the pontificate of Sixtus V (1585-90). The library was founded in the 15c by Nicholas V and moved to the Sistine Hall, built by Domenico Fontana in 1587-9. Through acquisitions and donations the library holds 70,000 manuscripts and about 800,000 printed books.

PINACOTECA VATICANA

The Vatican picture gallery was founded by Pius VI (1775-99) who soon had to surrender a large number of paintings to Napoleon in the Treaty of Tolentino, 1797. Of these, 77 were recovered after the Congress of Vienna (1815). Only the highlights are listed below.

ROOM 1 Byzantine school and Italian Primitives: the *Last Judgement*, which was commissioned by two 12c Benedictine nuns represented at the bottom on the left; *St Francis* by Margaritone d'Arezzo.

ROOM 2 **Giotto**'s *Stefaneschi Triptych*, commissioned by Cardinal Stefaneschi for the high altar of Old St Peter's. On the side walls are fine 14c-15c paintings, including Bernardo Daddi's *Madonna of the Magnificat* and works by Pietro Lorenzetti, Simone Martini, Sassetta, Lorenzo Monaco and Gentile da Fabriano.

ROOM 3 has works by **Fra Angelico** (*Life of St Nicholas of Bari*), Filippo Lippi and Benozzo Gozzoli.

ROOM 4 Melozzo da Forlì's *Sixtus IV and Platina*, a fresco transferred to canvas, showing the Pope appointing his librarian in the presence of his nephew Giuliano della Rovere (the future Julius II). By the same artist are the eight *Musician angels*, from the Ascension of Christ, formerly in the apse of the church of Santissimi Apostoli.

ROOMS 5-6 have 15c-16c paintings, including a *Pietà* by Lucas Cranach and polyptychs by Carlo Crivelli and Antonio Vivarini.

ROOM 7 15c Umbrian artists including Pinturicchio (*Coronation of the Virgin*) and Perugino (*Madonna and Child with Saints*).

ROOM 8 is entirely dedicated to **Raphael** and holds some of his masterpieces. The *Coronation of the Virgin*, painted in 1502-3 for the Oddi family in Perugia, belies his training under Perugino. To a more mature phase belong the *Madonna di Foligno*, painted in 1512 for Sigismondo de' Conti from Foligno, and the famous

Transfiguration, Raphael's last work, commissioned in 1517 by Giuliano de' Medici. Also here are the celebrated *tapestries of the Acts of the Apostles*, with ten scenes from the lives of Saints Peter and Paul. Intended for the lowest register of the Sistine Chapel, they were woven in Brussels after designs made by Raphael in 1515-6. Seven of the original cartoons were bought in 1630 by Charles I of England and are now in the Victoria and Albert Museum in London.

ROOM 9 Leonardo's *St Jerome* (1480) and Giovanni Bellini's *Pietà*.

ROOM 10 Titian's *Madonna of San Niccolò de'Frari* (1528) and the posthumous portrait of the *Doge Niccolò Marcello* (1542). The *Madonna of Monteluce*, painted in 1525 by Giulio Romano and Francesco Penni after Raphael's designs.

ROOM 11 paintings by Vasari, Federico Barocci (the *Rest on the Flight into Egypt*, 1573), and Ludovico Carracci.

ROOM 12 Baroque masterpieces, including **Caravaggio**'s *Deposition,* painted in 1604 for the church of Santa Maria in Vallicella; Domenichino's first major altarpiece, the *Communion of St Jerome* (1614); Guido Reni's *Crucifixion of St Peter*, commissioned by Cardinal Scipione Borghese. Most of the paintings exhibited here have micro-mosaic copies in St Peter's.

ROOMS 13-18 include works by Pietro da Cortona and Van Dyck, clay models by Bernini, including the *bozzetti* for the chapel of the Holy Sacrament and the Cathedra Petri in St Peter's.

GREGORIAN MUSEUM OF PAGAN ANTIQUITIES

The museum was established by Gregory XVI (1831-46) and housed in the Lateran until it was moved here in 1970. The collection comprises archaeological finds from the former Vatican territory.

To the right of the entrance are Greek originals, including a *Funerary stele of a Youth* (450 BC), a head of *Athena* (5c BC), and an Attic relief of *Dancing Nymphs* c 400 BC.

The following section has Roman works imitating Greek art such as the *Marsyas*, after a 5c BC bronze original by Myron, once part of a group described by Pausanias on the Acropolis of Athens. The satyr attempts to pick up a double flute that Athena has just invented and thrown away, but he is stopped by the commanding gesture of the goddess (here reproduced in a cast). The *Asaroton Mosaic* was found on the Aventine and shows a floor covered with the remains of a rich banquet. It is signed with the name Heraclitus, although it is a copy (2c AD) of a famous Hellenistic mosaic by Sosus of Pergamon. In a recess is the *Chiaromonti Niobid*, a Roman copy after a Greek original of the 4c BC.

The following sections contain Roman sculpture in chronological order. The large *Cancelleria reliefs* (named after the palace where they were found) date back to the Flavian period (AD 70-96) and represent the arrival of the Emperor Vespasian and the departure of the Emperor Domitian (whose portrait has been replaced by that of Nerva).

Further on are fragments from the *Tomb of the Haterii*, of the late Flavian period, unearthed outside Porta Maggiore, one of the gates of Rome. They include two niches with busts of the freedman Quintus Haterius and his wife, and reliefs of a woman's funeral (the only known Roman depiction of this subject).

Beyond a section with sarcophagi is a room dedicated to Roman mystery cults with *Mithras and the Bull* (3c AD), *Diana of Ephesus*, and *Asklepios* (2c AD). In a semicircular court is one of two mosaics discovered in the 19c in the Baths of Caracalla, with depictions of naked athletes and referees dressed in togas (3c AD). A walkway leads on to the Jewish lapidarium, with inscriptions from the Jewish catacomb at Monteverde (probably the oldest one in Rome). On the rest of the upper floor is the Pio-Christian Museum.

PIO-CHRISTIAN MUSEUM

The museum was founded in 1854 by Pius IX to house Christian antiquities found in catacombs. They were kept in the Lateran until 1963 and include important **sarcophagi** and one of the largest collections of **Christian inscriptions** in the world. The statue of the

Good Shepherd (3c AD) is one of the few free-standing sculptures of Early Christian art since they were regarded as a potential source of idolatry.

St Peter's

OPEN	Daily, April-Sept 7.00-19.00; Oct-Mar 7.00-18.00
	Treasury: open April-Sept 9.00-18.15; Oct-Mar 9.00-17.15
	Dome: April-Sept 8.00-17.45; Oct-Mar 8.00-16.45
	Papal tombs: April-Sept 7.00-18.00; Oct-Mar 7.00-17.00
	To visit the Necropolis apply to the Ufficio Scavi (left of St Peter's, beneath the Arco della Campana) Mon-Fri 9.00-17.00. **T 06 6988 5318**
	Mass is held on Sun at 9.00, 10.30, 11.30, 12.10, 13.00, 16.00, 17.45. Papal audiences are held on Wednesdays at 10.30 in the Piazza (April-Sept) or in the New Audience Hall, to the left of the basilica (Oct-March). Entrance tickets may be obtained (free of charge), at the Portone di Bronzo, in the colonnade to the right of St Peter's, on the Mon or Tues preceding the audience, 9.00-13.00
CLOSED	Visits are not permitted when the Pope is in the Basilica or in the Square for audiences (Wednesday mornings). The dome is closed 1/1, 1/5, 25/12 and Easter Sun and Mon
CHARGES	Free entrance except for the treasury (€5)
TELEPHONE	**06 6988 2019**
METRO	Line A to Ottaviano. Bus nos 64 and 40 Express from Termini Station, 46 from Piazza Venezia. All run through the city centre (Corso Vittorio Emanuele)

The Square - Gianlorenzo Bernini's architectural masterpiece - provides a fitting approach to the largest church of Christendom. Built in 1656-67 under Alexander VII Chigi it embraces the faithful with two semicircular colonnades topped by 96 statues of saints and martyrs. The 284 columns are divided into four rows that seem to merge into one when seen from the porphyry disks set into the floor at the sides of the obelisk. The latter provides

the focal point of the ellipse. It was brought from Alexandria in AD 37 and placed in the Circus of Caligula (to the south of today's church). In 1586, Sixtus V ordered the architect Domenico Fontana to move it here. To the right of the Basilica, behind the colonnade, is the papal residence, also built by Domenico Fontana. The Pope appears on Sundays, at midday, at the second to last window of the fourth floor, to recite the Angelus with the faithful.

THE BASILICA

In 324 the Emperor Constantine ordered the building of a basilica on the site of the tomb of St Peter. The structure was completed in 349 and comprised a nave with four aisles divided by columns and entered through a large courtyard with four porticoes.

By the middle of the 15c the basilica was considered unsafe and Nicholas V ordered its restoration by Bernardo Rossellino and Leon Battista Alberti. The Pope died in 1455 and work was suspended until Julius II decided on a complete reconstruction. The direction of the works was entrusted to **Donato Bramante**, who envisaged a centrally planned building in the shape of a Greek cross. His idea was to combine the largest known monuments of antiquity by erecting the Pantheon on top of the Basilica of Constantine. However, when Bramante died, in 1514, only the four piers and the arches supporting the dome had been completed. He was succeeded by a number of architects (including Raphael) who wavered back and forth between a Latin cross (with a long nave) and a Greek cross plan (with equal arms). Finally Michelangelo took over the direction of works in 1546, aged 72. He adopted Bramante's plan

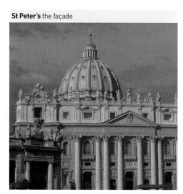

St Peter's the façade

but on an even larger scale. He replaced the piers by stronger ones and completed the dome (which he modelled on Brunelleschi's Florentine cupola) as far as the drum. After Michelangelo's death in 1564, Giacomo della Porta and Domenico Fontana finished the dome in 1590.

Subsequently, Paul V Borghese (1605-21) imposed a Latin cross ground plan, ordering Carlo Maderno to extend the nave by three bays. Maderno also added the portico and the façade, which were completed in 1614. The new basilica was consecrated in 1626. Once the architectural core was finished, Gianlorenzo Bernini, who took over from Maderno in 1629, was commissioned by Urban VIII to supervise the decoration of the vast interior which was covered in coloured marbles, stuccoes and sculptures by the artist and his followers.

ATRIUM In the entrance porch are two equestrian statues - (left) **Charlemagne** (who was crowned emperor in the basilica in 800) by Agostino Cornacchini; and (right) **Constantine** (the first Christian emperor) by Gianlorenzo Bernini (1670). Beyond the latter is the Scala Regia (the regal staircase) also built by Bernini for Alexander VII.

Five doors lead into the basilica, the last on the right being the Porta Santa which is opened only every 25 years during the Holy Year when the Catholic faithful come in pilgrimage to Rome for the remission of their sins. The central bronze door is from Old St Peter's and has reliefs of the 1430s by Filarete. Above the opposite wall is the heavily restored **Navicella** (symbolizing the role of the church), a celebrated mosaic made by Giotto for the first Holy Year (1300).

The church is 186m long and 137m wide (at the transepts). The diameter of the dome is 42m (1.5m less than that of the Pantheon) and its circumference 71m. The maximum height, from the ground to the cross at the top of the cupola, is 136m.

NAVE The nave is separated from the aisles by arches and colossal piers decorated with Corinthian pilasters and niches with statues of the founders of religious orders (18c-19c). On the pavement in front of the central door is a porphyry disk on which Charlemagne was crowned emperor by Leo III. The lengths of the principal churches of the world are marked on the floor. Against the last pillar on the right, seated on a marble throne, is a bronze statue of *St Peter*, also from the old basilica, ascribed to Arnolfo di Cambio (13c).

SIDE AISLES Bernini's lavish decorative scheme continues in the side aisles and transepts that contain numerous monuments of popes and important personalities in the history of the church. These include *Queen Christina of Sweden* (d. 1689) and *Countess Matilda of Canossa* (d. 1115), whose monuments, respectively by Carlo Fontana and Bernini, are in the right aisle.

There are no papal tombs in St Peter's except for those of Pius X (1903-14) and Innocent XI (1676-89), the last two popes canonized by the Catholic Church, whose remains are in the second chapels of the left and right aisles. However, 147 popes are buried in the Vatican Grottoes, beneath the basilica. They are entered from a door in one of the piers of the crossing. Most of the altarpieces throughout the church are mosaic reproductions of paintings now housed in the Vatican picture gallery.

In the first chapel of the right aisle is **Michelangelo's** *Pietà* of 1498-9, made when he was 23, and the only piece that he signed (on the ribbon across the Virgin's chest). One of the masterpieces of the Renaissance, it takes up a northern European theme but translates it into a highly idealized and innovative version. The body of Christ shows no suffering and the Virgin is portrayed as a young and beautiful girl, lacking the intense emotionalism of her precedents. The attention to detail and the highly polished surface place this work at the beginning of Michelangelo's career, while the frontal approach and the use of a single marble block are characteristic of the artist's method of sculpting. It has been restored and protected behind glass since it was damaged in 1972.

In the second passageway of the left aisle is the fine bronze *Monument to Innocent VIII* (1484-92) by Antonio del Pollaiolo, also from the old basilica.

THE CROSSING Against the piers supporting the dome are the statues of **St Longinus** (by Bernini, 1629-38), **St Helena** (by Andrea Bolgi), **St Veronica** (by Francesco Mochi) and **St Andrew** (by François Duquesnoy). The relics of each of these saints are preserved here (in the podium of the pier of St Veronica).

Beneath the dome is St Peter's tomb. Bernini's monumental **baldachin** was cast from bronze taken from the Pantheon and completed for Urban VIII in 1633. It has four spiral columns and a canopy decorated with bees of the Barberini arms. At the high altar below only the Pope may officiate.

APSE In the apse is the **Cathedra Petri**, or Chair of St Peter, symbolizing the Pope's authority and executed by Bernini in 1658-66. The throne encloses a wooden chair donated to Pope John VIII by Charles the Bald in 875. A circle of angels, clouds and rays of gilded stucco frame a stained glass window with the dove of the Holy Spirit. The composition epitomizes the Baroque in its drama and complexity, in the interplay of light and different materials, in the illusionist effects and the emotional intensity of the figures. Earlier in date and more subdued is Bernini's **Monument to Urban VIII** (d. 1644). The composition is clearly derived from the **Monument to Paul III** (1549) by Guglielmo della Porta opposite and from Michelangelo's Medici tombs in Florence.

In the passageway beyond the left transept is Bernini's last work, the **Monument to Alexander VII**. Completed in 1678, aged 80, he fully exploits the possibilities of marble to stress the contrast between the instability of life (Death with the hour glass) and the unshakeable faith of the praying pope.

In the passageway beyond the right transept is the **Monument to Clement XIII** (1784-92), one Antonio Canova's most important works, a Neoclassical re-interpretation of the 'standard' type of papal monument as defined by Bernini. Canova discards any Baroque exuberance and use of different materials and reverts to a more restrained composition. Sculpted entirely in white marble, the monument has a more intimate and serene character, with the pope kneeling in prayer rather than blessing from a throne.

TREASURY A door beneath the Monument to Pius VIII (in the passageway before the left transept) leads to the Treasury. Among the most important pieces are the *Crux Vaticana*, studded with gems, donated by Emperor Justin II in the 6c; a *ciborium* by Donatello (1432); Pollaiolo's *Monument to Sixtus IV* (1493); the *Sarcophagus of Junius Bassus*, prefect of Rome in AD 359, with scenes of the Old and New Testament.

From the entrance to the museum, a second corridor leads to the main **Sacristy**. The room to the left is the Sagrestia dei Canonici and is decorated with frescoes by Francesco Penni and Giulio Romano. The adjoining chapter house has 17c paintings by Andrea Sacchi.

THE DOME The entrance to the dome is outside the basilica, at the right end of the portico. A lift or staircase ascends to the terrace above the aisles. From here a fairly accessible staircase (330 steps) leads up to a circular gallery which commands an impressive view of the mosaics inside the dome as well as of the pavement below. A narrow spiral staircase (207 steps) climbs up between the two shells of the dome to the lantern, where a spectacular view of the city rewards the tired visitor.

on route

Castel Sant'Angelo Begun by Hadrian in AD 129 as a mausoleum for himself and his family, it was completed in 139 by his successor Antoninus Pius. Subsequently, all emperors and their relatives up to Septimius Severus (d. 211) were buried here. The original structure consisted of a square base, surmounted by a cylindrical structure and topped by a bronze quadriga driven by Hadrian represented as the sun god. During the Middle Ages it was transformed into a fortress which was enlarged in the 15c by Nicholas V and Alexander VI. The architect was

Castel Sant'Angelo

Antonio da Sangallo the Elder. Alexander VI also restored the medieval passageway which linked the Vatican directly to the castle (closed to the public). At the beginning of the 16c Julius II built the loggia facing the river. Pope Paul III (1534-49) had the interior decorated with frescoes by Perin del Vaga. In the 17c, Urban VIII armed the castle with cannons made of bronze taken from the Pantheon and commissioned Bernini to reinforce the outer defences.

Open Tues-Sun 9.00-19.00, closed Mon. €5; free for under 18s and over 65s, €2.50 for 18-25-year-olds from EU countries and with a valid ID card. *T* 06 3996 7600. Bus: 40 Express from Termini Station via Corso Vittorio Emanuele.

Ponte dell'Angelo Built on the site of the ancient 'Pons Aelius' built under Hadrian to connect his mausoleum with the opposite bank of the Tiber and reconstructed in the 16c-17c. The statues of angels holding the symbols of the Passion of Christ were designed by Gianlorenzo Bernini. The Angel with the Scroll and the Angel with the Crown of Thorns are copies of originals by Bernini himself.

Via della Conciliazione was built in the 1930s, for Mussolini, to provide a monumental approach to St Peter's. Like most Fascist projects, it involved the demolition of a substantial part of the pre-existing quarter, the so-called 'Borgo', dating back to medieval and Renaissance times.

eating and drinking

AT THE MUSEUMS

The cafeteria at the **Vatican Museums** is best avoided both in terms of quality and prices. The same applies to the touristy coffee bars and restaurants in the immediate surroundings.

RESTAURANTS

€ **Osteria dell'Angelo**, Via G. Bettolo 24, *T* 06 372 9470; open in the evening, Tuesday and Friday lunchtime; closed Sunday and in August. A little out of the way (Largo Trionfale) but worth the detour for its traditional Roman cuisine at good prices.

Pupina, Via Marianna Dionigi 37, *T* 06 32233. Unpretentious, good *trattoria*. Closed Sunday. Buses to Piazza Cavour.

€€ **Benito e Gilberto**, Vicolo del Falco 19, *T* 06 686 7769; evening only. Close to the Vatican, a very good fish restaurant at medium prices.

Dal Toscano, Via Germanico 58, *T* 06 3972 5717; always open. A popular restaurant serving Tuscan food.

Dante Taberna dei Gracchi, Via dei Gracchi 266, *T* 06 321 3126; closed Sunday, Christmas period and August. Classical Italian cuisine and good fish dishes.

Taverna Angelica, Piazza A. Capponi 6, *T* 06 687 4514; evening only; closed 10-20 August. Good and varied cuisine, close to the Vatican.

Velando, Borgo Vittorio 26, *T* 06 6880 9955; closed Sunday. Near the Vatican. North meets south: the owner from Lombardy joined forces with a chef from Apulia with excellent results.

Zen, Via degli Scipioni 243, *T* 06 321 3420; closed Monday and Saturday lunchtime. A good Japanese restaurant. Medium-priced if you choose the kaiten bar; more expensive if you order at a table.

€€€ **Il Simposio**, Piazza Cavour 16, *T* 06 321 1502; closed Saturday lunchtime and Sunday. Formerly an excellent wine bar, now a quality restaurant.

La Veranda dell'Hotel Columbus, Borgo Santo Spirito 73, *T* 06 687 2973; always open. A good restaurant two steps from St Peter's, inside the 15c Palazzo della Rovere (frescoed by Pinturicchio).

CAFÉS

Castroni, Via Cola Di Rienzo 196, *T* 06 687 4383, and at 55 Via Ottaviano, *T* 06 3972 3279; open 8.00-20.00. Excellent coffee, good *cornetti* (croissants) and *tramezzini* (sandwiches), but no seating.

Bar Latteria Giuliani, 48 Borgo Pio, *T* 06 6880 3955; open 8.00-20.00. An unpretentious *latteria* (milk shop) with tables outside (weather permitting) and good cappuccinos.

Franchi, Via Cola di Rienzo 204 . Next door to Castroni. The hot-spot deli to grab your take-away lunch. Try their deep fried *supplì* with rice and *crocchette* with potatoes or vegetables. No coffee or seating.

Il Papalino, Borgo Pio 170, *T* 06 686 5539. Close to the Vatican. Good coffee, *cornetti*, *tramezzini* and *panini*.

Sciascia dal 1922, Via Fabio Massimo 80, *T* 06 321 1580; open 8.00-20.00. An excellent coffee shop and bar roasting their own blend. Good *cornetti*.

ICE CREAM

Ottaviani, Via Leone IV 83-85, *T* 06 373 52003.

Pellacchia, Via Cola di Rienzo 103-107, *T* 06 321 0807.

Giovanni Fassi, Via Vespasiano 56, *T* 06 3972 5164.

WINE BARS

Del Frate, Via degli Scipioni 118, *T* 06 323 6437. An elegant and well stocked wine bar, open for brunch and lunch 11.30-15.30, and in the evening from 18.00-2.00. Closed Sunday evening.

LATE-NIGHT BARS

BarBar, Via Ovidio 17, *T* 06 6880 5682; open 19.00-3.00 except Monday. Stylish lounge bar with that NY feel, chill-out music and good cocktails.

Fonclea, Via Crescenzio 82a, *T* 06 689 6302. Food, wine and cocktails from 19.30-2.00. Live music.

Nuvolari, Via degli Ombrellari 10, *T* 06 6880 3018; open 18.30-2.00 except Sunday. Beer, wine, cocktails and snacks.

Shakti Bar, Lungotevere dei Mellini 33a, *T* 06 324 1401; open 19.30-2.00 except Monday. Oriental atmosphere, vegetarian food and ethnic or lounge music. Friday-Saturday, art and photographic exhibitions.

Sottovoce, Via P. G. da Palestrina 24, *T* 06 322 7837; open 22.30-4.30 except Sunday. A comfortable piano bar.

The Place, Via Alberico II 27-29, *T* 06 6830 7137. American bar, restaurant and music club. Creative food and wine from 21.00; live music from 23.00.

shopping

Most of the shops listed in this section are in Via Cola di Rienzo and the neighbouring streets. They can be reached by metro, station Ottaviano (Line A) and Bus 81.

ACCESSORIES

Antica Cappelleria Venanzoni, Via Ottaviano 5, **T** 06 3972 3532. Hats & Co. from a long established shop.

Furla, Via Cola di Rienzo 226, **T** 06 687 4505. Elegant bags, luggage and other accessories.

L'Arte del Cuoio, Via Alberico II 2, **T** 06 686 1724. Handmade leather bags and accessories to your own design and initials.

Mandarina Duck, Via Cola di Rienzo 272, **T** 06 689 6491. Functional bags with innovative designs.

ANTIQUES

High-Tech d'Epoca, Piazza Capponi 7 (Via Vitelleschi), **T** 06 687 2147. Owner Luisa is an architect with a background at the Yacht Restoration School of Newport. She now sells wonderful office furniture, and more, from the early 1900s.

BEAUTY

Bertozzini, Via Cola di Rienzo 192-194, **T** 06 687 4662. Perfumes, and more, since 1913.

Studio 13, Piazza Cavour 13, **T** 06 6880 3977. Makeup artists (theatre and film) get their stock here.

BOOKS

Gremese, 136 Via Cola di Rienzo, **T** 06 323 5367. An international library with a good art section.

Maraldi, 11 Viale Bastioni di Michelangelo, **T** 06 3972 3024. One of the best secondhand bookshops in town.

Mondadori, 81 Via Cola di Rienzo, **T** 06 322 0188.

CLOTHES

Antichi Telai 1894, Via Silla 102, *T* 06 3600 3944; open 10.00-19.30. Perfect cuts and the finest fabrics for dressing a gentleman. Everything from the suits and shirts down to the shoes is rigorously handmade. They receive by appointment.

Benetton, Via Cola di Rienzo 201-207. One of several stores in town.

Blunauta, Via Cola di Rienzo 303-309, *T* 06 3973 7336. Silk shirts and more at bargain prices.

Calvin Klein, 153 Via Cola di Rienzo 153, *T* 06 3211 1881. For your jeans and other basics.

Carbone, Via Leone IV 65, *T* 06 3972 5517. An award-winning tailor for the perfect gentleman's suit.

Carla G., Via Cola di Rienzo 134, *T* 06 324 3511. Trendy clothes for women.

Diesel, Via Cola di Rienzo 247. Funky clothes and accessories.

Gente, Via Cola di Rienzo 277, *T* 06 321 1516. Fashionable labels and new designers.

Kookai, Via Cola di Rienzo 146, *T* 06 687 6197. A favourite with girls.

L'Altra Moda, Piazza dell' Unità 56. Classic and affordable fashion for women.

Luisa Spagnoli, Via Cola di Rienzo 193, *T* 06 3600 3335. A long established favourite with ladies.

Max Mara, Via Cola di Rienzo 275, *T* 06 321 1268.

Tower, Piazza dell'Unità 57, *T* 06 321 1637. Stylish clothes for women.

Vesti a stock, Via Germanico 170a, *T* 06 322 4391. Designer labels (Armani, Valentino, Versace, etc) at 30%-50% discount.

DEPARTMENT STORES

Coin, Via Cola di Rienzo 173, *T* 06 3600 4298.

FLOWERS

Alicanti, Via Trionfale 80, *T* 06 3973 8302. Somewhat out of the way but still one of the best places for flowers (fresh and dried) in town. It is close to the flower market. Get there early.

Urbani, Via Cola Di Rienzo 115, *T* 06 321 4310.

FOOD

Castroni, Via Cola Di Rienzo 196, *T* 06 687 4383 and at 55 Via Ottaviano
T 06 3972 3279. Established in 1929, it sells freshly ground coffee by
the pound, and chocolate, preserves, candies, fine biscuits and
savoury specialities from all over the world.

Franchi, Via Cola di Rienzo 204; open 8.15-21.00. Next door to Castroni.
The hot-spot deli to grab your take-away lunch. Excellent cheese,
prosciutto and other charcuterie.

Giuliani, Via Paolo Emilio 67, *T* 06 324 3548. Pralines, fondants, fruit
jellies, candied fruits and, above all, the best marrons glacés in
Rome.

Makasar, Via Plauto 33, *T* 06 687 4602. The seat of the Italian Tea Club
and a shop with 150 tea varieties from all over the world.
Sophisticated accessories (cups, filters, Chinese teapots, trays, etc)
are on sale here too.

Mercato di Piazza dell'Unità. This covered marketplace sells every
possible seasonal produce.

HOMES

Italia Garipoli, Borgo Vittorio 91, *T* 06 6220 2196. The art of handmade
embroidery for your table and bed linens, and the best place to find
(or mend) grandmother's laces.

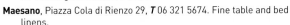

Maesano, Piazza Cola di Rienzo 29, *T* 06 321 5674. Fine table and bed
linens.

Vittorio Peroni, Piazza dell'Unità 29, *T* 06 321 0852. Pots, pans and
kitchenware to cook your pasta the Italian way and to make proper
coffee without spending a fortune.

KIDS

Brums, Piazza Cola di Rienzo 77, *T* 06 321 4449. Clothes for future
mums, babies and children from 0 to 14 years of age.

Iana, 211 Via Cola di Rienzo. Jeans and other basics for babies and
children.

Le Jardin des Enfants, Via Marcantonio Colonna 3. Bus 913, 492. Smart
clothes for babies, toddlers and children.

Petit Bateau, Via Cola di Rienzo 311. An excellent and versatile French
brand for 0-15-year-olds.

LINGERIE

Intimissimi, Via Cola di Rienzo 159-161, *T* 06 324 3137.

MUSIC

Doctor Music, Via dei Gracchi 41-43, *T* 320 0543. Renowned for its jazz
section, it covers other genres too. New and secondhand CDs and
vinyl.

SHOES

Antonio Arellano, Via del Falco 30. Solid handmade shoes by an
imaginative artisan.

Boccanera, 19 Via Vittoria Colonna 19, *T* 06 320 4456. For stylish Italian
shoes. Bus 913 and others via Piazza Cavour.

Brian Cress, Via Cola di Rienzo 166.

STATIONERY

Bottega di Calligrafia, Via Otranto 23, *T* 06 3751 1520. A master of ancient
calligraphy (of any form and sort), Maria Beatrice Cicchetti produces
little *chefs d'oeuvre* on Amalfi paper or parchment. Tasteful visiting
cards, menus, wine lists, labels, and personalized writing paper, as
well as announcement, greeting and invitation cards can all be
ordered here.

VINTAGE

40°, Via Virgilio 1o (at the corner with Via Boezio), *T* 06 6813 4612.
Vintage clothes and objects.

WINE

Enoteca Costantini, Piazza Cavour 16a, *T* 06 320 3575. A formidable stock
of the best Italian wines is kept in the cellar downstairs. Next door is
the restaurant **Il Simposio**.

entertainment

INFORMATION
TICKETS
THEATRE
CINEMA
MUSIC
BALLET, DANCE
SPECIAL EVENTS

INFORMATION

For information on exhibitions, concerts, theatre, live music, etc. consult *Roma c'è*, a weekly magazine (published on Wednesdays) which includes listings in English. Most hotels offer the free *Un Ospite a Roma* (in Italian and English) which lists events as well as opening times.

   Information is also available from Tourist Information Offices; their free leaflet, *L'Evento*, is published every two months. Alternatively, **T** 06 3600 4399 or consult *Wanted in Rome*, a weekly magazine for English speakers available at newsstands.

TICKETS

A toll-free line for the purchase of theatre tickets is available on **T** 800 907 080.

Agencies selling tickets for concerts are:

Box Office, Viale Giulio Cesare 88, **T** 06 372 0216. (**M** Lepanto)

Messaggerie Musicali, Via del Corso 472, **T** 06 6819 2349.

Orbis, Piazza Esquilino 37, **T** 06 482 7403.

THEATRE

Teatro Argentina, Largo di Torre Argentina 52, **T** 06 6880 4601 (tickets and information, Mon-Sat 10.00-14.00 and 15.00-19.00). This is the main theatre in Rome, staging classics to contemporary pieces (both Italian and international). During the summer, performances are held in the Roman theatre at Ostia Antica or in Hadrian's villa at Tivoli.

Teatro India, Lungotevere dei Papareschi (Viale Marconi-Piazzale della Radio). A branch of Teatro Argentina, this space is devoted to international avant-garde productions. It is outside the centre and best reached by taxi. For information, *T* 06 6880 4601.

Teatro Quirino, Via Marco Minghetti 1, *T* 06 679 4585. Italian and International drama in the Fontana di Trevi area.

Teatro Valle, Via del Teatro Valle 23, *T* 06 6880 3794. One of the historic theatres of Rome, it stages mainstream as well as interesting contemporary productions. Near Piazza Navona.

CINEMA

Arcipelago An annual festival of short films held in July on the Janiculum hill and in various cinemas of Rome. Check listings in the magazines mentioned on p 187.

Cinema Augustus, Corso Vittorio Emanuele II 203, *T* 06 687 5455. Films in English are shown on Tuesdays.

Cinema Pasquino, Piazza S. Egidio 10, *T* 06 581 5208. Films in English every day (four programmes 16.00-24.00).

Isola del Cinema Open-air cinema on the Isola Tiberina in July and August, *T* 06 583 33113.

Massenzio The main open-air cinema of the Estate Romana (p 191). The venue varies, but it is normally on the Celian Hill, opposite the Colosseum.

MUSIC
CLASSICAL AND OPERA

Accademia Filarmonica Romana, Via Flaminia 118, *T* 06 320 1752. Concerts are usually held at the Teatro Olimpico, Piazza Gentile da Fabriano 17, *T* 06 326 5991.

Accademia Nazionale di Santa Cecilia, Via Vittoria 6, *T* 06 802 42501. Their excellent concerts of chamber and symphonic music are held at the new Auditorium Parco della Musica.

Auditorium Parco della Musica, Viale Pietro de Coubertin, 30 (Parioli), *T* 06 802 411. Various genres, from classical to jazz, are performed in the three concert halls of the new auditorium designed by Renzo Piano. The open-air cavea is used in summer.

Concerti del Tempietto, Via del Teatro Marcello 44, *T* 06 8713 1590. Concerts are held in summer at the archaeological site of the Teatro di Marcello.

Concerts in churches Check newspaper or magazine listings for performances held in churches (Sant'Ignazio, Trinità dei Monti, Santa Maria degli Angeli, etc).

New Opera Festival This is held throughout the summer in the courtyard of the basilica of San Clemente. *T* 06 561 1519.

Opera Estate Concerts and opera are held in summer in the courtyard of Sant'Ivo alla Sapienza (Corso Rinascimento 40). *T* 06 8680 0125.

Oratorio del Gonfalone, Vicolo della Scimia, 1b (Via Giulia), *T* 06 687 5952. Well known for its great acoustics and the late 16c frescoes, the oratory houses concerts of chamber music from November to May, every Thursday at 21.00.

Teatro dell'Opera, Piazza B. Gigli 1 (Viminale), *T* 06 481 601. The opera theatre of Rome.

Terme di Caracalla, Viale delle Terme di Caracalla, 52. Opera productions are held during the summer season in the Baths of Caracalla. For information, *T* 06 481 601. For concerts organized by the Accademia di Santa Cecilia, *T* 06 6880 1044.

JAZZ, ROCK, POP, ETHNIC

Alexanderplatz, Via Ostia 9 (Vatican-Prati), *T* 06 3974 2171. An historic venue for jazz concerts. Dinner from 20.30, concerts from 22.30.

Big Mama, Vicolo San Francesco a Ripa 18 (Trastevere), *T* 06 581 2551. The address for blues in Rome, with mainly American artists; also jazz and funk concerts.

CafféLatino, Via Monte Testaccio 96 (Testaccio), *T* 06 5728 8556. Live music and dancing.

Café de Oriente, Via Monte Testaccio 36, *T* 06 574 5019. Latin American music, live concerts and dancing.

Fiesta! Ippodromo delle Capannelle, Via Appia Nuova, *T* 06 718 2139. A summer festival of Latin American fun, music, dancing and food. It takes place in the southern outskirts of the city.

La Palma Club, Via Giuseppe Mirri 35 (Tiburtino), *T* 06 4359 9029/4359 8626. Good concerts (jazz and more) are held in this fairly new space on the edges of town. *M* Tiburtina and taxi from there.

Testaccio Village, Via di Monte Testaccio 23. Held in summer in the former slaughterhouse of the Testaccio district, this is a music festival with a variety of concerts and exhibitions.

Villa Celimontana Jazz Festival, Piazza della Navicella (Celio),

T 06 589 7807. Set in the fine park of Villa Celimontana, this is one of the events you shouldn't miss if you're in Rome during the summer: live concerts (jazz, fusion, world) every night from mid-June to September.

World Music Festival, Laghetto di Villa Ada, Ponte Salario (Parioli). This open-air festival, with music from various parts of the world, is held during the summer in the park of Villa Ada. It is outside the centre and is best reached by taxi.

BALLET, DANCE

Cosmophonies The theatrical season (June-September) held at the Roman Theatre at Ostia Antica includes dance performances. See magazines for listings and details.

Invito alla Danza A festival of modern and contemporary dance held in July and August in the gardens of Villa Massimo, *T* 06 3973 8323 or 06 4420 2440.

Teatro Olimpico, Piazza Gentile da Fabriano 17, *T* 06 326 5991. The main venue for dance performances and ballet as well as concerts of the Accademia Filarmonica Romana (p 188).

Teatro Sistina, Via Sistina 129, *T* 06 4245 0675. This theatre specializes in musicals and dance performances.

SPECIAL EVENTS

Porta Portese The main flea market of Rome is held on Sunday mornings beyond Porta Portese. Tram 8 from Largo Argentina to Viale Trastevere.

5-6 January-Befana The Epiphany is celebrated in Piazza Navona, with the 'miraculous' midnight apparition of the witch-like Befana from one of the balconies. A favourite with children (stalls of sweets and toys line the entire piazza).

Shrove Tuesday Carnival is held in the streets and piazze - masks are worn and children dress up.

Concerto del 1 Maggio A huge pop concert with various guest artists is traditionally held on the first of May. The venue varies from year to year: Piazza del Popolo, Piazza San Giovanni in Laterano, etc. Check the newspapers for details.

Piazza di Siena The annual horse riding week takes place in early May in Piazza di Siena (Villa Borghese).

Estate Romana In the summer months Rome is brimful of life. Given the heat, Romans tend to go out only in the evening, filling the streets and squares until late at night. A variety of events - open-air cinema, concerts, opera, dancing, shows and exhibitions - are organized throughout the city. For further details, see the listings above and check in the magazines mentioned on p 187.

Festa de'Noantri A popular feast (literally 'Our Feast') celebrated on 15 July in the Trastevere district.

Roma Hip Hop Parade This is held in the first weeks of July in various venues throughout the city.

RomaEuropa Festival A two-month festival held in October and November in all the main theatres of Rome. It includes drama, dance and opera from all over the world.

Ostia Antica Roman theatre

planning

TOURIST OFFICES
GETTING THERE
GETTING AROUND
OTHER ESSENTIALS
PLACES TO STAY

TOURIST OFFICES

CANADA

Italian Government Tourist Board, 175 Bloor Street E., Suite 907 - South Tower, M4W 3R8 Toronto (Ontario), *T* 416 925 4882, *F* 416 925 4799, www.italiantourism.com, enit.canada@on.aibn.com

UK & IRELAND

Italian State Tourist Board, 1 Princes Street, London W1R 7RA, *T* 020 7408 1254, *F* 020 7493 6695, www.enit.it, italy@italiantouristboard.co.uk

USA

Italian Government Tourist Board, 630 Fifth Avenue, Suite 1565, New York, NY 10111, *T* 212 245 4822, *F* 212 586 9249, www.italiantourism.com, enitny@italiantourism.com

500 North Michigan Avenue, Suite 2240, Chicago 1, IL 60611, *T* 312 644 0996, *F* 312 644 3019, www.italiantourism.com, enitch@italiantourism.com

12400 Wilshire Blvd, Suite 550, Los Angeles, CA 90025, *T* 310 820 1898, *F* 310 820 6357, www.italiantourism.com, enitla@italiantourism.com

TOURIST OFFICES IN ROME

Azienda di Promozione Turistica di Roma, Via Parigi 5, *T* 06 488 991; open Mon-Fri 9.30-12.30; Mon and Thur also 14.30-16.30. A telephone service is available at *T* 06 3600 4399, Mon-Fri 9.00-19.00.

Tourist information desks can be found at Termini Station, Fiumicino Airport and in the city centre (Via del Corso, Largo Goldoni; Via dei Fori Imperiali; Piazza Città Leonina, St Peter's).

Websites The official website of the Rome tourist board is www.romaturismo.com. Other websites include www.romeguide.it and www.informaroma.it

GETTING THERE
BY AIR

Rome is served by Fiumicino airport (also called Leonardo da Vinci), 26km southwest of the city, which handles domestic, international and intercontinental flights. The smaller Ciampino airport, 13km southeast of Rome, is mainly used for domestic and charter flights.

Fiumicino airport, *T* 06 65951, www.adr.it

Ciampino airport, *T* 06 794 941, www.adr.it

FROM THE UK
Alitalia, *T* 0870 544 8259, www.alitalia.co.uk

British Airways, *T* 0870 850 9850, www.ba.com

easyJet, *T* 0871 7500 100, www.easyjet.com

Ryanair, *T* 0905 566 0000, www.ryanair.com

FROM THE REPUBLIC OF IRELAND
Aer Lingus, *T* 0818 365 000, www.aerlingus.com

Alitalia, *T* 01 677 5171, www.alitalia.co.uk

FROM THE USA AND CANADA
Air Canada, *T* 1 888 247 2262, from the USA 1 800 268 0024, www.aircanada.ca; from Toronto to Milan and Rome

Alitalia, *T* 1 800 223 5730, www.alitaliausa.com; from Atlanta, Boston, Chicago, Miami, Toronto to Milan; from New York, Toronto to Rome

Continental, *T* 1 800 231 0856, www.continental.com; from Atlanta, New York to Milan

Delta, *T* 1 800 241 4141, from Atlanta, Boston, Chicago, Miami, New York, to Milan; from Atlanta and New York to Rome

United, *T* 1 800 538 2929, www.ual.com; from Washington to Milan

USAirways, *T* 1 800 428 4322; from Philadelphia to Rome

GETTING TO THE CITY CENTRE FROM THE AIRPORTS
Trains run from Fiumicino airport to Stazione Termini in the centre of the city every 30 minutes, from about 7.00 to 21.00. They also go to Stazione Tiburtina (east of Stazione Termini) via Ostiense and Trastevere (every 15 mins from about 5.00 to 23.00).

There are night bus services to and from Stazione Tiburtina, but if you arrive at night it might be safer to take a taxi. Taxis charge an airport supplement in addition to the meter fare - expect to pay around €35.

Ciampino airport can be reached by metro line A to Anagnina station and from there by COTRAL airport bus, which runs from 6.00 to 22.00 (every 30 minutes). But it is quicker by taxi.

BY TRAIN
Trenitalia Information and tickets with station pick-up in Italy, www.trenitalia.it. Trenitalia Help Desk, *T* 0039 06 8833 9537, *F* 0039 06 8833 9613, helpdesk@sipax.com

FROM THE UK
European Rail Travel, *T* 020 7387 0444, *F* 020 7387 0888, www.raileurope.co.uk.

FROM THE USA AND CANADA
European Rail Travel, *T* 1 877 257 2887 in the US; *T* 1 800 361 RAIL in Canada, or www.raileurope.com

GETTING AROUND
BY BUS
As the centre has been closed to private traffic, apart from walking, which is the best way of getting around Rome, the orange ATAC buses are the quickest form of transport. Bus routes are displayed at bus stops and inside the buses. Most stops are request stops (*fermata a richesta*).

ATAC has a kiosk at Piazza dei Cinquecento, in front of Stazione Termini (open Mon-Sat 8.00-20.00), with free maps of the main routes. *T* freephone 800 431 784 (daily 7.00-20.00) or www.atac.roma.it

Useful bus lines (services from 5.30-24.00):

64 Stazione Termini - Via Nazionale - Piazza Venezia - Corso Vittorio Emanuele - Porta Cavalleggeri (for St Peter's) - Stazione San Pietro

85 Piazza San Silvestro - Piazza Venezia - Via dei Fori Imperiali - Colosseo - Via Labicana - San Giovanni in Laterano

87 Piazza Cavour - Corso Rinascimento - Piazza Venezia - Via dei Fori Imperiali - Colosseo - San Giovanni in Laterano

95 Piazza Bocca della Verità - Via Teatro Marcello - Piazza Venezia - Via del Corso - Via del Tritone - Via Veneto - Villa Borghese

Blue electric mini-bus services

Two services (116 and 117) follow a circular route through the city centre on weekdays from 7.40-20.00:

116 Via Veneto - Piazza Barberini - Via del Tritone - Piazza di Spagna - Piazza San Silvestro - Ponte Umberto I - Corso Rinascimento - Campo dei Fiori - Piazza Farnese

117 San Giovanni in Laterano - Colosseo - Via dei Serpenti (Monti) - Largo Tritone - Piazza di Spagna - Via del Corso

Tramlines

3 and 19 reach the Galleria Nazionale d'Arte Moderna, the Etruscan Museum and Villa Borghese.

3 Colosseo - San Giovanni in Laterano - Porta Maggiore - Viale Regina Margherita - Viale delle Belle Arti - Piazza Thorvaldsen (for the museums)

19 Piazza Risorgimento - Via Flaminia - Piazza Thorvaldsen (for the museums)

Late-night buses

Blue electric mini bus **116T** which runs 20.00-1.30 (except Sun) and connects the main theatres in the centre: Via Veneto - Piazza Barberini - Via Quattro Fontane - Via Nazionale - Piazza di Spagna - Piazza San Silvestro - Corso Rinascimento - Pantheon - Piazza Colonna - Via del Tritone - Via Nazionale

78N Piazza Cola di Rienzo - Piazza Cavour - Piazza Venezia - Via Nazionale - Termini

BY METRO

The metropolitana has two lines. The service begins at 5.30 and ends at 23.30. The last train on Saturdays is at 0.30.

Line A runs from Battistini (in the western suburbs) to Anagnina (to the south, beyond Cinecittà) via the stations Ottaviano (Vatican), Flaminio, Spagna, Barberini, Termini.

Line B connects Rebibbia (in the eastern suburbs) to EUR (in the south west) via Stazione Tiburtina, Termini, Via Cavour, Colosseo, Circo Massimo, Piramide (Stazione Ostiense).

TICKETS

Tickets and bus passes can be purchased at the ATAC kiosk in Piazza dei Cinquecento, at bars, newsstands and tobacconists or at the automatic, coin-operated machines at main bus stations. They cost €1, and are valid for 75 mins on any number of lines and for one metro journey. They must be stamped by the machines on board. Good options are the one-day ticket BIG (*biglietto giornaliero*), €4, or the weekly CIS (*carta settimanale*), €16. Beware of pickpockets (especially on line 64 from Termini station to St Peter's).

BY TAXI

Taxis are hired from ranks or by telephone; it is difficult to get cruising cabs. Make sure your taxi's meter is working. A small tip (generally a round up) is expected. Supplements are charged for late-night journeys and for luggage. There is a heavy surcharge when the destination is outside the town limits (ask how much the fare is likely to be).

Taxi telephone numbers: 06 3570; 06 4994; 06 6645; 06 8822

BY CAR

It is not a good idea to use your own car in Rome. The city centre is closed to private cars without a permit Mon-Fri 06.30-18.00, Sat 14.00-18.00. Access is allowed to hotels and for the disabled.

It is always advisable to leave a car in a supervised car park (under Viale del Muro Torto - Via Veneto, in the Ludovisi car park just off Via Veneto, or in Piazza dei Cinquecento by Termini Station). Parking is only permitted on kerbs marked by a blue line and costs €1 per hour (tickets from coin-operated machines or tobacconists). Never leave anything of value inside a parked car.

BY BICYCLE AND SCOOTER

Bicycles and scooters can be hired at stands in Piazza del Popolo, Piazza San Silvestro, Piazza di Spagna.

Scoot-a-long, Via Cavour 302, *T* 06 678 0206

Scooters for rent, Via della Purificazione 84, *T* 06 488 5485
St Peter's moto, Via Fosse di Castello 7, *T* 06 687 5714

OTHER ESSENTIALS
BANKING SERVICES
The best way to obtain Euros while in Italy is to use a cashpoint card or credit card: in most cities ATM are open 24hrs a day, require no waiting and offer the best exchange rates.

Banks are open Monday-Friday, 8.30-13.30, 14.30-16.00 and are closed on Saturday, Sunday and public holidays. The afternoon opening may vary from bank to bank, and many banks close early (about 11.00) on days preceding national holidays.

DISABLED TRAVELLERS
All new public buildings are now obliged by law to provide easy access and specially designed facilities for the disabled. Unfortunately the conversion of historical buildings, including many museums and monuments, is made problematic by structural impediments such as narrow pavements. Barriers therefore continue to exist in many cases. Hotels that are equipped to accommodate the disabled are indicated in the annual list of hotels published by the tourist board. Airports and railway stations provide assistance and certain trains are equipped to transport wheelchairs. Cars with disabled drivers or passengers are allowed access to the centre of town (normally closed to traffic), where special parking places are reserved for them. For further information, contact the information offices listed in this guide or consult www.tour-web.com/accessibleitaly.

EMBASSIES AND CONSULATES
Australia, Via Alessandria 215, *T* 06 852 721
Canada, Via G.B. de Rossi 27, *T* 06 445 981
Ireland, Piazza Campitelli 3, *T* 06 697 9121
South Africa, Via Tanaro 14, *T* 06 852 541

United Kingdom, Via XX (Venti) Settembre 80, ***T*** 06 4220 0001

United States, Via Vittorio Veneto 119, ***T*** 06 46741

HEALTH AND MEDICAL SERVICES

For all emergencies ***T*** 118 or ***T*** 06 5820 1030. For the Italian Red Cross, ***T*** 06 5510. First-aid services are available at all hospitals, railway stations and airports.

San Giovanni, Via San Giovanni in Laterano 1, ***T*** 06 77051, is the central hospital for road accidents and other emergencies.

The American Hospital in Rome, Via E. Longoni 69, ***T*** 06 22551 is a private English-speaking hospital which accepts most American insurances.

The International Medical Centre, Via Firenze 47, ***T*** 06 488 2371; at night and weekends, ***T*** 06 488 4051.

INTERNET POINTS

Internet Café, Via Cavour 213 (Monti), ***T*** 06 4782 3051

Internet Center, Via Fosse di Castello 8 (Vatican - Castel S. Angelo), ***T*** 06 686 1540

Internet Point, Corso Vittorio Emanuele II 312, ***T*** 06 6830 8823

Internet Point, Vicolo di Sant'Elena 1 (Largo Arenula, Largo Argentina)

Internet Point Trevinet Place, Via in Arcione (Trevi) 103, ***T*** 06 6992 2320

LOST OR STOLEN CREDIT CARDS

American Express, ***T*** 06 7290 0347

Mastercard, ***T*** 800 872 050

Visa, ***T*** 800 877 232

OPENING TIMES
GALLERIES, MUSEUMS AND CHURCHES

The opening times of museums and monuments have been given in the text, but they often change without warning. The tourist board keeps updated timetables of most museums. National museums and monuments are usually open daily 9.00-19.00, plus evening hours in summer. Churches open quite early in the morning (often for 6.00 Mass), but are normally closed for a considerable period during the middle of the day (12.00 or 12.30 to 15.00, 16.00, or 17.00). Some churches now ask that sightseers do not enter during a service, but normally visitors may do so, provided they are silent and do not approach the altar in use. At all times they are expected to cover their legs and arms, and generally dress with decorum. This rule is particularly strict in St Peter's.

SHOPS

Shops generally open Mon-Sat 9.00-13.00 and 16.00-19.30/20.00. Shops selling clothes and other goods are usually closed on Monday morning, food shops on Thursday afternoon.

PUBLIC HOLIDAYS

1 January
25 April (Liberation Day)
Easter Sunday and Easter Monday
1 May (Labour Day)
29 June (Sts Peter and Paul, patrons of the city)
15 August (Assumption)
1 November (All Saints' Day)
8 December (Immaculate Conception)
25 December (Christmas Day)
26 December (St Stephen)

SALES TAX REBATES

If you're a non-EU resident, you can claim sales tax rebates on purchases made in Italy provided the total expenditure is more than €150. Ask the vendor for a receipt describing the goods acquired and send it back to him when you get home (but no later than 90 days after the date of the receipt). The receipt must be checked and stamped by Italian customs on leaving Italy. On receipt of the bill, the vendor will forward the sales tax rebate (the present tax rate is 20 per cent on most goods) to your home address.

TELEPHONE NUMBERS

To reach an operator: AT&T, *T* 172 1011; MCI, *T* 172 1022; Sprint, *T* 172 1877.

For directory assistance, *T* 12 (for numbers in Italy) or *T* 176 (for international numbers).

TIPPING

A service charge of 15 to 18 per cent is added to hotel bills. The service charge is already included when all-inclusive prices are quoted, but it is customary to leave an additional tip in any case. As a guideline and depending on the category of your hotel, a tip of €1-2 is suggested for hotel staff except the concierge who may expect a little more (€2-3).

Restaurants add a service charge of approximately 15 per cent to all bills. It is customary, however, to leave a small tip (5-10 per cent) for good service. In cafés and bars, leave 5-10 per cent if you were served at a table (if the bill does not already include service) and 10-20 cents if standing at a counter or bar to drink.

At the theatre, opera and concerts, tip ushers 50c or more.

PLACES TO STAY
HOTELS

In this guide hotels have been classified by the official star system, reflecting level of comfort. In general for a double room you can expect to pay per night:

☆-☆☆ under €100

☆☆☆-☆☆☆☆ €100-300

☆☆☆☆☆ €300 plus

All of the hotels listed here (the price guides are for double rooms), regardless of their cost, have been chosen on the basis of their character or location. If you are travelling between May and October, try to book well in advance. If you cancel the booking at least 72 hours in advance you can claim back part or all of your deposit. Hotels equipped to assist the disabled are indicated in the tourist boards' hotel lists.

In all hotels the service charges are included in the rates. The total charge is displayed on the back of the hotel room door.

Breakfast is by law an optional extra charge. When booking a room, always specify if you want breakfast or not. Hotels are now obliged by law (for tax purposes) to issue an official receipt to customers: you should not leave the premises without this document.

CAMPIDOGLIO FORUM

☆☆ **Grifo**, Via del Boschetto 144, *T* 06 487 1395, www.italyhotel.com/it/roma/grifo. A basic but clean hotel in the lively Monti area. 21 rooms. €120-190.

Nardizzi, Via Firenze 38 (Termini), *T* 06 4880 0368, www.hotelnardizzi.it. A nice hotel for this price category. 18 rooms. €60-125.

☆☆☆ **Celio**, Via dei Santi Quattro 35c, *T* 06 709 6377, www.hotelcelio.com. A charming and quiet hotel close to the Colosseum. 19 rooms. €150-260.

Duca D'Alba, Via Leonina 14, *T* 06 484 471, www.hotelducadalba.com. A fine hotel in the Monti area. 26 rooms. €100-210.

Le Petit, Via Torino 122 (Esquilino), *T* 06 4890 7085, www.hotel-le-petit.com. Only 11 rooms (try to get room 3). €80-150.

Richmond, Largo C. Ricci 36, *T* 06 6994 1256, www.hotelrichmondroma.com. Right in front of the Forum, this small hotel has 13 rooms and a magnificent view from the roof garden. €160-190.

☆☆☆☆ **Britannia**, Via Napoli 64 (Viminale), *T* 06 488 3153, www.hotelbritannia.it. 33 rooms. €163-245.

Capo d'Africa, Via Capo d'Africa 54, *T* 06 772 801, www.hotelcapodafrica.com. Close to the Colosseum, the interior design is colourful and modern. 64 rooms. €255-300.

☆☆☆☆☆ **ES Hotel**, Via Turati 171 (near Stazione Termini), *T* 06 444 841, www.eshotel.it. The latest word in contemporary hotel design in Rome. €278.

Saint Regis Grand, Via Vittorio Emanuele Orlando 3 (near Stazione Termini), *T* 06 47091, www.stregis.com/grandrome. A grand hotel of international fame. 161 rooms. €595-755.

NAVONA PANTHEON

☆☆☆ **Casa Banzo**, Piazza del Monte di Pietà 30 (Campo dei Fiori), *T* 06 321 1783 (agency Latte & Miele, *T* 06 321 1783, info@aleepinitaly.com). B&B with fine rooms in a 16c palace decorated with frescoes. €110-120.

Due Torri, Vicolo del Leonetto 23 (Piazza Navona), *T* 06 687 6983, www.hotelduetorriroma.com. A delightful and comfortable hotel with 26 rooms. €175-218.

Portoghesi, Via dei Portoghesi 1 (Navona), *T* 06 686 4231, www.hotelportoghesiroma.com. A simple hotel set in a 17c palace. 25 rooms. €180.

Teatro di Pompeo, Largo del Pallaro 8 (Campo dei Fiori), *T* 06 6830 0170, web.tiscali.it/hotel_teatrodipompeo. A small hotel (13 rooms) above the ruins of the Theatre of Pompey (visible in the breakfast room). €100-190.

☆☆☆☆ **Locanda Cairoli**, Piazza Cairoli 2 (Campo dei Fiori), *T* 06 6880 9278, www.locandacairoli.it. A great address with 13 comfortable rooms set in a historic palace. Very popular so book well in advance. €232.

Tiziano, Corso Vittorio Emanuele II 110, *T* 06 686 5019, www.tizianohotel.it. A comfortable hotel close to Largo Argentina. 50 rooms with double-glazed windows. €170-300.

☆☆☆☆☆ **Grand Hotel de la Minerve**, Piazza della Minerva 69 (behind the Pantheon), *T* 06 695 201, www.hotel-invest.com. It has a stunning rooftop restaurant. 118 rooms. From €435.

TREVI SPAGNA

☆☆ **Marcus**, Via del Clementino 94 (Piazza Borghese), *T* 06 6830 0320, www.hotelmarcus.com. A small, family-run hotel with spacious rooms (some with antique fireplaces) and small bathrooms. 18 rooms. €108-144.

Parlamento, Via delle Convertite 5, *T* 06 6992 1000, www.hotelparlamento.it. A simple but comfortable hotel close to the parliament (and much frequented by politicians). 23 rooms. €99-150.

☆☆☆ **Fontanella Borghese**, Largo Fontanella Borghese 84, *T* 06 686 1295, www.fontanellaborghese.com. Set in a 16c palace, it has 24 pretty rooms. €185-245.

Locarno, Via della Penna 22, *T* 06 321 5249, www.hotellocarno.com. A fine hotel in an Art Nouveau style. 67 rooms. €130-310.

Piazza di Spagna, Piazza di Spagna 20, *T* 06 321 1783 (agency

Latte & Miele, *T* 06 321 1783, info@sleepinitaly.com). B&B over-looking the steps. Double rooms €110-196, apartment €154-284.

Scalinata di Spagna, Piazza Trinità dei Monti 17, *T* 06 6994 0896, www.hotelscalinata.com. A tiny hotel (16 rooms) at the top of the Spanish Steps. Recently refurbished. €250-320.

☆☆☆☆ **Art Hotel**, Via Margutta 56 (Piazza di Spagna), *T* 06 421 281, www.hotelart.it. New York style and very modern, this hotel is set in a historic palace (the lobby was formerly a chapel). Every floor is a different colour. The art exhibits are unexceptional. €387-490.

Dei Borgognoni, Via del Bufalo 126, *T* 06 6994 1501, www.hotelborgognoni.it. Between the Trevi Fountain and Piazza di Spagna, this is a quiet and elegant hotel. 50 rooms. €297-308.

D'Inghilterra, Via Bocca di Leone 14, *T* 06 699 811, www.hoteldinghilterraroma.it. The best address in this category of hotels. 90 rooms. €270-430.

Piranesi, Via del Babuino 196, *T* 06 328 041, www.hotelpiranesi.com. A recently opened hotel set in the delightful 18c Palazzo Nainer. 24 rooms. €310-350.

☆☆☆☆☆ **De Russie**, Via del Babuino 9, *T* 06 328 881, www.roccofortehotels.com. A splendid luxury hotel, with comfortable rooms, magnificent gardens and an 18c façade designed by Valadier. 102 rooms. €580-780.

Suite Condotti, Via Condotti 48,*T*06 6992 0803, www.suitecondotti.it. A newly established, beautiful hotel. €200-295.

VILLA BORGHESE

☆☆☆ **Oxford**, Via Boncompagni 89, T 06 420 3601, www.hoteloxford.it. The rooms have been recently refurbished in a simple and elegant style. 60 rooms. €166-212.

☆☆☆☆ **Barocco**, Via della Purificazione 4 (Piazza Barberini), *T* 06 487 2001, www.hotelbarocco.com. Comfortable and romantic rooms. € 284-325.

Rose Garden Palace, Via Boncompagni 19, *T* 06 421 741, www.rosegardenpalace.com. The name of this recently opened hotel derives from its inner rose garden. Comfortable. 65 rooms. €340-348.

☆☆☆☆☆ **Aleph**, Via San Basilio 15 (Via Veneto), *T* 06 422 901, www.aleph.boscolohotels.com. A recently opened, very refined designer hotel. 96 rooms. €340-561.

Excelsior Roma, Via Vittorio Veneto 125, **T** 06 47081. A completely refurbished landmark hotel. Luxurious ambience with antique furniture and gilded stuccoes. 321 rooms. €650-1250.

Regina Baglioni, Via Vittorio Veneto 72, **T** 06 421 111, www.baglionihotels.com. Set in a fine palace of the early 1900s, this hotel has 142 rooms with Art Deco furniture. €390-510.

Splendide Royal, Via di Porta Pinciana 14, **T** 06 421 689, www.hotelsplendideroyal.com. Luxurious and quiet rooms, a small fitness centre and an excellent rooftop restaurant with a magnificent view. 52 rooms. €600.

VATICAN ST PETER'S

☆☆ **Casa Valdese**, Via A. Farnese 18 (Piazza Cola di Rienzo), **T** 06 321 8222, www.italmarket.com/hotels/casavaldese. A simple but clean hotel. 34 rooms. €96-105. **M** Lepanto

☆☆☆ **Arcangelo**, Via Boezio 15, **T** 06 687 4143, www.travel.it/roma/arcangelo. 33 comfortable rooms and a delightful roof garden with a view of St Peter's dome. €155-210.

La Rovere, Vicolo di Sant'Onofrio 4, **T** 06 6880 7062, www.hotellarovere.com. Its location near Trastevere and within walking distance of both Piazza Navona and St Peter's make this charming hotel a special place. 20 rooms. €124-188.

☆☆☆☆ **Atlante Star**, Via G. Vitelleschi 34, **T** 06 687 3233, www.atlantehotels.com. Check out the view from the rooftop restaurant Les Etoiles. 80 rooms. €170-299.

Bramante, Vicolo delle Palline 25, **T** 06 687 9881. Charmingly located in the historic Borgo, a few steps away from St Peter's.

Columbus, Via della Conciliazione 33, **T** 06 686 5435, www.hotelcolumbus.net. Set in a 15c palace close to St Peter's, it also has a very good restaurant. 90 rooms. €237-307.

Dei Consoli, Via Varrone 2d (Piazza Risorgimento), **T** 06 6889 2972, www.hoteldeiconsoli.com. A recently opened and charming hotel. 26 rooms. €130-290.

Farnese, Via A. Farnese 30 (Piazza Cola di Rienzo), **T** 06 321 2553, www.hotelfarnese.com. A tasteful and elegant hotel set in a building of the early 1900s. 22 rooms. €201-270. **M** Lepanto

art glossary

Algardi, Alessandro (1595-1654). A pupil of Lodovico Carracci in Bologna, the sculptor was called to Rome in 1625 by the Bolognese cardinal Ludovico Ludovisi whose collection of antique sculpture he restored. Algardi represented Bolognese classicism in opposition to Bernini's exuberant Baroque. Examples of his work can be seen in Santa Maria del Popolo (Mellini Chapel), Chiesa Nuova, St Peter's (Monument to Leo XI), Sant'Ignazio, the Capitoline Museums, Galleria Borghese and Galleria Doria Pamphilj.

Basilica In Roman architecture a basilica was a large rectangular hall used for public meetings (it often functioned as a law court or market place). The term may derive from the Greek *basileos* (royal) and the shape from the main hall of Hellenistic palaces. From the time of Constantine (306-337) the basilica was utilized for churches. Christian basilicas often have a transept and are preceded by a quadriporticus (foursided court) and a narthex (entrance porch). The earliest basilicas were St John the Lateran, St Peter's and St Paul's in Rome, all erected under Constantine.

Baroque A style that developed during the 17c and is generally characterized by a high degree of drama and movement which aimed at the emotional involvement of the spectator. Early Baroque painters include Annibale Carracci, Domenichino, Guido Reni and Guercino. Their art remains more classical and restrained than the work of later Baroque artists whose paintings featured illusionistic effects and daring foreshortening, as exemplified by the ceilings of Palazzo Barberini and the Chiesa Nuova (by Pietro da Cortona), Sant'Andrea della Valle (by Lanfranco), the Gesù (by Gaulli) and St Ignazio (by Andrea Pozzo). The greatest Baroque sculptors in Rome were Gianlorenzo Bernini and Alessandro Algardi. In architecture, Baroque found its greatest expression in the work of Pietro da Cortona, Bernini and Borromini whose buildings are enriched by a variety of curves, forms and tonal contrasts that give the surface an impression of constant transformation.

Bernini, Gianlorenzo (1598-1680). The leading figure in Roman Baroque art, Gianlorenzo Bernini was born in Naples and settled in Rome in 1605. A versatile genius, he was a sculptor, architect, set designer and, occasionally, a painter. Already famous by the age of twenty (his earliest sculptures are in the Borghese Gallery), he rose to undisputed primacy during the pontificate of Urban VIII (1623-44), when he was involved in all of the main commissions in Rome. In sculpture, his work evolved from the spiral compositions typical of Mannerist artists: his figures are shown from multiple viewpoints, at the moment of action, and with a strong emotional intensity. His many assignments demanded the help of numerous assistants. The theatrical quality of his work, combining different colours and materials, the use of focused rather than diffused light, and the representation of a fleeting moment rather than an eternal image are the main elements of his art and the fundamental principles of Baroque.

Borromini, Francesco (1599-1667). The most original architect of Baroque Rome, Borromini began his career in Milan before settling in Rome in 1619. He worked as a stone-carver for Carlo Maderno when he was chief architect at St Peter's. After 1629 he became Bernini's assistant, contributing to the decoration of St Peter's and Palazzo Barberini. An excellent craftsman and a solitary genius, who ended his life with suicide, Borromini despised his rival Bernini's technical weaknesses as much as his extroverted character and easy success. His first independent commission came in 1634 with the revolutionary church of San Carlino alle Quattro Fontane. Subsequent commissions included Sant'Ivo alla Sapienza (1643-60), with its star-hexagon plan, the interior of San Giovanni al Laterano (1646-9), the façade of Sant'Agnese in Piazza Navona (1653-7) and the imaginative dome and lantern of Sant'Andrea delle Fratte. His palace designs include the Oratory of St Philip Neri (1637-50), the trompe-l'oeil gallery at Palazzo Spada, the grand *salone* at Palazzo Pamphilj and the Collegio di Propaganda Fide (1654-62).

Bramante, Donato (1444-1514). Palladio said that he was 'the first to bring good architecture to light'. Trained at the court of Urbino, his first works, in Lombardy, experiment with perspective and show the influence of Leon Battista Alberti and Brunelleschi. In

1499, the French invasion and the fall of Lodovico Sforza forced him to flee to Rome where he built the cloister at Santa Maria della Pace (1500), with superimposed orders derived from the Colosseum, and the circular Tempietto in the courtyard of San Pietro in Montorio (1503). In its perfectly balanced proportions, the Tempietto was the first expression of the High Renaissance in architecture. For Pope Julius II he designed the Belvedere Courtyard in the Vatican and planned the construction of the new St Peter's. Bramante's last works in Rome were the choir of Santa Maria del Popolo (1505-9) and Palazzo Caprini, later acquired by Raphael and extensively altered.

Caravaggio, Michelangelo Merisi da (1571-1610). The most important painter in 17c Italy is known by the town near Milan where he came from. He arrived in Rome around 1592 and entered the workshop of Cavalier d'Arpino as a painter of still lifes. During the 1590s he painted several genre subjects for Cardinal Del Monte and through him received the commission to decorate the Contarelli Chapel in San Luigi dei Francesi (1599-1602). From the same period are his two paintings for the Cerasi Chapel in Santa Maria del Popolo (1600-1) and the *Madonna di Loreto* in Sant'Agostino (1604). Other works by him in Rome can be seen in the Vatican, Capitoline, Borghese, Doria Pamphilj, Corsini and Barberini galleries. In 1606 Caravaggio was accused of murder and fled from Rome. He went to Naples, Malta and Sicily before receiving papal forgiveness. In 1610, on his way back, he died, possibly of fever. His art is characterized by a dramatic use of light and shade (chiaroscuro) and a marked realism, with characters taken from the street and dressed in contemporary costumes. His disregard for the conventions of the Counter-Reformation often led to the rejection of his altarpieces which, though criticized for lack of decorum, found ready buyers among cardinals and aristocrats. Much admired and imitated by his contemporaries, he was forgotten in the 17c-18c and only rediscovered after 1950.

Carracci family Agostino (1557-1602), Annibale (1560-1609), Ludovico (1555-1619). Agostino and Annibale were brothers, Ludovico was their cousin. Together they founded a teaching Academy in Bologna (1582) in reaction against the contrived and repetitive formulas of late Mannerism. They favoured a return to the classical naturalism and balance of form and content achieved by the great masters of the early 16c. The academy became the most important of its kind and trained a whole generation of painters, including Domenichino, Reni and Guercino, many of whom followed Annibale to Rome, where he was summoned, in 1595, to decorate the great Gallery of Palazzo Farnese.

Cavallini, Pietro (active 1273-1308). The main painter and mosaicist active in Rome in the late 13c, he is documented as working on all the main commissions of the time, although comparatively little by him remains. His surviving masterpieces in Rome are the mosaics with the *Life of the Virgin Mary* in the apse of Santa Maria in Trastevere (1291) and the frescoes in Santa Cecilia (1293). Together with Cimabue, Arnolfo di Cambio and Giotto, he was among the protagonists of the profound revolution in art at the end of the 13c. Discarding the established Byzantine manner, he looked back to the classical tradition and imbued his compositions with a new sense of space and volume.

Classical art Although it is often used generically to describe ancient Greek and Roman sculpture, the term identifies a particular period of Greek art, from about 480 BC to 323 BC, when a revolutionary change took place leading to a greater naturalism of form. The key artists working at that time were the sculptors Myron, whose best known work is the *Dyscobolos* (460 BC), Polykleitos with his *Doryphoros* (440 BC), and Pheidias, active in Athens at the time of Pericles (c 490-429 BC). The main qualities associated with Classical art are an absolute harmony of composition and the idealization of the human figure. During the 4c BC artists began to introduce greater naturalism and a sense of movement, evident in the sculpture of Skopas and Praxiteles whose statues, such as the *Aphrodite of Knidos*, *Hermes*, *Apollo Sauroktonos* and *Satyr,* were extensively copied in the Roman world (examples can be seen in the Vatican and Capitoline Museums). Lysippos, active at the court of Alexander the Great and famous for his portraits, was responsible for introducing a strong psychological characterization which anticipated Hellenistic art.

Classicism The term identifies any style or aesthetic approach derived from antique precedents. The most notable examples occur during the Renaissance (15c-16c) and the Neoclassical period (18c), when antique culture and history were re-discovered and Classical art and architecture deliberately imitated.

Cosmati A conventional name given to marble and mosaic workers in Rome between the 13c and 14c, many of whom were named 'Cosma' and belonged to the same family. They decorated pavements, parapets, pulpits, candelabra, columns (in cloisters) and other church furnishings with inlays of coloured stone and glass.

Domenichino (1581-1641). Byname of Domenico Zampieri. A pupil of the Carracci, in 1602 he joined Annibale in Rome to work at Palazzo Farnese. Following the teaching of his masters, his art emulated Raphael's classicism. His main works in Rome are the *Stories of St Cecilia* (1611) in San Luigi dei Francesi, the *Communion of St Jerome* (1614) in the Pinacoteca Vaticana, the *Hunt of Diana* (1616-7) in the Borghese Gallery and the frescoes in the choir and pendentives of Sant'Andrea della Valle (1624-8). Together with Annibale Carracci, and Elsheimer and the Bril brothers from northern Europe, he was among the first in Italy to experiment with landscape painting (examples hang in the Galleria Doria Pamphilj).

Dughet, Gaspard (1615-75). This French landscape painter lived and worked in Rome where his art was eagerly collected in the 17c and 18c. He is often called Poussin, after his more famous brother-in-law whose pupil he was in 1631-5. His idealized images of the Roman countryside combine Claude Lorrain's warm and diffused light with Nicolas Poussin's classicism.

Early Christian Art The art of the first centuries of the Christian era was closely related to that of Classical Antiquity from which it borrowed themes, imagery and forms. Geographically it covered all the territories under Roman rule both in the West and the East (although in the East many buildings were destroyed or entirely reconstructed under Byzantine rule). It is conventionally divided into four periods: before Constantine's Edict of Milan (313, when Christians were granted freedom of worship - it was at this time that most of the catacombs were decorated); the Constantinian period (4c); and the age of Teodosius (5c) and of Justinian

(6c). The end of the Early Christian period in art coincided approximately with the death of Gregory the Great (601).

Guercino (1591-1666). Byname of Giovanni Francesco Barbieri. Born near Bologna he was at first influenced by Venetian painting and Ludovico Carracci, and later by Caravaggio. In 1621 he was called to Rome by Gregory XV to decorate the Casino Ludovisi with the illusionistic ceiling fresco of *Aurora*, one of his masterpieces. Shortly afterwards (1622-3) he painted the *Burial of St Petronilla*, a large altarpiece for St Peter's now in the Pinacoteca Capitolina. Other works are exhibited in the Doria Pamphilj and Borghese galleries, in the Pinacoteca Vaticana and in the Galleria Nazionale d'Arte Antica (p 90). He left Rome after the death of the pope (1623) and moved to Bologna in 1642 to take over Guido Reni's workshop. His later style, heavily influenced by Reni's devotional pictures, lapsed into a repetitive and sentimental classicism devoid of the vigour and inventiveness of his Roman period.

Hellenistic Art This defines the art of the period between the death of Alexander the Great (323 BC) and the Roman conquest of Egypt (31 BC). The visual arts, and particularly sculpture, moved away from the quest for ideal beauty typical of the Classical period (5c-4c BC) and become more naturalistic and individualistic. New themes were explored, including trivial scenes, genre and grotesque characters as well as old age and youth. There was an interest in depicting movement and also a marked sense of pathos evident, for example, in the *Laocoön* and the *Torso Belvedere* (Vatican Museums), or in the *Galatian Committing Suicide* (Palazzo Altemps).

Lanfranco, Giovanni (1582-1647). Born near Parma, where he studied Correggio's paintings, he was a pupil of Agostino Carracci and followed Annibale to Rome, where, in 1621-4, he decorated the Loggia of the Casino Borghese (now the Borghese Gallery). His frescoes in the dome of Sant'Andrea della Valle (1621-7) are among the earliest expressions of High Baroque illusionism. They were painted in competition with the more classical Domenichino who was employed to decorate the apse below. From 1634 he was in Naples, where his work marked the transition from the Caravaggesque tradition to Baroque painting. In 1646 he returned to Rome where he died after completing the apse of San Carlo ai Catinari.

Mannerist Art The style that developed in Italy between 1520 and 1600 is known as Mannerism. The term comes from *maniera*, an expression already used by Vasari to describe artists (like himself) who followed the 'great manner' of Michelangelo or Raphael. While Michelangelo was praised for *disegno* (drawing) and *invenzione* (invention, complexity), Raphael had codified ideal beauty for generations to come. Subsequent artists could either emulate or adapt their vision. Many continued to focus on the human figure but chose to elongate or manipulate it into artificial poses. Grace, complexity and variety are the characteristics most frequently associated with Mannerist art. Form generally prevails over content and paintings are treated like demonstrations of technical virtuosity rather than narratives. Among the early Mannerists active in Rome were Raphael's pupils Giulio Romano and Perin del Vaga, as well as Rosso and Parmigianino. These were followed by a number of Tuscan artists, such as Francesco Salviati, Daniele da Volterra and Giorgio Vasari. The last generation of Roman Mannerists included Taddeo and Federico Zuccari and Jacopo Zucchi. In architecture, Mannerism subverts the Classical rules. The first to do so was Michelangelo himself, emulated in Rome by Giacomo della Porta and Vignola whose most notable works are Villa Giulia and the Gesù.

Michelangelo Buonarroti (1475-1564). The sculptor, painter, architect and poet is universally regarded as the greatest genius of the Italian High Renaissance. Trained in Florence at the court of Lorenzo de' Medici, he moved to Rome in 1496 where he sculpted the *Pietà* for St Peter's. In 1505 he was commissioned to make a huge funerary monument for Pope Julius II, which he was never allowed to complete, leaving just a few statues such as the *Moses* in San Pietro in Vincoli (1514). Between 1508 and 1512 he painted the Sistine Ceiling, one of the most famous art works in the world. Subsequently, he worked in Florence until returning to Rome in 1534, where he remained for the rest of his life and where he painted the *Last Judgement* (1536-41; Sistine Chapel) and two frescoes for the Pauline Chapel (Vatican). During the same period he was increasingly active as an architect, redesigning the

Capitoline Hill (1538), working on Palazzo Farnese (1546), supervising the construction of St Peter's, transforming the Baths of Diocletian into the church of Santa Maria degli Angeli (1562) and providing designs for the Gate of Porta Pia (1561-4). Michelangelo was celebrated by his contemporaries for his absolute mastery of anatomy, drawing, compositional inventiveness and the feeling of *terribilità* (intensity) which characterized his figures.

Pietro Berrettini da Cortona (1596-1669). A painter and architect, Pietro da Cortona was one of the leading personalities of the High Baroque. His first commissions in Rome included paintings for the Sacchetti family, now exhibited in the Capitoline Pinacoteca. Soon afterwards he entered the service of Urban VIII Barberini whose palace he decorated with the *Triumph of Divine Providence* (1633-9). His later paintings include the *Stories of Aeneas* in Palazzo Pamphilj and the magnificent frescoes in the Chiesa Nuova (1647-65). As an architect he reconstructed the church of Santi Luca e Martina near the Forum (1635-50) and built the façades of Santa Maria della Pace (1656-7) and Santa Maria in Via Lata (1658-62). In his paintings he combined Raphaelesque narratives and figure types with a Venetian sense of colour. His illusionistic works, based on multiple perspectives and daring foreshortening, set the standard for subsequent ceiling decorations and had numerous followers.

Poussin, Nicolas (1594-1665). Together with Claude Lorrain he was the most important French painter working in Rome in the 17c. He arrived in 1624 and entered the studio of Domenichino whose rational compositions and cool colour exerted a lasting influence on his art. In 1628 he was commissioned to paint an altarpiece for St Peter's (the *Martyrdom of St Erasmus*, now in the Vatican Pinacoteca). A serious illness in 1629-30 brought about a marked change in his style. He abandoned religious subjects and fashionable Baroque grandiosity and turned to smaller compositions inspired by Classical art and Raphael. After a short stay in France (1640-2) he returned to Rome, where he remained, developing a marked interest in landscape painting. His landscapes are highly idealized and exemplify his theories on painting: each picture should be constructed with clarity and simplicity; colour should be subordinated to the overall composition; everything should be geometrically balanced in a perfect unity of vision.

Raphael (1483-1520). In Italian, Raffaello Sanzio. Raphael was trained by Perugino, whose influence is evident in his early works. In Florence he absorbed the art of Leonardo and Michelangelo. By 1508 he was in Rome decorating the Apartment of Pope Julius II. From 1514 he was working on the frescoes of the Villa Farnesina (Trastevere), the building site of St Peter's and designing the cartoons for the Vatican tapestries. His last painting was the *Transfiguration*, now in the Pinacoteca Vaticana. When he died, at the age of thirty-seven, he was praised as one of the greatest masters of his time. His art is characterized by serene and balanced compositions with classically poised figures embodying ideals of perfect beauty. His colours are rich but never overwhelming and his designs graceful and clear. In contrast to Michelangelo, the solitary genius, Raphael was the perfect courtier, elegant and refined, on friendly terms with cardinals and princes, a position never before attained by an artist. He had numerous followers and a prolific school of artists (Giulio Romano, Francesco Penni, Giovanni da Udine) who developed his style into Mannerism. There are paintings by Raphael in the Pinacoteca Vaticana, Galleria Borghese and Galleria Nazionale d'Arte Antica.

Renaissance The term means 'rebirth' and conventionally identifies the period between the 15c and the early 16c. This period was influenced by Humanism, which placed man at the centre of universe, and saw the rediscovery of Classical Antiquity. In the visual arts it developed a high degree of naturalism, and in architecture it adhered closely to Classical forms. The Renaissance originated in Florence and rapidly spread throughout Italy and Europe. Tuscan artists were soon called to the papal court. The walls of the Sistine Chapel were decorated in the early 1480s by Perugino, Botticelli, Ghirlandaio, Pinturicchio, Signorelli and their assistants. Pinturicchio continued to work in Rome, decorating the palaces of Cardinal Della Rovere, Alexander VI's apartment in the Vatican and the choir of Santa Maria del Popolo. The climax was reached at the beginning of the 16c with the art of

Michelangelo and Raphael and the architecture of Donato Bramante. These masters set the standard of artistic perfection for years to come and were extensively imitated.

Reni, Guido (1575-1642). Coming from Bologna, Reni was first trained by the Flemish artist Denis Calvaert and later by the Carracci. Around 1600 he went to Rome where he studied the work of Raphael and, in 1614, painted the *Aurora* in the Casino Pallavicini-Rospigliosi, which is regarded as his masterpiece. Reni's patrons, Paul V and Scipione Borghese, employed him at San Gregorio al Celio, the Quirinal Palace and the Pauline Chapel in Santa Maria Maggiore. After a short trip to Naples in 1622 he returned to Bologna where he became a prolific painter of sentimental religious subjects.

Rococo The last phase of Baroque, in the early 18c, is known as Rococo. It was initiated in France as a reaction to the pompous splendour of Versailles. The term derives from *rocaille*, meaning shell-like rock-work, and describes a type of decoration characterized by playful scrolls and countercurves. Although it originated in the decorative arts, it was soon taken up in painting, sculpture and architecture, which became increasingly lighthearted and purely decorative. The best examples of Rococo in Rome are the Spanish Steps by Francesco de Sanctis (1726), Piazza Sant'Ignazio by Filippo Raguzzini (1728), Nicola Salvi's Trevi Fountain (1732-62) and the façade of Santa Maria Maddalena (1735; near the Pantheon) by Giuseppe Sardi.

Rubens, Peter Paul (1577-1640). Among the most important northern European painters of the 17c, Rubens was born in Flanders and travelled to Italy around 1600. By 1606-8 he was in Rome where he made three paintings for the Chiesa Nuova. He collected antiquities, read the classics, wrote a book on the customs of the Romans and signed his name in Italian (Pietro Paolo). While in Rome he bought Caravaggio's *Death of the Virgin* and closely studied both his revolutionary works and the achievements of the Carracci. His art is also indebted to the great masters of the Renaissance and, above all, to Titian whose sense of colour he inherited, giving rise to a famous debate between the Poussinistes and the Rubenistes about the role of colour in painting. After his return to Antwerp in 1608, he rose to extraordinary fame and ran a large and prolific studio. His works can be seen in the Vatican, Capitoline, Borghese and Corsini galleries.

Sangallo, Antonio da (the Younger) (1484-1546). Born in Florence, he was the most notable member of the Sangallo family of architects (the nephew of Antonio the Elder and Giuliano, who worked mainly in Tuscany). He became the leading architect in Rome after the death of Raphael (1520), working at St Peter's and designing Palazzo Sacchetti and Palazzo Farnese. He was also employed as military engineer on the fortifications around Rome.

Titian (1488/90-1576). In Italian, Tiziano Vecellio. The greatest of Venetian painters, he was apprenticed to Bellini and Giorgione but soon developed a personal style marked by a strong sense of colour, loose brushwork and free compositions, which make him the precursor of modern art. Acknowledged by his contemporaries as one of the greatest living masters, he worked for dukes, popes and cardinals, even Emperor Charles V and his son Philip II. His painting of *Sacred and Profane Love* (1514) in the Borghese Gallery exemplifies his early style still influenced by Bellini.

Vanvitelli (1653-1736). Original name Gaspar van Wittel, but known in Italy as Vanvitelli. Originally from the Netherlands, in 1674 he settled in Rome where he produced a series of topographical drawings of the river Tiber. From these he derived his precise *vedute* (views) of Rome, Venice and Naples which made him the precursor of Canaletto and Panini. His paintings can be seen in the Galleria Nazionale d'Arte Antica and in the private apartments of Palazzo Colonna. He was in Naples in 1700, when his son Luigi, the great Neapolitan architect, was born.

Zuccari, Taddeo (1529-66) and **Federico** (1543-1609). The Zuccari brothers represent the latest development of Mannerism in Rome. Taddeo's main works are the Sala Regia in the Vatican and the Farnese Deeds in the villa at Caprarola. These were completed by his younger brother, Federico, who later worked with Vasari in Florence and travelled extensively throughout Europe. In 1593, Federico re-founded the Academy of St Luke at his palazzo at Trinità de' Monti. He is best known for his treatise, *L'idea de'scultori, pittori e architetti*, of 1607.

First edition 2004
Published by A&C Black Publishers Ltd
37 Soho Square, London W1D 3QZ

ISBN 0-7136-6697-8

Published in the United States of America by
WW Norton & Company, Inc
500 Fifth Avenue, New York, NY 10110

ISBN 0-393-32596-2

Published simultaneously in Canada by
Penguin Books Canada Limited
10 Alcorn Avenue, Ontario M4V 3B2

Series devised by Gemma Davies
Series designed by Jocelyn Lucas
Editorial and production: Gemma Davies, Jocelyn Lucas, Lilla Nwenu-
Msimang, Miranda Robson, Kim Teo, Judy Tither

Maps by Mapping Company Ltd

Photographic acknowledgements

Front cover and inside front cover: *Rest on the Flight into Egypt* (1596-7; detail
on front cover) by Caravaggio, Galleria Doria Pamphilj, Rome
© Photo: akg-images/Pirozzi
Back cover photograph: The Colosseum, courtesy of Lisa Hirst
Insides: pp 12, 24, 33, 50, 65 by kind permission of Lisa Hirst; pp 6, 29, 34, 37,
39, 58, 67, 72, 86, 96, 99, 104, 146, 175, 180, 191 courtesy of the Rome Tourist
Board; p 121 *Apollo and Daphnis* (1621; detail) by Gianlorenzo Bernini, Galleria
Borghese © Photo SCALA, Florence - courtesy of the Ministero Beni e Att.
Culturali, p 168 *Delphic Sibyl* (1508-12) by Michelangelo, the Sistine Chapel ©
Photo SCALA, Florence - courtesy of the Ministero Beni e Att. Cultural

Printed and bound in Singapore by Tien Wah Press (Pte.) Ltd.

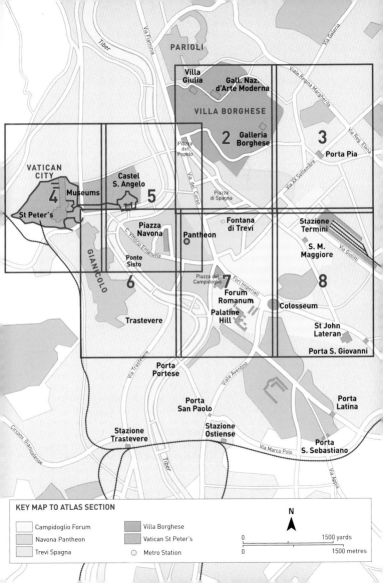

PARIOLI

Villa Giulia

Gall. Naz. d'Arte Moderna

VILLA BORGHESE

2 Galleria Borghese

3

Porta Pia

Piazza del Popolo

Piazza di Spagna

VATICAN CITY

4 Museums

Castel S. Angelo

5

St Peter's

Fontana di Trevi

Stazione Termini

Piazza Navona

Pantheon

S. M. Maggiore

C. Vittorio Emanuele

Ponte Sisto

6

Piazza del Campidoglio

7

Fori Imperiali

8

Forum Romanum

Palatine Hill

Colosseum

Trastevere

St John Lateran

Porta S. Giovanni

Porta Portese

Porta San Paolo

Stazione Ostiense

Porta Latina

Stazione Trastevere

Porta S. Sebastiano

KEY MAP TO ATLAS SECTION

☐ Campidoglio Forum	☐ Villa Borghese	
☐ Navona Pantheon	☐ Vatican St Peter's	
☐ Trevi Spagna	○ Metro Station	

N

0		1500 yards
0		1500 metres

2

Viale G. d'Annunzio

Viale Bruno Buozzi

Viale d. Belle Arti

Austrian Academy

V. d. Nibani

Via A. Gramsci

Via G. Mangili

Via Ulisse Aldovrandi

Via G. Rossini

Via Mercadante

Via Carissimi

Museo Civico di Zoologia

S. Eugenio
V. d. Villa Giulia

British School

Galleria Nazionale d'Arte Moderna

Giardino Zoologico Bioparco

Villa Poniatowsky

Museo Etrusco di Villa Giulia

Piazza Thorvaldsen

Viale d. Belle Arti

Viale del Giardino Zoologico

Entrance

Viale dell'Uccelliera

Piazza Firdusi

Pza. Paolo Borghese

Villa Strohl Fern

Via di Valle Giulia

Via Bernadotte

Museo Canonica

EXPLORA

VILLA BORGHESE

Pza. d. Fiocco

Giardino d. Lago

Piazza di Siena

Via dei Cavalli Marini

Viale Pietro Canonica

Viale Fra Papazzi

Fontana dei Cavalli Marini

Stazione Roma Viterbo

Via Flaminia

Viale Washington

Pza. U. Hugo

Viale la Guardia

Via Pietro Canonica

Piazza di Canestre

Viale di Paggi

Via del Museo Borghese

Metro Flaminio

Piazzale Flaminio

V. le d. Muro Torto

Umberto I Monument

Viale Goethe

Porta d. Popolo

S.M. d. Popolo

Pincio

V. dell'Obelisco

Piazzale Napoleone

Piazzale dei Martiri

Viale delle Magnolie

Goethe Mon.

Viale di S. Paolo del Brasile

Casina delle Rose

Piazza del Popolo

Via G. d'Annunzio

S.M. di Miracoli

Via d. Penna

S. in Montesanto

Viale del Muro Torto

Galoppatoio

Piazzale Brasile

Corso d'Italia

Porta Pinciana

Via Pinciana

Via del Corso

Goethe Museum

Via Margutta

Via Laurina

Casina Valadier

Viale Trinità d. Monti

Villa Medici

Via di Porta Pinciana

Via Lazio

Via Lombardia

Via Emilia

Via Marche

Via Sicilia

Via Campania

Ch. Lutera

Via del Vantaggio

All Saints' Anglican Ch.

Via d. Greci

Via Aurora

Casino dell' Aurora

Via Ludovisi

US Embassy

S. Giacomo

Via A. Canova

Via del Babuino

Viale F. Alberti

Via d. Sebastian

Spanish Steps

SS. Trinità dei Monti

Via Vittorio Veneto

Via Boncompagni

S. Isidoro

Palazzo Margherita

Via d. Frezza

Mausoleum of Augustus

Via Vittoria

Via Mario de' Fiori

Via della Croce

Keats' House

Via Gregoriana

Via Francesco Crispi

Via Sistina

S.M. della Concezione

Via d. S. Basilio

Ara Pacis

Largo degli Schiavoni

Via d. Carrozze

Palazzo d. Spagna

Pza. di Spagna

Spagna

Coll. di. Propag. Fide

Via Capo le Case

Gall Comunale d'Arte Moderna

Barberini

Via S. Nicola da Toler

Via Barberi

Palazzo Borghese

Via di Ripetta

Via Tomacelli

Via della Vite

Via della Mercede

S. Andrea delle Fratte

Via del Tritone

Piazza Barberini

Palazzo Barberi (Galleria Nazionale d'Arte Antica)

Pal. Ruspoli

Largo Carlo Goldoni

Via Frattina

S. Silvestro

Via d. Nazar.

Fontana del Tritone

Via delle Quattro Fontane

S. Lorenzo in Lucina

Pal. Fiano

Via del Corso

Piazza S. Silvestro

Via del Tritone

L. Go Tritone

Via Rasella

Piazza Nicosia

Via d. Prefetti

Piazza del Parlamento

QUIRINALE

Mercato

V. Giov. Bovio

Via Rodi

Via della Giuliana

Via Angelico

Via Camozzi

Viale delle Mili

Via S. Pellico

Viale Angelico

Via B. Telesio

Circonvallazione Trionfale

Via Savonarola

Via Giord. Bruno

Via T. Campanella

Via Trionfale

Via Legnano

Viale delle Milizie

Largo
Trionfale

Viale d.
Medaglie d'Oro

Viale delle Milizie

Via Barletta

Ottaviano

Piazza
degli Eroi

Via Andrea Doria

Via Santamaura

Via Ostia

Via Famagosta

Viale Giulio Cesare

Via Caio Mario

Via Mocenigo

Via Tunisi

Via degli Scipioni

Via Vespasiano

Via Ottaviano

Via Germanico

Via dei Silla

Via Vitt. Pisani

Via Candia

Via Vespasiano

Via dei Gracchi

Piazza
d. Unità

Via Cipro

Viale Vaticano

Via Cola di Rienzo

Via Merc. Bragadin

Via Ang. Emo

Via Leone IV

Via Crescenzio

Via Properzio

Entrance

Piazza
Risorgimento

Borgo Angelico

Via S. Porcari

Piazza
A. Capponi

Via d. Porta Angelica

Vatican

V. del Pellegrino

Via d. Falco

Borgo Vittorio

**Vatican
Gardens**

**Vatican
Museums**

**Vatican
P.O.**

Via d.
Belvedere V. S.
d'Anna

Via d. Plauto

Borgo Pio

Stradone

VATICAN CITY

Via d. Corridori

**Palazzo
Torlonia**

**Sistine
Chapel**

Via di Fondamenta

Piazza
S. Pietro

Piazza
Pio XII

Via d. Conciliaz

**Pal. dei
Penitenzieri**

St Peter's

Pza.
d. Prot.
Romani

Borgo S. Spirit

**Stazione
Vaticano**

Piazza
S. Marta

V. d. S. Uffizio

**S. Spirito
in Sassia**

Viale Vaticano

Largo
di Porta Cavalleggeri

Trafora del
Principe Amedeo

**Porta
S. Spirito**

Via Aurelia

Porta Cavalleggeri

Pia
d. Ro

Via Aurelia

Via Aurelia

Via di Porta Cavalleggeri

Via di Stazione d. S. Pietro

Via Gasperi

Via S. Maria

**American
College**

Via Gregorio VII

Via Paolo II

Via Nicolò III

Via Innocent. III

Gianicolo

Via d. Cava Aurelia

Via d. Cava Aurelia

S. Gregorio VII

**Stazione
S. Pietro**

Viale delle Mura Aurelie

Via d. Fornaci

S. Onof

GIANICOLO